THE EIGHTH GENERATION

UNDER THE EDITORSHIP OF
GARDNER MURPHY

THE EIGHTH
GENERATION

CULTURES AND PERSONALITIES
OF NEW ORLEANS NEGROES

Editors: JOHN H. ROHRER
MUNRO S. EDMONSON

Co-authors: HAROLD LIEF
DANIEL THOMPSON
WILLIAM THOMPSON

HARPER & BROTHERS, PUBLISHERS, NEW YORK

Dedicated to
ALLISON DAVIS AND JOHN DOLLARD
Whose generosity made this study possible

CONTENTS

A C K N O W L E D G M E N T S

This volume reports a research project carried out during the years 1953–1956 at the Urban Life Research Institute of Tulane University. The idea of making the study and the responsibility for its direction rested with Dr. John H. Rohrer. In other respects it would be misleading to attempt to indicate individual contributions, which were closely coördinated activities of the co-authors who constituted the basic project staff: Dr. Daniel C. Thompson, Staff Sociologist; Dr. Munro S. Edmonson, Staff Anthropologist; Dr. John H. Rohrer, Staff Psychologist; and Drs. Harold I. Lief and William C. Thompson, Staff Psychiatrists.

The study was made possible by the generosity of Drs. Allison Davis and John Dollard, who made available to us all the original interview records from which they derived their book, *Children of Bondage*, published in 1940. In gratitude, we are dedicating this follow-up study to them.

The initial attempt to gauge the feasibility of making this study rested with Dr. Daniel C. Thompson and Mr. Frank Cherry, who spent the summer of 1952 relocating the scattered subjects. As a result of their successful search we applied for and received a grant, subsequently renewed, from the National Institutes of Health,[1] that enabled us to carry out the full study.

Miss Hazel Long joined the staff and did all of the local clinical testing. Her sudden death in 1956 was a saddening blow to all of

[1] This investigation was supported by a research grant, M 729, from the National Institutes of Health, Division of Research Grants, U.S. Public Health Service; John H. Rohrer, Principal Investigator.

us, and a severe loss to her profession in New Orleans. Mrs. Joyce-
lyn Hart worked with us for a time as staff social worker. When
she found it necessary to leave, she proved irreplaceable.

Dr. Rutherford Stevens graciously accepted an invitation to
spot check our subjects, probing for color factors in the psychiatric interview situation. He took leave of his own practice in New
York City for the summer he spent in New Orleans. Dr. Joel
Handler of the Chicago Psychoanalytic Institute helpfully interviewed for us some subjects residing in the Chicago area who
would otherwise have been lost. Dr. Samuel J. Beck, in his usual
coöperative manner, agreed to do the psychological testing of
these same subjects. Dr. Sumner Ives joined the staff during the
second year of the study to carry out the linguistic analysis of the
speech recordings we had obtained. Dr. George Jacobson did
some psychiatric interviewing for us with a subject living in upper
Louisiana, for which we are most grateful.

In analyzing the mass of data accumulated, Dr. E. Lee Hoff-
man and Dr. Thomas Ktsanes ably assisted us in the solution of
several statistical problems. In addition, a number of graduate
students from Tulane's Departments of Sociology, Anthropology,
and Psychology worked on the study for varying periods of time.
Among these were Mr. Paul Kay, Mrs. Evelyn Kimura, Mr. Paul
Zopf, and Miss Audry Jennings. Mrs. Sarah Harmon Sledge did a
number of analyses and is primarily responsible for the analysis of
the "Adoption Study" data in Appendix 3. Fourteen undergraduate students enrolled at Dillard University worked for various
periods of time on the study, and Mr. Leon Johnson gathered
much of the linguistic material.

In transcribing and typing nearly three file drawers of material,
Mrs. N. Donnelly performed a laborious and invaluable service.
Mrs. Hazel Erickson contributed her ability, energy, and all but
incredible precision to the preparation of the numerous drafts of
the manuscript, and particularly to the painstaking production of
a final copy. Mrs. Camilla Morgan expertly assisted us in bringing
together the semifinal draft.

The Committee on Social Issues of the Group for the Advancement of Psychiatry generously devoted a two-day period at their meeting in 1954 to a discussion of our project. We hope this volume reflects the benefits gained from the valuable suggestions made at that meeting.

We are grateful to Prentice Hall, Inc., for permission to quote from *Satchmo: My Life in New Orleans,* by Louis Armstrong, and to Doubleday and Co. Inc., for permission to quote from *His Eye is on the Sparrow,* by Ethel Waters and Charles Samual.

We are also grateful to the Mona Bronfman Sheckman Foundation for a grant which enabled us to complete the manuscript in its final form, and to Tulane and Dillard Universities who supported our research in many tangible and intangible ways.

Finally, to the people we studied, our "subjects," we extend our heart-felt thanks for the time they spent with us, their trust in the worthwhileness of the study, and their tolerant attitude toward our odd and sometimes painful probing.

JOHN H. ROHRER
Georgetown University

MUNRO S. EDMONSON
Tulane University

THE EIGHTH GENERATION

CHAPTER 1

Introduction

The limited success of the behavioral sciences in founding new research ventures on previous solid achievements has been noted with various degrees of despair by many critics. We are confident of the cumulative quality of the research that lies behind this book, because it has been designed and executed as a follow-up study, taking up where Allison Davis and John Dollard left them almost twenty years ago, the lives of the *Children of Bondage*.[1]

Davis' and Dollard's report may fairly be considered a classic of modern social science. Our study follows it and is indebted to it in more ways than can easily be acknowledged or described. We have started from Davis' and Dollard's ideas and they have generously furnished us with a complete file of their data; we have followed them at the respectful distance of half a generation to many of the same New Orleans doorsteps, and to many of the same interpretative findings and conclusions. This book is an account of our research efforts.

Our active pursuit began in 1953, when, furnished with a list of addresses known to be fifteen years out of date, we set out on a preliminary effort to locate the former teen-agers Davis and Dollard had studied. We started from a file of interviews of 277

[1] Allison Davis and John Dollard, *Children of Bondage,* Washington, American Council on Education, 1940.

1

individuals. We attempted to find 107 of them, selecting those cases that were most fully covered in the initial study in 1937–1938 (including all 76 of Davis' and Dollard's "intensive cases").

The process of relocating the subjects was an adventure in itself. If the address proved useless and the telephone book and the city directory provided no helpful leads, we questioned neighbors, looked at school or police records, or returned to the original case records for other hints. One man, a successful entertainer, was sunk without a trace until we tried his old nickname on the neighbors: "Why, everybody knows 'Little Bit.' " One trail led to an obscure house on a little-known street where the subject's sister told us the youngster we were looking for had been killed at Pearl Harbor fourteen years before. Another search brought us to a state penitentiary where we were able to establish definitely that the man we sought had been discharged the week before, after several years' residence. There was no forwarding address. At one home Davis and Dollard left the mother of a little girl of the lower class rocking on the porch and smoking a corncob pipe. There we found her, still rocking, still smoking. Many of the subjects had moved away—to Chicago, Los Angeles, New York. One was fighting in Korea. Many were still in school, struggling to complete an education delayed by financial need, the war, or early marriage. They were clerks, salesmen, hospital attendants, disc jockeys, teachers, domestic workers, prostitutes, firemen, doctors, and business executives. Sometimes we hit blind alleys; often there was some suspicion that we might be bill collectors or agents of the law. One man questioned had the utmost difficulty recalling his step-daughter's name until he had finished probing our intentions. Despite these problems we were usually able to continue the search on another tack. In the end we were able to locate 90 of the 107 subjects we looked for.

The scattered and seemingly random social placement of the subjects was reassuring, and speaks well for the representativeness of the original sample. Davis and Dollard had selected the subjects, mostly from the schools, with an eye to a representative sample from different social classes.[2] To the degree we could, we tried to subselect them on the same basis. We early discovered that only a strenuous effort to locate and interview subjects of the lower class would keep our sample in balance in class terms. We also tried to select for intensive interviewing equal numbers of men and women, and we made every effort to include the subjects most extensively interviewed in 1937–1938. Necessarily, however, the practical consideration of availability loomed large in our selection of cases.

The subjects' motives in agreeing to the considerable investment of time needed for our program of interviews and tests were seemingly diverse. Almost all of them had some reservations. Most of them recalled the original interviews, and for some this was sufficient to make them feel committed to "helping out again." In some cases there were altruistic reasons (e.g., "if my troubles can help anybody else"), or a desire for free psychotherapy, or a feeling that the study might help the Negro. In some cases the scientific importance of the study was a relevant symbol, and in many cases the prestige names of Tulane and Dillard Universities served both to allay anxiety and to provide a status motive for participating. Most of the subjects were given money, sometimes to cover the cost of transportation, baby sitting, or even loss of income which the interviewing program might entail for them. One was frankly paid to participate, although in the absence of other inducements, money alone proved a surprisingly poor motivator. We experimented throughout with ways to present the project to different subjects, and especially to those of the lower class, but we end the study without the information that might have been given by one lower class woman who persisted in disappearing over the back fence whenever one of us reached the front door of her mother's home.

We actually interviewed 47 of the 90 people we had traced, and we selected 20 of these, ten men and ten women, for a more

[2] See p. 48 for discussion of social classes in New Orleans.

intensive program of testing and interviewing. The degree to which 20 individuals can be a representative sample of a population of 200,000 would seem to be an academic question. On the basis of a content analysis of the case records, however, the status context of these 20 lives seems to reflect fairly satisfactorily that of the city at large. There is some measure of "middle-class bias" still to our selection,[3] but the distortion is not great.

Because our work was cut out for us by Davis' and Dollard's selection of subjects, our additional attempts to control the sample were actually less a matter of sampling than of rapport. Recognizing that our mode of treatment of a given subject would unquestionably affect his participation in the study, we were forced to manipulate this rapport as a sampling mechanism, and to work harder on some subjects precisely because they were harder to work on. Class differences loomed large among the rapport problems we encountered. Color differences loomed small. Although we expected some differentiation of the subjects' reactions to Negro and white interviewers, we found almost none, and in only one case did we encounter a refusal on color grounds to be interviewed by whites. We cannot, of course, be sure of the motives of the subjects we could not recapture. In some cases we suspect psychopathic conditions. Fear because of involvement in illegal activities is likely in at least two cases, and some status anxiety and concern over privacy may be indicated in another. Some fear of the label "psychiatry" was expected, but did not appear, and it is worthy of remark that several of the subjects had had psychotherapy of one or another type before we recontacted them. In a sense we did not really "sample" from Davis' and Dollard's list of subjects, for we did not reject anyone who could be interviewed easily. We did spend different amounts of time and energy on different subjects and groups of subjects, and by this means we have tried to manipulate the composition of our final "sample." Our actual rejection rate was low: we were unsuccessful in interviewing only four of those whom we tried hard to interview.

[3] See Appendix 1.

Our program of interviewing began with the relocation of the subject. Usually a formal questionnaire was completed at that time, covering briefly but comprehensively the subject's present social position and participation. This initiated a series of informal contacts of a participant observation type in the home, on the job, or in other natural contexts. Most of these interviews were by a sociologist, a psychiatric social worker, or an anthropologist, and they aimed at a natural account of the subject in his own milieu.

A major aspect of the home interviewing was the pursuit of the interest in the training of children that was the central focus of Davis' and Dollard's study. We wished not only to discover what had happened to the "Children of Bondage," but also to find out whether they were perpetuating in their relations with their own children the methods by which they themselves had been trained. Ten of the 20 subjects have children, 29 in all. Much of our home interviewing was devoted to observation of these children and discussion of their upbringing with their parents. Six of these children were also included in the psychological testing program. Usually the subject had been visited several times in this way before seeing the psychiatrist.

Scheduling psychiatric interviews proved, indeed, to be a major hurdle in our research program. Motivating the subject to initiate and then to continue these contacts required the utmost patience and ingenuity on the part of the entire staff. Most of the subjects, of course, were not therapeutically motivated, and in that respect differed importantly from patients. It seems scarcely accidental, however, that the most stable and prolonged psychiatric contacts were maintained with the five subjects who could also be considered patients. When only brief psychiatric contacts were possible, the psychiatrist attempted to gain a general impression of each person's current adjustment. When the contact was more sustained, the scope of the interviewing was broadened and deepened to include analysis of personal problems and therapeutic attempts to deal with them, with consequent enrichment of the record. It is worth underlining that only five of the subjects attempted to establish any kind of therapeutic relationship with the psychiatrist, even though some of the others completed as many as 20 hours of psychiatric interviewing.

In one major respect the psychiatric data were experimentally controlled. After about five or six interviews the two psychiatrists presented general summaries of a particular case at a staff meeting. Until this time the psychiatrist who was seeing the subject worked "blind," without having read the recorded account of the subject's adolescence. The other psychiatrist worked only with the old record, and in ignorance of the tenor of the current interviews. Complete control over the information available to the psychiatrists was not possible, since staff discussions inevitably included some premature remarks about subjects who had not yet been "staffed." This procedure, however, tended to sharpen very usefully our perception of continuity or discontinuity in the subject's adjustment, and invariably raised further questions to be pursued in the interviews, with consequent benefit to the precision of the interpretations.

After the study was well under way, a second psychiatric control was introduced by inviting a Negro psychiatrist to spot-check a group of the subjects who had already seen the white psychiatrists. He was able to interview nine persons, most of them several times, and provided a useful if largely negative check on the role of color in these interviews.

Before each subject was discussed in general staff meeting, he was asked to take a battery of psychological tests, including the Rorschach, TAT, Machover Draw-a-Figure, and Wechsler-Bellevue. One or more of his children were tested at about the same time, and the test results and interpretations were presented at the staff meeting and discussed. In what is perhaps a unique arrangement among recent studies of this type, our psychiatrists worked "blind," while our psychologists did not. The final psychodynamic descriptions, of course, make use of all the available materials.

In preparing for the first general discussion of a case, our sociologist and anthropologist assembled a general report on the subject's social background. A complete list of the individuals mentioned in both the older and contemporary files was compiled, each individual being identified in terms of every status he was known to have occupied. A status history of the subject was also prepared, including an assessment of his class position and background, and a summary interpretation of the social dynamics of his adjustment and the character and values of his social world.

It may be imagined that coördination of these various activities and directing their convergence on a particular date proved a somewhat delicate operation, which heightened the excitement inherent in this phase of the work and punctuated the regular weekly meetings of the staff with a periodic intensity that often generated new questions and enduring enthusiasm. At times, indeed, it has seemed that the staff meetings themselves were as interesting a phenomenon as the data they were instituted to discuss.

As has become usual in this period of interdisciplinary teamwork in science, our staff was heterogeneous and complex. Its core included two psychologists, a sociologist, an anthropologist, and two psychiatrists who are both psychoanalysts and graduates of psychoanalytic institutes. An imposingly random array of birthplaces was represented: Missouri, Louisiana, California, New York, Georgia, and Arizona. To this basic staff must be added for varying periods of time five secretaries, two psychiatric social workers, three additional psychiatrists, seven interviewers, a third and fourth psychologist, four graduate students, and a linguist. In all, 19 whites and 11 Negroes worked on the project. Such a staff constitutes a social system in its own right, and we were early made aware of some of the special problems of organization and communications that this system imposed upon us.

Involving as they do important questions of language and belief, the differing disciplines to which we have been trained are perhaps the most generally important factor in these problems.

The situation may be caricatured, but not altogether distorted, by referring to an early discussion in which we aired our preferences for thinking of the people we were studying as *patients, respondents, informants, clients,* or *subjects.* The differences implied are real and they are persistent. Although we reached a formal decision in favor of the sociopsychological term *subjects,* that did not altogether eliminate the social worker's desire to help them, the psychiatrists' interest in their medical and adjustment problems, or the anthropologist's urge to use each one as an information source. Nor did it eliminate the social-psychological tendency to see the subjects as the *respondents* or *interviewees* to whom questionnaires are administered. The results are a more or less harmonic compromise. We have helped, treated, quizzed, and administered questionnaires to our subjects. We have also recorded their speech, analyzed their folklore and their reactions to inkblots, and questioned them formally about child care. But our agreement on a term did symbolize an emerging concensus on our common goals.

The maturity of this concensus came only after trial and error. Perhaps the most clearly marked error was the phase in which we cross-identified with one another and attempted with indifferent success to play each other's professional roles. Possibly this is a necessary psychological step to the fuller acceptance by each of us of the others' several and distinct functions. Once we began to see this heterogeneous activity as a real and efficient contribution to a homogeneous goal, we began to experience less difficulty of communication in defining that goal. We do not believe that we have found a method for integrating research activities. We are not even sure that one exists. But there is perhaps no context of modern life in which the gentle art of compromise must be so delicately practiced as in this endeavor. To be a party to the effort is one of the less frequently cited rewards—and one of the more refined punishments—in the scientific life.

In addition to the carefully timed and elaborately organized preparation of the record of each subject's history and current adjustment, we made a special effort to get background information on the environing society. This led us to the library and the history of Louisiana, to the newspapers and especially the Negro press (the *Louisiana Weekly* and the Louisiana edition of the *Pittsburgh Courier*), to the burgeoning literature on the American Negro, to source books and the U.S. Census, and to the theses of students at the universities of Louisiana and other states. And in three cases it led us into special studies of our own, on language, folklore, and child training.

Because language is usually a sensitive index of general cultural organization, and because it had not been carefully studied in this context, we embarked on the collection of a sample of speech suitable for dialect analysis. Our aim was to examine the relationship between dialect and social class, and initially we had hoped to use all the subjects of the original study for this purpose. When this proved impossible, we added additional subjects to a total of 52, recorded their speech on tape, and let our linguist do a "blind" analysis of the dialect features. We then compared the dialect characteristics of the sample with data on their social placement.

Because we felt an increasing need for documentation of the subcultural differences among the segments of the Negro community, especially in relation to motivational patterns, we undertook a content analysis of selected "folklore" media from three such segments. The words of jazz songs, Creole folk songs, and newspaper editorials were selected. These were scored in terms of generic motivational content, and then compared.

In order to focus more sharply on the methods of child training among New Orleans Negroes, we designed a questionnaire, ostensibly about adoption, and administered it to a random, areally selected, class-stratified sample of 105 Negro women. The questionnaire was particularly directed toward discriminating different practices or attitudes within the Negro community, and made possible comparison of groups differing by class, ethnic origin, and family type.

As the project developed the regular staff meetings carried an ever heavier freight of cases, some of which were "staffed" three or four times. It also became possible to introduce more and more of our developing fund of social information into the discussion. At the same time we were able to test more sharply hunches and hypotheses we had carried along from the beginning, which could now be provisionally accepted or rejected. From this matrix our research findings have emerged. Helped (and at times hindered) by evenings spent groping for more explicit theory, by special research reports and staff memoranda, we have gradually come to see our findings as we here present them.

An aura of particular interest has attended this research since the momentous desegregation decision of the Supreme Court burst upon us in the second year of our study. A period of rapid social change has now given way to one of crisis. While these developments obviously intensify the interest of the research worker, however detached and scientific, they have seemed to us to impose a special burden of scrupulousness in differentiating our findings from our fancies. Social science studies were given important recognition in the arguments before the Court. With some of these earlier studies our findings disagree. We do not believe that this alters in any relevant respect the question the Court was called on to decide, or the moral rightness of its decision. In any event, the issue lies beyond the scope of this investigation.

Approximately seven generations have come and gone since the first Negro slaves were landed at New Orleans. Our ex-teenagers are the eighth. Their ancestors of the fifth generation were primarily slaves; their grandparents were the freedmen of a bitter Reconstruction. Their parents of the seventh generation appear in these pages as embattled adults, products of the most restrictive phase of the white supremacy of the early twentieth century and of the hardships of our worst depression. For the eighth generation there are many unprecedented problems and opportunities, but we cannot but be impressed by the evidences that assail us in our research of the continuity of development of their social life and of their psychological adaptation. The remainder of this book is dedicated to an examination of these continuities, in the expectation that this may also be a contribution to the understanding of the ninth generation.

11   Introduction

our research of the continuity of development of their social life
and of their psychological adaptation. The remainder of this
book is dedicated to an examination of that adaptation and
standing of the ninth generation.

CHAPTER 2

New Orleans Negro Society

The social background of the lives to be described and interpreted in this volume cannot be merely the recording of their contemporary settings. Such backgrounds of modern New Orleanians
are formed in patterns that can best be understood as the precipitates of history, for it is true of New Orleans, possibly more than
of some American cities of more volatile development, that its
past continues to live in its present. A survey of the nature of
contemporary New Orleans social institutions is liable to gross
misinterpretation if the eight generations of historical development that have structured the New Orleans present are not examined in broad time perspective.

This is all the more important because during the lifetime of
the individuals we have studied the environing society has undergone changes which, at least in recent years, approximate the
revolutionary. The memory of living people spans the period of
perhaps both the nadir and the zenith of conflict and harmony in
Southern race relations. The issues of segregation and integration
have been framed and have reached a level of popular significance and mass participation substantially since 1920. The social
changes brought about in recent years have a new and accelerat-
ing tempo, and have raised consequent problems for a Negro society that is, in its detailed structure at least, only beginning to
take definite form.

Creole New Orleans: The Eighteenth Century

New Orleans has been a multiracial community almost from its founding. The town itself, a small provincial outpost in the swamps during the much-romanticized period of French domination, began as a military camp with a small population of colonist-landholders, soldiers, traders, and slaves, surrounded and outnumbered by the Natchez, Choctaw, and other Indians who lived in communities almost as large as New Orleans. For a long time it was not even the chief European town in the province, Biloxi and Mobile being older and larger settlements. The Indians continued to be a serious military challenge to the settlers until only a decade or so before the Louisiana Purchase.

The social structure that developed in the colony under French rule was a distant provincial reflection of metropolitan France, conditioned by the subtropical setting, the military circumstances, and, above all, by slavery. Increasingly the importation of slaves from Africa or Santo Domingo led the colonists to rely on Negroes for the bulk of heavy labor, setting a pattern and elaborating a code which continue as factors in Louisiana life to this day.

Under the conditions of slavery, and over a period of time, the African social structure of the Negro slaves was all but destroyed. Basic features of their social life in the New World came to be patterned after European models, most frequently under laws especially adapted to their slave status. In folklore, in belief, in art forms (notably in music) there continued to be African influence, and the Africanism of these aspects of nonmaterial culture cannot be said to be gone from New Orleans Negro culture even yet.[1] In the eighteenth century, certainly, they were massively important.

The first Negro slaves were brought to New Orleans within a

---

[1] See, for example, Richard Alan Waterman, "African Influence on the Music of the Americas," in Sol Tax, ed., *Acculturation in the Americas*, Chicago, University of Chicago Press, 1952, pp. 207–218.

year or so of its founding (1718), and as early as 1721 they appear to have constituted between a third and a half of the total population of the city. Labor was to prove the chronic problem of the colony, and may even have been its fatal weakness before the nascent "manifest destiny" of the expanding United States. Slavery and subsidized colonization were the primary French and Spanish solutions to the problem, and both were used extensively.[2]

By 1763 the institution of slavery was firmly rooted in Louisiana, and the division of labor among the slaves had begun to result in the social differentiations that were to have lasting importance in New Orleans Negro society. The bulk of the slaves were used for heavy manual labor: as field hands, stevedores, and porters. A more fortunate minority were trained for skilled jobs or used as household servants, and a scant few among these were given some education, even in *belles-lettres*, and became the cooks, valets, housemaids, wet nurses, laundresses, baby sitters, teachers, and personal servants to the wealthy whites and their children.

In Louisiana, as elsewhere, slavery issued from rights of capture as well as purchase. Considerable numbers of captive Indians were absorbed into the Negro slave population of Louisiana during the eighteenth century. This development, incidentally, set the pattern for Indian-white relations in Louisiana, and the process of assimilation of Indians to Negro status is still going on with groups of so-called "Red Bones" and "Sabines" in isolated areas of the bayou country.[3] At the same time the purchase of freedom was a regular legal procedure, and the slow growth of a small but

[2] See C. Richard Arena, "A Social Study of the Land Tenure System in Spanish Louisiana," unpublished Master's thesis, New Orleans, Tulane University, 1954.

[3] For a general placement of these and other marginal population groups in modern Louisiana, see Alvin L. Bertrand, *The Many Louisianas: A Study of Rural Social Areas and Cultural Islands*, Baton Rogue, Louisiana State University Agricultural Experiment Station, June, 1955, 496:44.

critically important group of free Negroes or *gens de couleur* began under the French. The changing fortunes of this group constitute a sensitive index to the shifting condition of the Negroes
and to the nature of Negro society under the French, Spanish,
and American regimes.

The Spanish administration of New Orleans (1763–1801) was
marked by population growth and economic expansion. New
groups of immigrants arrived: the Isleños, Canary Islanders whose
descendants are still identifiable in the city's rural environs, the
refugee Acadians from Nova Scotia who came to populate all of
rural south Louisiana and to give to the area its enduring provincial French imprint,[4] the Spaniards, mostly soldiers and officials,
French Creole refugees from the slave rebellions in Santo Domingo, and at the turn of the century the first of numerous political refugees from France itself reached Louisiana. To all of these
may be added the small but significant number of "Kaintucks,"
American flatboat men, and colonists who took advantage of the
relaxation of immigration and trade policy in a Spanish colony
desperate for settlers and for commerce.

The Negro population doubled and redoubled. Further importation of slaves from Africa and the Antilles added to the natural
increase, and by 1800 the city's polyglot white population of perhaps 7,000 was more than matched by the Negro population. The
importation of the Code Noir by the French and its strict application by the Spanish may have prevented slave revolts of the Santo
Domingo type, but it also fostered the steady growth in numbers
of the *gens de couleur,* who probably represented more than a
tenth of the Negro population at the time of the Louisiana Purchase.

The Creole society that grew up under the French and Spanish
in colonial Louisiana set a pattern for social structure that was
to be modified only slowly during the century and a half of Amer-

[4] See Oscar Winzerling, *Acadian Odyssey*, Baton Rouge, Louisiana State
University Press, 1955.

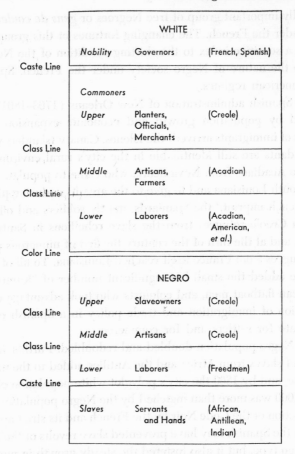

Figure 1. Creole Social Structure, 1800.

icanization following the Louisiana Purchase. The system was essentially a biracial society of three culture-castes (or semicastes) and three classes. The arrangement can be represented diagrammatically as in Figure 1.

This structure ignored other racial differences than those between white and Negro. The local Indians came to be classified as Negro (in an indefinite and ambiguous way), just as, later, Orientals came to be classed as white. The relationships be-

tween the two recognized races was that of endogamy modified
by the special legalization of hypergamous concubinage known
locally as *plaçage*. The legal and political rights of free Negroes
were not differentiated from those of free whites, although in informal social relations custom enforced a structure of white superiority. It should be noted that despite these barriers there was
no legal ceiling at this stage in history (*circa* 1800) to the achievement aspirations of free Negroes in the occupational sphere. The
system was not unlike the *evolué* system of modern French colonies in Africa.

The Noble caste was endogamous and inherited its rank within
the framework of French and Spanish nobility, but it should be
mentioned that this was a period in which nomination to the nobility was widely used in Spain to reward services to the crown,
so that social mobility was not totally lacking. Similarly, slavery
was not immutable, there being a standard legal practice of man-
umission by purchase or grant. The evidence seems to indicate
that this was fairly extensive, especially under the Spanish.

In addition to the white Noble caste and the Negro Slave caste,
there was a middle caste of white and Negro Commoners divided
into approximately three classes. The free Negro population
tended to be concentrated in the skilled trades, although there
were a few Negro slaveowners during the latter eighteenth century. Because the Negro slaves furnished most of the heavy labor,
it would appear that the number of whites and free Negroes in
the laboring class was relatively small.

There was some tendency for ethnic as well as racial differences
to become important within this framework. During the Spanish
period the American-born Spaniards and Frenchman of the
upper class of Commoners (planters, merchants, and officials)
were known, as elsewhere in colonial Latin America, as *criollos*
(French, *créoles*). The term is surrounded with controversy and
confusion. Apparently its initial significance emphasized reference to European descent, American birth, and upper-class status.
Possibly because the free Negroes came to include a large pro-

portion of "Negroes" who were also partly European by descent, born in America, and upper class in status, the term *Creoles* early came to be applied to them as well as to the upper-class whites. The white Commoners of the middle class were, by the end of the Spanish period, predominantly "Cajuns," Acadian farmers, trappers, and fishermen who have come to outnumber the other immigrant groups and have culturally absorbed them. The white lower class appears to have included "Cajuns" as well as "Kaintucks" from upriver, and no doubt remnants of the Spanish and French garrisons, men from the crews of the ships stopping at New Orleans, and Indians or *mestizos* from Latin America brought in as servants by the Spaniards.

The Negro Creoles, at least as they used the term, were predominantly mulattos of French or Spanish and African descent, born in Louisiana, and occupied as artisans, or in a few cases as slaveowners and property holders. The term was not ordinarily applied to free Negroes of the lower class (those without a "profession") or of pure or nearly pure African descent, nor to those brought in from English colonies, nor was it commonly applied to slaves, even though these were French in speech and culture and sometimes light in color.

The term "Creole" came to denote the entire society of Louisiana in the French and Spanish colonial periods, and is used today in Louisiana, as throughout the Caribbean area in English, French, Portuguese, and Spanish, in ambiguous ways, now meaning the indigenous white aristocracy, especially of French or Spanish culture, now referring to upper- or middle- (and sometimes lower-) class Negroes of French or Spanish culture. The modern New Orleans whites use the term in the first sense, the New Orleans Negroes in the second.

The Creole society of colonial Louisiana was, by law and custom, a Roman Catholic society. It was overwhelmingly French in speech and, despite 40 years of Spanish rule, in culture as well. It was highly stratified, ethnically and racially complex, with a growing plantation economy augmented by small farming, fishing, trapping, handicraft industries, and river and ocean trade. By 1800 New Orleans had a population of about 15,000, and had acquired the ideological stamp and formed the social structure that have been its romantic and aristocratic fame in the century and a half of subsequent history.

Dixie: The Nineteenth Century

During the century that followed the Louisiana Purchase there were sweeping changes in the composition of the population, the economy, and the culture of New Orleans that came finally to modify even the basic fabric of the social organization of the city. Although the structure changed, however, it was never entirely subverted, and the changes were mainly gradual and general rather than sharply defined and revolutionary. The population expanded and, during the first half of the nineteenth century at least, the economy flourished. The growth of the great cotton and sugar plantations and the river trade made New Orleans into the metropolis of the Confederacy and one of the great cities of the world. The Negro population of the city at the time of the Civil War was still about equal to the white population.

From the very beginning of the Americanization of New Orleans a shift in the caste-class-race structure of society began to appear. The disparity of power between the races, between the classes, and between the castes became accentuated. New definitions of the relations of these parts of society to each other began to be formed. Progressively, during the antebellum period, the purchase of freedom by slaves was inhibited. The economic and political rights of the free Negroes were limited. The immigration of free Negroes from other states was restricted and then outlawed. Despite disenfranchisement and economic pressure, the free and Creole Negroes gave ground but slowly, and they were never eliminated as a group.[5] Up to the time of the Civil War the direc-

[5] See Donald E. Everett, "Free Persons of Color in New Orleans, 1803–1865," unpublished doctoral dissertation, New Orleans, Tulane University, 1952.

tion of evolution of the society of the Old South was toward the creation of two color (or racial) castes, with gradual depreciation of the distinction between slave and free Negroes together with gradual augmentation of the social distance between Negro

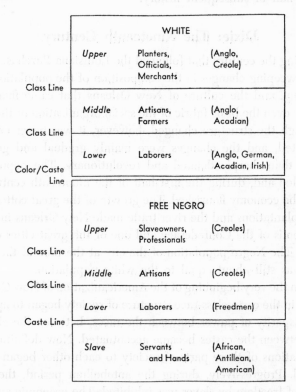

	WHITE	
Upper	Planters, Officials, Merchants	(Anglo, Creole)
Middle	Artisans, Farmers	(Anglo, Acadian)
Lower	Laborers	(Anglo, German, Acadian, Irish)
	FREE NEGRO	
Upper	Slaveowners, Professionals	(Creoles)
Middle	Artisans	(Creoles)
Lower	Laborers	(Freedmen)
Slave	Servants and Hands	(African, Antillean, American)

Figure 2. Social Structure of the Old South, 1850.

and white. The racial endogamy of the Franco-Spanish system was kept, but the hypergamous custom was reduced to a nonlegal status, thus robbing the Negro woman of the sanction and protection of law and custom that *plaçage* had guaranteed. By 1850 the social structure had reached the form diagrammed in Figure 2.

The Louisiana Purchase meant the immediate disappearance of the nobility from positions of political power in New Orleans. Socially, the city continued to recognize the European nobility just as did other American cities. By 1859 it had incorporated mock nobility and royalty into its famous Mardi Gras celebration. The caste system was reduced to two castes: slave and free. There was already a foreshadowing of the system of race castes that a defeated South was to substitute for slavery in the Reconstruction, since strenuous efforts were made to limit or eliminate the free Negroes.

The white upper class continued to be made up of the planters, merchants, and officials who constituted the economic and political leadership of the city, with the Anglo-Americans vigorously competing with the old Creole aristocracy for economic and political mastery. This was the period in which Canal Street divided the French Quarter from Anglo-Saxon New Orleans in a literal rather than an allegoric or architectural sense. German immigrants swelled the ranks of the white middle and lower classes and were gradually absorbed into the Acadian and Creole cultures of south Louisiana, as had been the Isleños before them. In the middle class, as in the upper class, the Anglo-Americans grew gradually to numerical dominance. The polyglot lower class of Creole days was swamped by the tide of Anglo, German, and Irish laborers who came in increasing numbers to the city on the eve of the Civil War.[6]

Despite the restrictions of their changing social positions, the Negro Creoles in this period went through a modest "golden age," publishing a literary review and a collection of poetry written in metropolitan if stuffy French.[7] The waning of the French influence among the whites was not matched by its decline among the free Negroes, since the legislation of the period tended to limit

[6] On this period particularly, see Roger W. Shugg, *Origins of Class Struggle in Louisiana*, Baton Rouge, Louisiana State University Press, 1939.

[7] See C. B. Rousseve, *The Negro in Louisiana: Aspects of His History and His Literature*, New Orleans, Xavier University Press, 1937, and R. L. Desdunes, *Nos hommes et notre histoire*, Montreal, Arbourt Dupont, 1911.

additions to the free Negro population from among the English-speaking slaves or freedmen of adjacent states. While declining in numbers relative to the rest of the Negro population, the Negro Creoles continued to be dominant in the upper and middle classes of free Negro society.

The slave population of New Orleans grew from around 8,000 in 1800 to about 70,000 in 1850. Slaves continued to be brought from Africa and the West Indies, but a considerable interchange of slave population took place between Louisiana and neighboring states as well. Thus the French-speaking slaves began to give way to those of English speech. The French dialect of the earlier Negro population, closely related to the "Creole" dialect of Haiti, continued to be the speech of a diminishing number of slaves and of their descendants in the New Orleans area. Associated with the "Creole" dialect was the practice of "Voodoo," first as an Afro-American public cult, later as an unsystematized set of magical beliefs and practices. Both the dialect and the cult have all but disappeared in New Orleans, though occasional echoes of voodoo may be found in family superstition, and a small number of speakers of "Creole" remain, mostly in the older generation.

The Creole society of two races, three castes, and three classes changed gradually into the society of the Old South, a system of two race-castes divided into three classes each. The ethnic complication of the social system and the growth of the city's population had begun to change the configurations of the classes, but the society of 1850 had in no way revolutionized the technology, occupational structure, or, apparently, the values of the classes. The city remained aristocratic and romantic, adding Greek Revival "cottages" and spacious plantation hospitality to the magic of grillwork balconies and provincial French *hauteur* of the legendary (but partly historical) "city that care forgot."

The Civil War and the occupation of New Orleans by Federal troops put a definitive end to slavery. The postwar administration of Louisiana affairs by governments sustained by federal rather than local power did not, however, overthrow the social structure of the city, and the eventual reassertion of "white supremacy" in the generation and a half of Reconstruction completed the evolution of the social form that had been interrupted by the Yankee invasion. The social structure of New Orleans became a system of two racial castes of three classes each, with the freed slaves taking their place in the Negro lower class. Furthermore, the bitterness generated by the war and the carpetbag reconstruction led to more conflict, hostility, and fear between the two racial castes, and to more repressive measures on the part of the white caste towards the Negro.

In the white reaction to the temporary Negro freedom of the immediate postwar period, the complete political disenfranchisement of the Negro was matched by legal and extralegal means of economic and occupational control. The tendency was toward a society in which every Negro would be politically and economically subordinate to every white. Under a legal theory of "separate but equal" Negro and white societies, much of the practice tended to reinforce the constitution of separate but ranked racial castes, as illustrated in Figure 3. The implementation of this system was not fully incorporated into law until after the turn of the century.

A consistent racial caste system was never achieved in the South. Attempts to give such a system a convincing Scriptural basis were never wholly satisfactory. Scientific or pseudo-scientific rationalizations of the system based on evolution and race theories gained widespread acceptance but proved in the long run to be untenable intellectually. Furthermore, the proliferation of occupations and the complication of the economy rendered the old class system obsolescent in the face of the industrial revolution, which had begun to catch up with the South. In the political and social ideology of the white South there remained the germ of the "integration" movement. There continued to be Negroes who were the status equals (and potential competitors) of whites in class terms (education and occupation) despite the

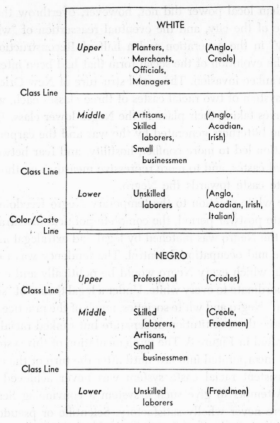

			WHITE	
	Upper	Planters, Merchants, Officials, Managers	(Anglo, Creole)
Class Line				
	Middle	Artisans, Skilled laborers, Small businessmen	(Anglo, Acadian, Irish)
Class Line				
	Lower	Unskilled laborers	(Anglo, Acadian, Irish, Italian)
Color/Caste Line				
			NEGRO	
	Upper	Professional	(Creoles)
Class Line				
	Middle	Skilled laborers, Artisans, Small businessmen	(Creole, Freedmen)
Class Line				
	Lower	Unskilled laborers	(Freedmen)

Figure 3. Social Structure of Reconstruction, 1900.

segregation of the races. Some of the most violent and deplorable racial incidents in Southern history have centered on the treatment of these Negroes, often defined as "uppity," but the group continued to exist.

The Crescent City in the Twentieth Century

The model of a society of two race-castes of three classes each continued to be descriptive of most of the facts and of the direction of movement of New Orleans society through the beginning of the twentieth century.[8] Between 1910 and 1920, however, the society changed its course. Subtly and imperceptibly at first, and with increasing tempo later, the caste barriers began to be removed and the nature of New Orleans society began to alter. After stumbling beginnings in the nineteenth century, Negro education became well organized on a broad basis in New Orleans in the twentieth. Slowly and ponderously the doors of occupational opportunity were opened to Negroes, and chances for vocational training became available. Some labor unions became interracial. More recently, since the legal supports of segregation have begun to fall, Negro participation in politics has become less dangerous. The "etiquette of race relations" has been loosened, and public segregation has been publicly broken with increasing frequency. Interracial activities have increased, and some churches have explicitly opposed religious segregation. Important civic figures, still in the unpopular minority among New Orleans whites, have taken an open stand favoring some types of integration. Segregation in public schools and state universities has been declared unconstitutional.

Societies change slowly. But contemporary New Orleans is a society in relatively rapid change. The childhood of the individuals whose lives we are describing was passed in the atmosphere of a race-caste system. Their adult life has the atmosphere of transition, with increasingly rapid elimination of the caste structure. New Orleans society began as a biracial society; it is still bi-

[8] Through the 1940's the term *caste* was used by specialists to describe briefly the social structure of race relations in the deep South. We have kept the usage, necessarily with more reservations than our predecessors, to refer to the hierarchical system of organization formerly typical of interracial social relationships. This facilitates our relating our research to the relevant classics in this field, four of which are particularly important in relation to New Orleans: Allison Davis and John Dollard, *Children of Bondage*, Washington, American Council on Education, 1940; Allison Davis and Burleigh B. and Mary R. Gardner, *Deep South: A Social Anthropological Study of Caste and Class*, Chicago, University of Chicago Press, 1941; John Dollard, *Caste and Class in a Southern Town*, New York, Harper, 1937, and Hortense Powdermaker, *After Freedom*, New York, Viking, 1939.

racial. The "integration" and "segregation" issue, which has turned
primarily on public and legal questions, is being increasingly re-
solved in favor of integration. The social structure of the city in
1950 is no longer that of a caste society. Neither is it that of a society without racial distinctions. It is essentially a biracial society
of three classes, as illustrated in Figure 4.

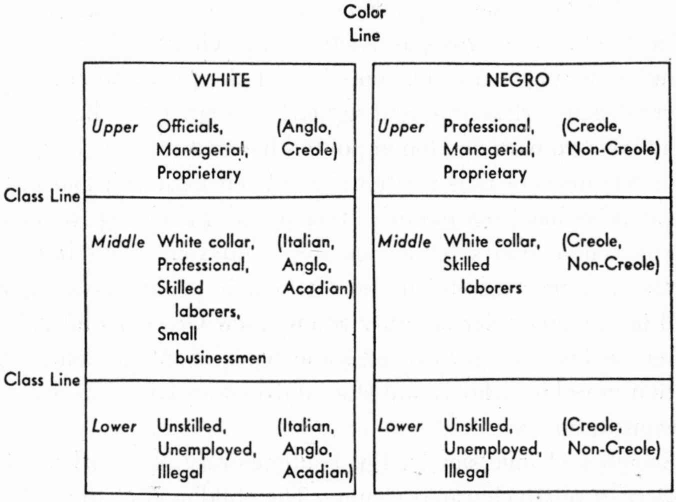

Color
Line

		WHITE				NEGRO	
Class Line	*Upper*	Officials, Managerial, Proprietary	(Anglo, Creole)		*Upper*	Professional, Managerial, Proprietary	(Creole, Non-Creole)
Class Line	*Middle*	White collar, Professional, Skilled laborers, Small businessmen	(Italian, Anglo, Acadian)		*Middle*	White collar, Skilled laborers	(Creole, Non-Creole)
	Lower	Unskilled, Unemployed, Illegal	(Italian, Anglo, Acadian)		*Lower*	Unskilled, Unemployed, Illegal	(Creole, Non-Creole)

Figure 4. Social Structure of the New South, 1950.

As might be expected, the change from a race-caste, three-class
system to a biracial three-class system is taking place in complex
ways in the complicated operations of a society that has become
modern, urban, and pluralistic. The present period of transition
has created confusion and anomalies of pattern, but the direction
of change is nonetheless uniform. Thus, for example, some labor
unions are racially mixed; others are still segregated, and some
are contemplating integration. Some schools (and some colleges
or departments in the universities) are integrated; others are
not. The disposition of the public school system is an unresolved
question in practice if not at law. The number of Negro voters in

Orleans Parish is rising steadily, although more opposition to Negro registration has been encountered in some of the other parishes.[9] Some of the churches are segregated; others are integrated. Even within denominations individual churches vary in this respect. Special boards and commissions of the city and the Southern region have come to include prominent Negroes with some regularity; others have remained segregated. These developments in a broad area of social organization are unlikely to be nullified by purely legislative action, and seem to represent the basic trend of custom and attitudes.

Perhaps the most important structural aspect of these changes for the overall form of society is the fact that there are increasingly frequent contacts of class equals across racial lines. Under the caste system, the pattern of relations was such that whites met Negroes overwhelmingly as social inferiors: the upper-class whites met lower-class Negroes as servants; the upper- and middle-class Negroes were particularly isolated from white contacts. Increasingly today, Negro leaders are meeting white leaders, especially in educational and political contexts, and the desegregation of unions, of churches, and of schools tends to extend this relationship to other class levels. Thus, while the society has become a biracial class society, the social definition of what "race" implies is still in process of reformulation.

A dramatic illustration of the changing structure of society in New Orleans was a recent united protest of Negro parents in the city against continued segregation of school children at the McDonogh Day observance.[10] John McDonogh, a Baltimore-born New Orleanian and a wealthy slaveowner of the antebellum period, in 1850 left his considerable fortune to the public school systems of New Orleans and Baltimore. The generosity of the bequest is customarily celebrated by New Orleans school children in

[9] Surprisingly there are rural parishes in which Negro registration is proportionally higher than in New Orleans, too. See John H. Fenton, "Negro Voting in Louisiana," *Research in Action,* October, 1956, pp. 1–6.

[10] The account that follows draws largely on the *Louisiana Weekly, passim,* January–May, 1954.

an annual observance at City Hall. In January, 1954, a group of
Negro parents protested the segregated "white children first" arrangement of the customary celebration, and preliminary plans
were laid for Negro and white children to march simultaneously
in two separate lines past the McDonogh monument facing City
Hall. The abrogation of this agreement by the school board, allegedly at the instance of the city Chief of Police, brought strong
protests from Negro leaders, and occasioned unified action by the
PTA Council of the Negro schools, the Orleans (Negro) Principals' Association, the New Orleans League of (Negro) Classroom
Teachers, representatives of the Louisiana State Conference for
Labor Education, the New Orleans branch of the NAACP, the
Orleans Parish Progressive (Negro) Voters' League, the Teamsters' Local 965, and the Interdenominational (Negro) Ministerial Alliance, as well as local professional people and the Negro
press. A movement to boycott the observance gained headway,
and on McDonogh Day (May 14) only 34 of approximately 32,-
000 Negro children in the public schools attended the ceremonies.

Since this represents the first occasion in the history of New Orleans on which its Negro population has ever done anything
spontaneously as a group, it is particularly revealing of the social
changes that have already taken place. The individualistic atomism that characterizes Negro society through most of the United
States, weakening Negro organizations and isolating the Negro
individual, has been overcome in this instance by organized
group action. Only in the last generation have the Negroes of
New Orleans built the social system that has made this symbolic
action possible. The organization of the protest deserves closer
scrutiny, since it reveals a great deal about the Negro society that
twentieth-century New Orleans has created.

Contemporary Social Institutions

As we have seen, the structure of New Orleans society in its
broadest aspects is the end product of a long, slow evolution from
the more or less rigid culture-caste system of the eighteenth-cen-

tury Creole society, which was based upon national and cultural differences, through the even more rigid racial caste system of the Old South, the Confederacy, and nineteenth-century Reconstruction, to the more flexible class and color system of the twentieth century. In this broad aspect, modern New Orleans society has considerable time depth.

In striking contrast with the mature growth and development that have taken place in New Orleans society generally, the most characteristic feature of Negro society in the city is the recency of its organization in one institution after another. With few exceptions, the more detailed institutional forms of Negro society in New Orleans—the family, the schools, the churches, political factions, labor unions, business enterprises, social clubs and fraternal organizations, and the neighborhoods—are predominantly the products of twentieth-century growth and development. Few indeed of the organizations peculiar to New Orleans Negro society can trace their founding to before 1910.

It is important, also, to note that many Negro institutions and organizations have not developed naturally as means of satisfying the indigenous needs of Negroes as such, but for the most part have borrowed their structure, ritual, and form from white society. However, the institutional and organizational forms that were effective in white society frequently proved to be relatively ineffectual in satisfying the peculiar needs of the socially and economically submerged Negro masses. Consequently, as we shall see, many of the borrowed social forms have had to be modified in order to meet these needs effectively. In discussing the organization and development of contemporary social forms in the Negro community it is important to keep in mind the fact that their structure has been strongly conditioned, at first by slavery, and later by the social, economic, and political restrictions that are still features of the biracial society of New Orleans.

THE FAMILY IN NEW ORLEANS

A strong and stable Negro family was difficult or impossible to achieve under the system of slavery. Slaveowners frequently sold more men than women because women were valuable both for their work and for childbearing. It was hardly possible for the slaves to maintain the lifelong pledge of loyalty and fidelity to one mate that is the very foundation of the Western European family. Some masters did attempt to safeguard the virginity of their slaves and even insisted upon marriage between sexual partners, but more often slavery fostered promiscuity and left Negro women unprotected before the sexual exploitation of both Negro and white males. The slave woman alone was responsible for the welfare of her children. She had no choice but to assume the role of mistress of her cabin and her wishes in regard to her child and household were paramount.[11]

Slavery, then, gave rise to a matriarchal type of family among Negroes. Even after emancipation the differential impact of racial discrimination upon Negro men and Negro women made a stable patriarchal family difficult to achieve. The Negro man has had little incentive to accept the burdening responsibilities of a husband and father. Economically he has continued to be severely restricted. Thus throughout the latter part of the nineteenth century (and in some places well into the twentieth) the majority of Negro mothers were forced to support themselves and their children without outside help. Today, after decades of legal freedom, many Negro men are still reluctant to assume full responsibility for the support of their wives and children, while many Negro matriarchs evince unwillingness to surrender the independence to which they have grown accustomed. The matriarchs follow in the footsteps of their mothers, and the matriarchal family remains prevalent among New Orleans Negroes, especially in the lower class.

The matriarchal family is held together by at least two very strong bonds: economic interdependence of mothers and daughters, and emotional ties forged by recurrent personal and family crises. Among the cardinal mores in Negro society is the guarantee that mothers will always provide for and protect their children,

[11] E. Franklin Frazier, *The Negro Family in the United States*, Chicago, University of Chicago Press, 1939.

and that daughters will care for their aged mothers. Even a starving mother who abandons her children is regarded as having "committed an unpardonable crime against the natural dictates of the human heart,"[12] and the emotional bonds between daughter and mother are usually stronger than those between wife and husband. Sometimes the Negro matriarchs are ambitious for their daughters, regarding them as a form of old age insurance. Mothers have been known to make great sacrifices to get their daughters well married, or educated—doubtless an important factor in the preponderance of women among Negro college graduates.

Since many of the circumstances that influenced the structure of the Negro family during slavery and the crisis period following emancipation are still present and are still experienced in some measure by all Negroes regardless of their social class, the New Orleans Negro family at all levels is considerably more matricentric than the New Orleans white family. However, the middle- and upper-class Negro family tends more and more to approximate that of middle-class whites: a nuclear kinship unit held together by a relatively stable marriage and rarely including other relatives. It seems certain that with increasing economic security the Negro male will tend to assume greater and greater authority over the family. The middle-class family, in which both the husband and wife are usually employed in stable white-collar or professional jobs, may best be described as egalitarian. It is much more stable than the lower-class family because it is supported by an explicit ideology opposing divorce and equalizing both the rights and responsibilities of husband and wife. Though both parents are regarded as responsible for the rearing of the children, the husband is regarded as the chief provider, and the wife as the main homemaker.

THE CHURCH

Aside from the family, perhaps the oldest and best-established institution in New Orleans Negro society is the church. New Or-

[12] *Ibid.*, p. 143.

leans is unique among American cities in having a large proportion of Catholics in its Negro population. The Americanization of
the city introduced both the white and the Negro populations of
the first half of the nineteenth century to religious diversity. The
splitting of the Northern and Southern Protestant churches before
the Civil War led to the pattern of independent Negro churches,
the Baptist and Methodist denominations engaging the loyalties
of the vast majority of Southern Negroes. This pattern of segregation was followed variously by the Presbyterian, Episcopalian,
Lutheran, Congregational, and Christian Science churches in the
South. In the Roman Catholic church, on the other hand, there
was no actual break although segregation of whites and Negroes
within individual churches came to be the universal practice,
and in some cases particular parishes became more or less formally "Negro" or "white." Segregated Negro attendance at white
churches other than the Catholic was continued, but was distinctly
a minor mode in the religious organization of New Orleans.

The leadership of Negro Protestant ministers came to be the
most reliable social form in Negro society outside of kinship during the latter part of the nineteenth century and continues to be
a major feature of a society widely renowned for deep religious
feeling. The Catholic Church has begun to provide a similar religious outlet through the ordination of local Negro priests in recent years, but very few of these serve local parishes, and none
has become a local leader. The Catholic Church has not only
maintained its organizational independence of the caste system
(by not setting up an African Catholic Church); it has provided
real leadership among the whites, especially recently, in the "integration" of New Orleans society. This is of particular importance for New Orleans, where the Catholic Church has the largest white membership of any denomination. Within Negro society,
Catholic influence has been exerted primarily through white
priests and Negro laymen. The Negro ministers in the Protestant denominations, and especially the Baptist and Methodist
Churches, have come to be important leaders even in the political sphere.

In a real sense the church is the oldest and most effective Negro "uplift" organization, and several separate uplift movements have been, to a greater or lesser degree, nurtured by the churches. Although members of the lower-class Negro churches have not as much social consciousness and are not as vocal about bettering the lot of Negroes as are members of the middle class, all Negro churches concern themselves with racial advancement.

It is difficult to derive an accurate estimate of the religious affiliations in any population. Alternatives of counting membership, church attendance, or individual profession of choice give widely differing results. For the Negro population of New Orleans, furthermore, no explicit figures are available. The New Orleans Negro population that is religiously active is predominantly Baptist (over 300 churches, possibly 100,000 "members"), and Methodist (over 170 churches, possibly 34,000 "members"). Probably some 10 percent of New Orleans' 300,000 Catholics are Negro. (The Negro population of New Orleans in 1950 was 181,755.)[13] Even these crude figures should be interpreted with caution. Shifting or ambiguous religious allegiance is relatively common. Some individuals have been joining the Protestant sects in recent years to escape the rigor of the Catholic Church with respect to divorce. Many children of Protestant families attend Catholic schools. Different religious affiliations among the members of the same family are common, and in some cases individuals will be simultaneously Catholic and Protestant, attending churches of either denomination or using forms drawn electically from both. Deep religious feeling and staunch church membership are widespread. So is religious indifference.

Many of the churches serve as centers of organized social activity, and the elaboration of institutions—of choirs, men's societies, ladies' aid societies, teen clubs, vestries, etc.—reaches considerable proportions. One large Baptist church (recently completed at a reported cost of $295,000) is organized around a deacon

[13] A reliable religious census has not been taken in New Orleans in many years. The figures cited constitute an informed guess, based on Stuart O. Landry, ed., *Louisiana Almanac and Fact Book, 1953, 1954,* New Orleans, American Printing Co., 1954, p. 545.

board, two deaconess boards, a missionary society, a Busy Bee Club, a senior choir, a young people's choir, a midweek choir, two usher boards, a Sunday School, a youth group, a young women's league, and a Beautification Club. Not all the churches are as wealthy nor as elaborately organized, of course, but a considerable part of the organized social life of the Negro community is structured in organizations of this type.

The structure of the one church just mentioned is elaborate, but characteristic of the organizations to be found in individual congregations. Broader organizations unify some of these: the youth groups (Hi-Y, Junior Hi-Y, Gra-Y), the sodalities (organized into the New Orleans Union of Sodalities) of the Catholic churches, and in the Protestant denominations such nationally affiliated groups as the Wesleyan Service Guild, the National Baptist Laymen, the Baptist Young People's Union, the American Alliance for the Development of Christian Culture, the Freedmen Baptist Association, or the Women's Society of Christian Service.[14]

THE SCHOOL

In Creole New Orleans education was little organized and narrowly distributed in the population. Nevertheless, it appears that some of the free Negroes were able to achieve a measure of education. In a few cases they were sent to France to complete specialized training. For most of the Negro population, however, education was well out of reach, and the mass of the population, white as well as Negro, remained illiterate. This pattern continued into the nineteenth century, and the first public schools (1841) did not admit Negroes. At one point (1830) it was made illegal to teach a slave to read or write. Private instruction remained the primary source of education for the few Negroes who could afford it until the Civil War, although the founding of the "Couvent School" in 1848 presaged a gradual growth in private

[14] For a description of a Catholic Negro parish, see Charles Palazzolo, "Corpus Christi: a Sociological Study of a Catholic Negro Parish in New Orleans," unpublished Master's thesis, Baton Rouge, Louisiana State University, 1955.

schools during the latter part of the century. The first public schools admitting Negroes were organized by the Federal Army during its occupation of the city (1861–1865), but even during its stay the organization of the system was erratic and the attendance relatively small.

Negro education developed slowly in New Orleans, and it was not until the present generation that schooling became a part of the normal experience of most Negro children. Increasingly, however, New Orleans Negroes came to value education as a path to success and social mobility, if not to salvation itself, and the schools have continued to grow and to improve. In 1954, at the time of the Supreme Court decision on public school segregation, they were still separate, and still not equal, despite very extensive building and remodeling. The use of the same buildings by two "platoons" of school children a day was still common, the physical plants of many of the schools were still in serious disrepair, and the school board and principals struggled with the problem of maintaining and raising standards against widespread absenteeism and the pressures of economic necessity on both the students and the school administrators.

Despite these problems in New Orleans Negro education, events have conspired to give the teachers in the schools an extraordinary voice in the affairs of the Negro community. The Negro teachers receive an income appreciably more secure and more nearly adequate than that of the bulk of the Negro population. They enjoy higher prestige, not being swamped, as in white society, by a large number of better paid professionals, businessmen, officials, and the like. There is evidence that where white parents tend to hold strong views about what the teacher should and should not do to and for their children, many Negro parents, especially in the large lower class, are sensitively respectful to the teachers' opinions and attitudes as relayed by their children. The importance of the teacher as a social leader is underlined by the McDonogh Day protest.

The tradition of private and parochial school education is well established in New Orleans. In 1950 Negroes were 32 percent of the total population of the city, but Negro children were 38 percent of the children in public school. About half of the white children and a fifth of the Negro children were in private schools, almost all of these being Catholic schools. Wholesale attendance at school, even despite some inadequacies in the school system, has worked and is working a nearly revolutionary change in New Orleans' social life. Only in the last few years have high school educational facilities even approximated adequacy for the Negro children of the city, but there is a growing pressure to find jobs for young people who are getting more training. Vocational career clinics at some of the high schools have indicated realistically the occupational areas in which Negro graduates may seek employment: agricultural and industrial research, the armed forces, photography, building trades, business administration, clerical occupations, hospital trades, home economics, medicine, law, radio, social work, teaching, art, athletics, beauty culture, entertainment, music, and nursing. The "even if" argument sometimes heard from white employers is being rendered obsolete by the growth of special training in a more adequately educated Negro population.

Political turmoil has come to center on the public schools as a phase of the segregation and integration battle. Louisiana's legislature has passed extreme legal measures to preserve the structure of segregation. There are signs, however, that regardless of the detailed arrangements made in New Orleans to fulfill the requirements of the federal courts, both white and Negro New Orleanians will continue the trend toward broader application in practice of the universal free and public education theory. There is probably no other aspect of social life that engages more completely the attention and interest of the Negro population: it is no accident that the McDonogh Day protest focused on the schools.

In addition to the formal organization of the schools themselves, there is an extensive organization of student clubs and extracurricular activities. The Y-teen clubs are particularly noteworthy.

There is a further proliferation of organizations to incorporate the parents of students, alumni, and others outside the formal school organization. These include the Parent-Teachers Associations, and other parents' associations (even of dance schools or high school bands), the alumni associations, especially of Dillard and Xavier Universities and some of the older high schools, and such action groups as the Modern Schools Development Association or the Citizens' Committee for Grade A Schools. The activities of the PTA organizations are consolidated in the city-wide PTA Council. The university organizations are partly coördinated by such associations as the Inter-Alumni Council and the local chapter of the National Association of College Women.

The emergence of these synthetic associations is perhaps the clearest indication of growing structure and stability in New Orleans Negro society. One such organization, United Clubs, Inc., which started as a voluntary effort on the part of five Mardi Gras clubs and a musicians' union in sponsoring a charity ball for the United Negro College Fund, has developed in strength and influence and is now a significant racial uplift organization. The influence of this organization was dramatically illustrated during the 1957 Carnival season when its members led a "blackout of Negro entertainment" in sympathy with Negroes in Montgomery and Tallahassee who were then boycotting streetcars and buses. A member of this group coined the slogan that "It is immoral for New Orleans Negroes to dance while Montgomery Negroes walk." Carnival clubs were asked to contribute whatever money they had budgeted for balls to some organization fighting for civil rights, such as the NAACP, and almost all of them did so.

THE NEIGHBORHOOD

Residential segregation of the races in New Orleans is a recent and restricted phenomenon. The complex pattern of growth forced on the city by its swampland site and the early custom of quartering slaves on the premises of their masters has led to a modern population distribution in which few neighborhoods are exclusively white or exclusively Negro.[15] Political or school district gerrymandering can have but little reference to the racial division of the population.

The growth of significant neighborhood groupings within the Negro population, however, is a salient feature of its social life. The broadest of these divisions is that between Uptown and Downtown, the former being stereotypically associated with the Negro servants of the white Garden District, the latter being equated with the Negro Creoles.[16] Negro "Main Street" might be said to be Dryades Street, although historic Rampart Street shares in this honor. Many of the local and neighborhood divisions of the city, such as the West Bank or the Carrollton area, are significant regionally for both white and Negro society. Others, such as Milneburg, Girt Town, or Fazendeville, are primarily Negro groupings.

To some degree the neighborhoods are class-defined: London Avenue, certain sections of the Uptown area, Pontchartrain Park, and the vicinity of Dillard University might be considered upper or middle class. Many of them are homogeneous by class but racially mixed.[17] Amicable interracial neighborhood relations and racial gang warfare among older children are both found with some frequency in the mixed lower-class neighborhoods.

The significance of neighborhood groupings, at least historically, is indicated by the pattern of violence (found also in other

[15] See Harlan W. Gilmore *et al.*, eds., *New Orleans Population Handbook: 1950*, New Orleans, Urban Life Research Institute, Tulane University, 1953.

[16] On the Uptown neighborhood see George A. Hillery, "The Presence of Community among the Urban Negro: a Case Study of a Selected Area in New Orleans," unpublished Master's thesis, Baton Rouge, Louisiana State University, 1951; and George A. Hillery, "The Negro in New Orleans: a Demographic Analysis," unpublished doctoral dissertation, Baton Rouge, Louisiana State University, 1954. For a study of one segment of Creole society see Kara F. Rousseau, "Cultural Patterns of Colored Creoles: a Study of a Selected Segment of New Orleans Negroes with French Cultural Orientations," unpublished Master's thesis, Baton Rouge, Louisiana State University, 1955.

[17] An extended account of residence patterns is given in Forrest E. La-Violette and Joseph Taylor, "Negro Housing and the New Orleans Community," Berkeley, Commission on Race and Housing, 1958, mimeographed.

parts of the Caribbean area) among carnival gangs—in New Orleans the "Indian tribes" and the "Baby Dolls"—although the violence has disappeared from this activity in the present generation. Some 25 "Indian tribes," organized primarily on a neighborhood basis, still appear occasionally on Mardi Gras in gorgeously sequinned Sioux costumes, and dance through the streets to traditional calypso war chants. The Baby Dolls, Zigaboos, and Gold Diggers who often accompany them are apparently the relic of historic rival gangs of uptown and downtown prostitutes, who "walk raddy" (a sensuous undulation) and "shake on down" as they parade informally on Mardi Gras.[18]

Most of the school- and church-centered activities are also structured by neighborhood, and regionalism is important in the constitution of such political action groups as the Ninth Ward Civic Improvement Association, and of many of the social clubs. Regionalism and neighborhood groupings are important in both Negro and white social structure. The groupings overlap, never being completely segregated and autonomous spatially, and never completely coinciding. Significant interracial contacts in neighborhood groups appear to be more common between the white and Negro lower classes than between the upper and middle classes of the two groups.

THE BUSINESS FIRM

As has been roughly indicated in the diagrams of New Orleans' changing class structure, there has been in recent years a considerable expansion and complication of the occupational organization of the city, and Negroes have shared in this on an increasing scale. This is a recent development, restricted perhaps to the present century, for heavy manual labor, domestic work, and the small industry of the artisan have made up, historically, the bulk of the employment of Negroes in New Orleans.

The organizational forms of this economic system have tradi-

[18] A somewhat oblique description is given in Robert Tallant, *Mardi Gras,* Garden City, Doubleday, 1947.

tionally centered on individual enterprise, individual ownership, and individual competition. There is little mention of business companies, partnerships, guilds, or unions in historical accounts of the life of New Orleans' free Negro population. There seems to be a legacy of this atomism even in the modern organization of Negro business, though this is changing. Corporate organization of businesses has not yet resulted in any overwhelming concentration of economic power. The funeral-life insurance companies prominent in the Negro business world still tend to be primarily family-owned and directed, and both their financing and their management are dependent on the dominant individuals who found and expand them. Orderly transmission of wealth and economic power through inheritance or incorporation has yet to become a tradition. Litigation within the family for control or ownership is not uncommon. As is true to a considerable extent of the individual Protestant church communities, Negro companies appear to be the creation of individuals rather than quasi-public institutions. To the traditional occupations of the skilled trades, the middle- and upper-class Negroes have added small-scale trade (largely retail), and some "service" businesses (such as night clubs, hotels, and Negro taxi services). Dealerships and agencies for white companies are becoming common. An independent Negro press, radio, university, and hospital have been established, and there has been some talk of a Negro bank.

The business structure of the Negro community is still primarily local and, by comparison with large state and national corporations, extremely simple and small scale. Exploitation of the potential Negro market is vigorously contested by white enterprises, while Negro business makes no corresponding dent on the white market. Efforts on the part of the Negro Business League and individual Negro leaders to encourage support of Negro concerns have had little direct effect, but many white-operated companies have demonstrated their sensitivity to these efforts by substantially increasing the number of Negro salesmen and public relations representatives they employ. The vast majority of Negroes

are still employed in institutions and agencies owned and oper-
ated by whites, and the stability of much of the local economic
system makes it likely that this will be true for some time to come.

THE UNION AND THE GUILD

Just as the organization of business corporations, partnerships,
dealerships, and other enterprises has been modest and recent
among the upper- and middle-class Negroes of New Orleans, the
organization of guilds and the labor union movement in the middle and lower class is late and limited. Nonetheless, labor unions,
trade guilds, professional associations, and similar societies may
be said to have burgeoned in New Orleans in the last decade. In
addition to the unions of teamsters, longshoremen, construction
workers, hotel and club employees, postal employees, sleeping
car porters, beauty operators, musicians, bricklayers, and clothing
workers, there are important associations of classroom teachers,
principals, coaches, druggists, funeral directors and embalmers,
practical nurses, and doctors. In most cases the founders and original leaders of these organizations are still living; in many cases
they are still the leaders of the groups.

Despite their recency and the as yet limited success of the
movement toward occupational organization, the unions and
professional societies have already come to play an important role
in Negro society. Partly, no doubt, because of the relative fluidity
of class lines and the absence of strong Negro managerial associations, the leaders of the labor unions have become important
social leaders. Their prominence in the organization of the Mc-
Donogh Day action is noteworthy, and they are almost equally
conspicuous in a broad range of community affairs outside of
strictly union business.

That union members expect more than a good contract arrangement from their leaders is illustrated by the platforms of the
candidates in a hotly contested campaign for the presidency of
one of the longshoremen's unions held in 1956 (a union, incidentally, considered to be the strongest Negro local in the country).

The campaign was won by a fighter who kept himself in the headlines through vigorous opposition to the "right to work" (anti-closed shop) bill pending before the state legislature, and through indignant protests over the procedures of the unemployment compensation office. Several candidates indicated sensitivity to members' desires for age and death benefits, college scholarships for longshoremen's children, medical care, and rank and file control of the local. The unions tend to take on "social" and recreational functions, though these are sometimes distinct, as in the Nurses' Aide Birthday Club or the Estelle Hubbard Nurses' Club.

THE FACTION

As has been true of modern white Louisiana, Negro politics in New Orleans constitutes a politics of faction rather than of party.[19] During the last decade, the number of registered Negro voters has risen from almost zero to about 27,000 and the Negro press and NAACP are striving for a New Orleans vote of 50,000. Encouraged by the election of Negroes to public office elsewhere in the South (including two councilmen in Crowley, Louisiana), New Orleans Negroes have begun to run for governor, state representative, and city councilman. Twenty-seven thousand Negro voters hold the political balance of power in New Orleans in a close election, and although the factional division of the Negro vote reduces its potential racial significance somewhat, white candidates seek the public endorsement of prominent Negroes and Negro organizations with increasing frequency. In the 1956 elections an unusually united stand by Negro voters made their votes the margin of victory in both the gubernatorial and presidential elections in New Orleans.

Important in the growth of political machinery are such hetero-

[19] An excellent discussion of the general character of Louisiana politics is given in V. O. Key, Jr., *Southern Politics in State and Nation*, New York, Knopf, 1949, pp. 156–182. For New Orleans see Leonard Reissman, K. H. Silvert, and Cliff W. Wing, Jr., *The New Orleans Voter: a Handbook of Political Description*, New Orleans, Tulane Studies in Political Science, Vol. 2, 1955.

geneous organizations as the Ninth Ward Civic and Improvement Association, the People's Republican Club, the Seventeenth Ward Dunbar Community Improvement Association, the People's Defense League, the Orleans Parish Progressive Voters' League, the Second Ward United Voters' League, and surprisingly, the Interdenominational Ministerial Alliance. None of the Negro political associations can yet be called a true pressure group, but some associations have programs which tend in that direction: e.g., playground associations, better schools clubs, and such other organizations as the Better Jobs for Negroes in New Orleans Association.

THE LODGES

Among the clubs not primarily associated with one or another of the institutions already treated are the fraternal lodges and their associated (or independent) auxiliaries. The primary lodge organizations are the Prince Hall Masons (and the associated Order of Eastern Star), the Elks Club, the Knights of Pythias, the Scottish Rite Masons, the Odd Fellows and Daughters of Ruth, the Knights of Honor of America, the Benevolent Daughters of Louisiana, and the (Catholic) Knights of Peter Claver and its auxiliary. Masonry in particular enjoys an old if schismatic history in Negro Louisiana, the Grand Consistory of Louisiana of the Ancient Accepted Scottish Rite of Freemasonry, for example, dating from 1814. Many of these groups have numerous chapters within New Orleans. The Prince Hall Masons have 15 lodges and an estimated membership of 2,000 in the city.

In addition to their recreational and ritual activities, all the organizations listed above make some contribution to the "uplift" movement in Negro society. Most, perhaps all, of their regional and national bodies have adopted resolutions condemning racial segregation and discrimination. Further, they have pledged themselves to one or more specific uplift programs: scholarships are provided for potential Negro leaders and professional students (especially in medicine); leadership training institutes are organized and supervised; and mass meetings are held to stimulate racial consciousness and pride, support Negro businesses, and encourage wider participation of Negroes in the political life of their communities through voting and candidacy in local, state, and national elections.

FRATERNITIES AND SORORITIES

Organized mainly around the universities are a number of fraternities and sororities. Among these are: Alpha Kappa Alpha, Alpha Phi Alpha, Delta Sigma Theta, Zeta Phi Beta, Kappa Alpha Psi, Sigma Gamma Rho, Phi Beta Sigma, Phi Delta Kappa, and Omega Psi Phi (this last with an "auxiliary" called the Quettes). The Panhellenic Boule, composed of outstanding fraternity members, is a special, high-prestige superfraternity. The alumni chapters of these organizations are particularly active in social and uplift activities. The veterans' organizations are also fraternal in type, although they frequently act as political pressure groups as well. The American Legion, Veterans of Foreign Wars, and Spanish American War Veterans are all represented. Among youth groups, the Boy Scouts also have the fraternal type of organization; it would appear that their membership is not large.

THE "SOCIAL" CLUBS

A large number of clubs in the city have diffuse recreational, "cultural," insurance and benefit, or hobby interests. Although various of these related purposes are expressed in the titles or stated aims of the organizations, the vast majority of them appear to be primarily recreational. They are mainly small and ephemeral groups with an average membership of around fifteen. A large number of the purely "social" clubs, including some of the longest-lived and highest-prestige clubs, make a point of holding a masquerade ball at Mardi Gras, but most of them are not uniquely Carnival organizations.[20] News of the doings of more

[20] It is worthy of special mention that the well-known Zulu Aid and Pleasure Club, while important in its own right, is neither typical of these organizations nor particularly prominent in Negro social life.

than 140 of these clubs is carried in the Negro newspapers. Almost 70 percent of them are women's organizations and most of the remainder include women members. Teas, parties, luncheons, and balls are typical activities. Seven bridge and whist clubs (pokeno is also popular), two garden clubs, two art clubs, and a music club should be mentioned as additional "social" clubs. A few of these organizations emphasize a dedication to thrift (The Ellen Christmas Savings Club or The Sons and Daughters of Zion Social and Savings Club). There are good indications that the "social" clubs are class-stratified to a considerable degree.

ATHLETIC ORGANIZATIONS

Both participation and spectatorship in many sports are widely popular among New Orleans Negroes. On the local scene football, basketball, and track are organized primarily around the schools and colleges, and around the YMCA, YWCA, and the New Orleans Recreation Department. These include league competitions within the city, the state, and the region, and are largely segregated. Baseball, swimming, amateur boxing, tennis, and some minor sports are similarly organized. There is one local private athletic club, and a professional Negro baseball team, and professional boxing and wrestling are also popular. These sports endeavors are more or less commercially organized. Much recent controversy has centered on the segregated organization of some of these sports, particularly baseball and boxing. A recent and controversial state law attempted to resolve the anomalies by an affirmation of total segregation, but it has been ruled unconstitutional.

Spectatorship and other passive participation in sports is of course subject to somewhat less legal or customary control, especially since the advent of television, and national sports contests are closely followed. The Negro press reports scrupulously the careers of Negroes who have attained stardom in sports and large numbers of fans appear to follow the press with equal care. Attendance at most local arenas, stadiums, and playing fields is still usually segregated. The organization of horse racing is in white hands, but legal and illegal betting on the races is an old and popular diversion for Negro as well as white New Orleanians.

In addition to sports as such, recreational activities in the Negro community are stimulated by the schools and colleges, the YMCA and YWCA, and the New Orleans Recreation Department in arts and crafts, drama, and similar fields, and annual celebrations are organized by such agencies as the Louisiana State Fair Committee, the New Orleans Creole Fiesta Association, and the New Orleans Mardi Gras Association.

COMMUNITY SERVICE ORGANIZATIONS

Community service agencies tend to be primarily organized around the churches and the schools. There is a community betterment plank, however, in the constitution of many other groups: the labor organizations, the business clubs, the lodges, the political groups, and even a great many of the purely "social" clubs. Some organizations, such as the Universal Negro Improvement Association, the Cercle de Service, and the Community Volunteer Service, emphasize this as a primary aim. Generally Negro organizations participate in the March of Dimes, the United Fund, and similar community campaigns.

In addition to these, an increasing number of Negro leaders are beginning to participate in governmentally sponsored programs of welfare and community service. Such organizations as the Advisory Committee on the Children's Bureau Adoption Program, the Mayor's Housing Study Committee, the Advisory Safety Committee, and the Department of Public Welfare have come to include Negro participation. Nevertheless Negro leaders complain that they are still generally ignored in basic community planning.

The facilities currently available for care of the Negro needy— orphans, the aged, the indigent, cripples, invalids, unmarried mothers, and so forth, are not yet adequate, and there is little development of specifically Negro institutions for this purpose.

The main burden falls on the governmental services and on a few private social work agencies, and it is a very heavy burden indeed.

In the field of community service, however, the contribution of the Negro YMCA and YWCA is unique and invaluable. As a center for athletics, dramatics, handicrafts and hobbies, discussion groups and supervised play, the "Y" is highly organized and involves participation of a broad section of all classes. It has become almost an institution rather than one organization among many, and the annual drives for membership and support for the "Y" program attract the attention of the whole community.

THE STATE AND THE NATION

Formal participation of Negroes in the political organization of Louisiana has not existed in this century. It is no surprise, therefore, to find the organization of Negro society at the state level somewhat restricted. When we recall the recency and fragility of more local institutions, it is perhaps surprising that there is any statewide organization of Negro society at all. Extension of organization to a regional or a national base is *a fortiori* noteworthy and important. Increasingly, state, regional and national organizations are coming to play an important part in Negro life.

This broader organization has taken place primarily in relation to the hierarchies and laymen's organizations of the "African" churches, the nationally affiliated labor unions, the regional and national professional organizations, the national councils of lodges, fraternities, and sororities, regional and national programs in athletics, and, above all, the National Association for the Advancement of Colored People. The role of the Negro press in shaping these broader affiliations is uniquely important.

The potential significance of these organizations would be hard to overestimate, especially in a period when power and issues seem more and more displaced to the national stage. It is worth noting, therefore, that there are weaknesses as well as strengths to this structure. The lack of large corporate businesses (despite the existence of business associations, for example, for life insurance executives) and the fragmentation of political organization (with the partial exception of the 1956 presidential election) are perhaps the most salient of these. It remains true that prominent individual Negroes may still speak for "the Negro" with as much authority as representative officials of a duly constituted formal organization. Ralph Bunche or Jackie Robinson or Adam Powell may carry as much weight in some respects as even so widely respected an official as Thurgood Marshall.

Though the significance of wider geographic integration of Negro society is potentially very great, it remains more potential than actual. Many Negro associations are going through crises of leadership and organization, and few indeed have managed to relate themselves firmly to local communities. For most New Orleans Negroes, therefore, these higher echelons of institutional life tend to be relatively peripheral and unimportant.

Class Cultures

The importance of "classes" in modern complex civilizations is that they represent cultural constellations, rising and falling, solidifying and changing with the ebb and flow of social movements, in a framework of social structure. They thus approximate the independence of development—what might be called the historical autonomy—of temporally or geographically distinct cultures. That this autonomy is never really complete is perhaps the most massive induction that can be made from the facts of culture history. Yet even a partial historical autonomy has recognizable concomitants.

In the constitution, emergence, decline, and disappearance of class cultures, one of the clearest social elements is the rule of marriage and descent. Classes become distinct as they become endogamous. They maintain their distinctness through the inheritance of status. It is correspondingly true that classes become blurred when social mobility increases, whether through mobile marriage or the recognition of individual achievement. Class represents, in this sense, a synthetic configuration of social and biological inheritance, and it is because we perceive the correlation of the social-historical factors with the biological framework that we find it useful to isolate a "class" as a "culture."

We have seen that the biological makeup of the New Orleans "Negro" group can be traced to African, European, and American Indian ancestors, in that order of genetic importance. Furthermore, racial mixture has occurred in structured ways: hypergamously between white men and Negro women, promiscuously between Negro slaves and Indian slaves, preferentially (in *plaçage*) between upper-class white men and Negro Creole women. Nor has mating been random within the changing "Negro" group, the social structure of the time having an important bearing upon mating choice in each historical period. Class, caste, and color have played an important part.

The broad outlines of the social continuity corresponding to this biological continuity have been sketched. Briefly, we may say that the two correspond in the creation of the culture of the Creole Negroes around the middle of the eighteenth century, and that the breakdown of class endogamy and of transmission of class prerogatives by inheritance in the later nineteenth century have resulted in the modern scattering of the Creoles as a class: they have not been displaced, wiped out, nor eliminated. They have simply been dissipated. "Creoles" in many different senses still exist among the Negroes of New Orleans, but they are no longer a distinct cultural, biological, or social group. Rather, the division of New Orleans Negroes in Civil War times into "Creoles," "Freedmen," and "Slaves" has grown into a new structure of middle and lower classes. The new structure is related to the old by both biological and social heredity, but it has involved a redefinition of the classes, a redistribution of individuals. Today, therefore, each social class in Negro society contains descendents of all major divisions of antebellum society.

These are the social influences that have shaped the modern

life of New Orleans Negroes. They are the precipitates of a dramatic history that has come to express itself in the wide variety of social institutions of an ever more complex society. Stability and continuity are largely lacking in this history, and we have seen that the organization of Negro society is in a state of restless change, expansive development, and increasing community-wide integration. It is a society in formation, rapidly gaining precisely the elements of stability and continuity that it has so conspicuously lacked in the past. From these threads of a volatile past and a dynamic present come the trends, attitudes, and issues from which individuals in this society weave their lives. We have repeatedly described the class structure as "fluid," "loose," and "flexible." Thus it is not easy to describe the differing classes of the population since it is simply the case that they are not well defined in reality.

THE QUESTION OF THE UPPER CLASS

Virtually all descriptions of Negro society in the United States agree that the Negro upper class, however defined, is very small. New Orleans is no exception. Furthermore, there is a virtual absence of the dependably inherited status and means everywhere identified with the upper class. Every society has, of course, a top leadership, as does Negro New Orleans, but not every society segregates this leadership to the same degree and in the same manner from other social levels. Social mobility is widespread—one might almost say rampant—in Negro society in New Orleans, and there are few evidences of fixity of status from one generation to the next. Even the best families have little past.

Perhaps the most accurate way to describe this situation is to say that the Negro upper class is still relatively undifferentiated from the larger middle class. It has not yet pulled away from the middle class in terms of social participation, intermarriage, or occupational values. When we regard "class" as a continuum of social rank, we may perhaps arbitrarily speak of the top of the continuum as an "upper class," but we should remember that this does not imply cultural autonomy or social discontinuity. It is, thus, no accident that many observers have chosen to consider people of the Negro upper and middle classes together.

Very few of the associations of New Orleans society described above even approximate a membership of upper-class people exclusively. Two or three of the social clubs with overlapping membership, the Junior League, the Jack and Jill Club, one or two of the neighborhoods, and perhaps a few of the churches have a tendency in this direction, but it is a tendency only. The case of the country club once under consideration is instructive. The original intent of a limited and apparently upper-class membership was frustrated by economic limitations. Accordingly, the class barriers had to be let down, the original desire to be exclusive was destroyed, and eventually the project was abandoned altogether.

The values of the upper class are not yet significantly different from those of the middle class. Their family structures are similar or identical. Their occupations and educational attainments overlap, and their religious affiliations and ethnic identifications are more or less the same. Aside from the symbolic value of a few individuals and families widely recognized as leaders of top prestige, there is no differentiated "upper class" in New Orleans Negro society.

THE MIDDLE CLASS

By contrast there is an emphatic bipolarity between the middle and lower classes in terms of education, occupation, religious participation, family structure, neighborhoods, political activity and associational memberships. The nascent upper class may be considered as the prestige and power leaders of the middle-class group, but its way of life is, as has been mentioned, the same.

The middle-class family is based upon relatively stable monogamous marriage, neolocal residence, an ideal of economic dominance of the husband and father, relatively rigid discipline of

children and strict interpretation of the Judaeo-Christian code of
sexual morality. Occupationally the middle class is heterogeneous.
The men of the middle class receive stable incomes as businessmen, skilled workers, owners of property, managers, salesmen,
white-collar workers, and professionals. The women are house-
wives, or, if they work, "professionals": schoolteachers, nurses,
stenographers, beauticians. The children of the wealthier families
attend the "better" public schools, if possible, and significant
numbers of them complete a high school education, and go on to
vocational training or college degrees. A few attend the "better"
private finishing schools and colleges in the North. They live on
the quieter streets and avoid the rough neighborhoods. They are
extremely active organizationally, joining church societies, PTA
groups, social clubs, lodges, professional societies and some unions, civic service and betterment associations. They tend to be
staunch supporters of the churches, and are especially prominent
in the Congregational, Lutheran, Methodist, Presbyterian, and
Episcopal denominations, though they are strongly represented
in the Baptist and Catholic churches as well.

It will be seen that there is no abrupt and complete discontinuity between the middle and the lower class. A person of the
middle class is likely to meet other middle-class people socially,
in school, or as status equals in business, as neighbors, or as
relatives. On the other hand he is likely to meet lower-class people
in church, in political groups, in the veterans' organizations, as
clients, customers, or associates on the job. He is likely even to
have some lower-class relatives, at least by marriage.

The relative distinctness of middle- and lower-class society,
however, both in its institutional forms and in terms of participation, has tended to result in differing norms and values. People
of the middle and upper class prize those values by which they
explain their own privileged position: their economic and social
success, their thrift and caution, their inhibition of aggression and
sexuality, their ambition, initiative, and manners. And since they
view their own past through these glasses they cling all the more

staunchly to these values in order to keep and to extend their conquests. Eager for social change that will better the race, they are still not revolutionary, but prefer a conservative gradualism to the forcing of risky changes. Some middle-class individuals who are more eager to hasten change are particularly frustrated by the apathy of the lower class and the conservative attitudes of many leaders.

The Negro middle class has the defects of its virtues, but the virtues should be noted nonetheless. It has often been taxed with Uncle Tomism in its accommodative leadership, but the accusation is not the whole truth. Its own values emphasize peace, politeness, and amicable relations among people, and it has done its best to maintain these values even under the frustrations of segregation and discrimination. If its leadership has been accommodative, it may well be arguable that historically nothing more was possible. Certainly, Negro leaders have been neither slow nor timid in speaking for their people in the time of rapid change that has arisen.

The ideology of the middle class is overwhelmingly individualistic. Racism is decried on the grounds that a man should be judged as an individual rather than by color. The implications of this credo are never *race* progress, but *individual* progress regardless of race. We have seen that this is changing. The degree of coördination of community activities and of organization of the lives of individuals is increasing, and the development of a more solidary in-group ideology is both cause and result of this change.

The way of life of the middle class corresponding to the structure we have outlined cannot be extensively described in the compass of this chapter. It is eagerness to succeed and good table manners; it is afternoons at the bridge club and worries over the church finances; it is hushed gossip about sexual delinquency and regular trips to the dentist; it is having a daddy with a steady job and seeing mamma respect him. It involves worry about the future, Sunday school, and home ownership. It means speaking carefully without an accent, and extending one's vocabulary and knowledge of the world. It implies coming in early from dates, a new dress for a friend's wedding, and an allowance for extras. It means not going hungry. It means drinking only in moderation, if at all; birthday parties and contributions to community fund drives; indoor plumbing and respect for adults; a taste for good music; a Christmas tree; and saying you didn't want to be president of the fraternity anyway. And in all of this it means remembering that you have a position to maintain and that you don't want to disgrace your family or your friends or your club. In short, the middle-class way of life is a distinct culture.

THE LOWER CLASS

The lower (and larger) class in Negro society differs from the middle class in the organization of most, but not all, of its social forms. Briefly, it has a different family structure, lives largely in different neighborhoods, participates in business only as an employee or customer, forms the backbone of some of the labor unions but not of professional societies, joins political movements but not uplift organizations, creates and abandons an enormous number of ephemeral clubs, gangs, and bunches, constitutes the bulk of the membership of innumerable Baptist and some Catholic churches, experiments constantly in spiritualist and fundamentalist store-front cults, and queues up patiently in the endless waiting rooms of government offices and charitable organizations for aid and rehabilitation.

Broadly speaking, the social structure of the lower class is less organized, less stable, and less coördinated than that of the middle class. Its family life is predicated on unstable (frequently "common law") marriage and frequent desertion. The mother is often the chief breadwinner, augmenting her own earnings with what she can wheedle or extort from her current husband, and the discipline exercised over the children is apt to be harsh and inconsistent, with both parents frequently out of the home. The men of the lower class are unskilled laborers, often unemployed, frequently involved in illegal activities in one sense or another. Multiple jobs are common. The women work at menial or manual labor in factories and stores, or, most commonly, in domestic occupations. The children attend public school somewhat erratically, with frequent retardation and absenteeism, though some manage to finish high school and even college. This is significant since education is the main path to social advancement. Lower-class families live almost entirely in crowded and inadequate houses and undesirable neighborhoods. Home ownership is rare. They are likely to be members of a church and its affiliated organizations, and in some occupations they will be union members, but otherwise their organizational affiliations are few. Their social clubs are largely organized by women, and do not often last more than a few years.

It must not be thought from this description that there is *no* stability in lower-class life. The general poverty and the disruptive pressures place an even greater premium on the reliable institutions that do exist, and there is good evidence that the church clubs, the unions, the family, the government agencies, and even the "aid and pleasure" or "sewing and saving" clubs enlist the steadiest loyalty of many lower-class people. Furthermore, the more steadily employed members of this class are increasingly aware of middle-class stability and values, and strive to emulate them.

For the bulk of lower-class people, however, a wide range of habits and patterns is oriented to social norms and values different from those of the middle class. For them life is a web of fiery and apocalyptic sermons, wheedling money out of your half-sister's husband for a movie, threatening to have your husband drafted for nonsupport, and painting "Bad Dog" on your gate to keep out the violence of the bar next door. It means "playing the dozens" with the gang from down the street, missing meals or eating alone, answering the door with caution because it might be the bill collector, walking "raddy" just to prove you can do it, and listening to religious music or jazz and jive talk on the radio while you do the laundry. It means precocity in sexual knowledge, constant "fussing" within the family, gambling, putting on a show of destitution for the "committee" from the Welfare Department, and maintaining one's dignity by fighting for it. It means placing a high valuation on the visible signs of success: the chartreuse Cadillac, the "sharp" clothes, and night life, but having the most elementary sensitivity to the cost of social mobility in terms of control and inhibition.

THE SHADOWS

The sharp difference of culture between the middle and the lower class is blurred by the fact of social mobility. Individuals who are in every stage of transition between the two are numerous. Nonetheless, it is noteworthy that the society is structured in a bipolar manner, so that, while social mobility is frequent, it is impossible for any large number of people to remain permanently in the social limbo between the classes. The social forms for this do not exist. The actual organization is discontinuous at a number of points: either you send your child to a public school or to a private one; either you are accepted by a "social club" or you belong to an "aid and pleasure" or "saving" club; either you have a "professional" job or you do not; either you "finish" your education or you do not. Most people will fit consistently into one class or the other on the basis of these and kindred criteria.

A taxonomic problem of considerable importance is posed, however, by the existence of some social groups that are significantly outside the class structure (and sometimes even the caste structure) in at least some respects. The entertainment world and the underworld are two important examples of this kind of grouping, and significant numbers of people live most of their lives in the shadows of these cultures. For the lower class, indeed, "respectability" is identified with the lack of a police record—the ability to "stay out of trouble."

It should be noted, of course, that for individuals in "the

shadows" some parts of life may be in a nonclass context while others are not. The professional life of an entertainer may involve the relatively easy white-Negro familiarity of the jazz musician or a glorification of semicriminal slang and shady activities (in the words to the "blues" or the "jive" talk of the disc jockey), while he simultaneously maintains a class-bound home life and strives to educate his children. In the last analysis, these shadow areas of society do not operate under different rules from the rest of society, but their ideology is emphatically different, and their social life is markedly distinct from that of the bulk of the social order.

SELF-EXPRESSION OF NEW ORLEANS NEGRO CULTURES

Enough has been said to indicate the complexity of influences, past and present, on the contemporary social life of Negro New Orleans. From a cultural standpoint we may summarize the most general level of organization of these influences by differentiating three distinct cultural traditions, those of the Creoles, of the modern middle class, and of the lower class. In order to explore the general motivational dimensions of these traditions we have selected a sample of literature or folklore characteristic of each of them and analyzed its motivational content. As a sample of middle-class expression we used editorials from the *Louisiana Weekly*. For the lower class we sampled from the lyrics of New Orleans jazz songs. Our Creole materials are a sampling of traditional folk songs.

The materials selected are not rigorously comparable. The editorials are highly contemporary, while jazz lyrics date largely from the last generation, and the Creole folk songs from the last century. There are obviously important differences in function between the editorials and the songs, and even between the dancing and marching songs of the jazz tradition and the jingles and lullabies of the Creoles. Despite these differences we may reasonably suppose that each of the genres selected is a fair representation of the self-expression of its own subculture and that the structure and content of the medium is related to the structure and content of the culture or subculture that created it. The case for this viewpoint is somewhat stronger than may be obvious, in that each of these media is more or less uniquely important. Indeed, among the types of literary or folkloristic expression available to us, we have omitted only the tradition of hymns and spirituals and the self-conscious literature of profes-

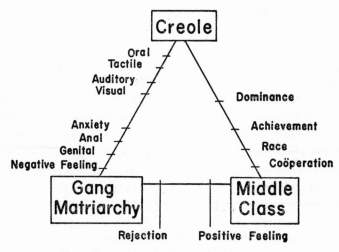

Figure 5. Diagnostic Significance of Folklore Themes.

sional Negro writers, and we have made these omissions only because neither of these is particularly associated with New Orleans. We have, then, analyzed all the materials we could find that appear to involve some genuine self-expression of New Orleans Negroes.

A detailed account of the results from the formal analysis of these literatures is included in the Appendix.[21] The accompanying diagram (Figure 5) expresses the general findings by placing the psychological terms used in the analysis in positions illustrating their relevance as descriptions of each of the three groups. The

[21] See Appendix 2.

differences among the groups are amply confirmed and even somewhat sharpened by this additional information.

Middle-class literature is far more optimistic, race-conscious, and coöperation- and achievement-oriented than either type of folk song. It is also more inhibited in its use of all kinds of sensory imagery, and it is less anxiety-laden than either of the other forms. All this seems thoroughly congruent with what we know of the middle class. We might suppose that this description holds only for relatively superficial aspects of middle-class self-expression, and certainly newspaper editorials are a rather formal and controlled medium, leaving little scope for the projection of more buried feelings. On the other hand it seems hardly accidental that the middle class chooses this inhibitory form for expressing what are, after all, its most cherished public ideas. While we may legitimately infer that the rosy feeling tone that pervades the editorials may well conceal much more anxiety than is expressed, there would appear to be no grounds for assuming, as some observers have done, that the restrictive character of middle-class emotional expression is *ipso facto* evidence that it is more anxious at some deeper level than is the less inhibited lower class.

The lower-class literature is overwhelmingly negative in feeling tone. It also includes more anal and genital imagery than the other forms. Even in the jazz songs these types of imagery are rare, although we are suspicious that they may be underrepresented in our sample of lyrics, many of which have been at least partly bowdlerized by the exigencies of public performance, recording, or publication. The themes of rejection and anxiety are frequent in the jazz songs, as they are in the Creole ones, but there is very little representation of dominance relationships in comparison with either of the other media. This last finding would seem to suggest that the frequent imputation of strong status awareness to the lower class seriously needs reëxamination. Again it is likely that deeper levels of motivation would reveal patterns not overtly apparent, but from the general structure of lower-class literary expression we would expect these to be more concerned with sexuality than with status.

On most of our dimensions of measurement the Creole folk songs are intermediate. They are race-conscious, but not as much so as the editorials; they are anxious, but so are the jazz songs. They do manifest less concern over rejection than either of the other media. Their most outstanding positive attribute is their general use of "colorful" imagery: they make more use of oral, tactile, auditory, and visual imagery than do the other genres. It may be, as the limited thematic use of rejection suggests, that the relatively stable familism of the Catholic Creole tradition actually provides more psychological security than the other ways of life, but the concern with dominance and the frequent expression of anxiety seem to indicate that the Creoles have paid some psychic price for their equivocal intercaste position in historic times.

All the differences in thematic content we have cited are statistically significant $(p < .01)$. We can conclude that even the gross divisions of Negro society with which we have been concerned here differ markedly in the manner and content of their self-expression. In this finding we can read the warning that interpretation of the sociocultural environment of individual New Orleans Negroes must necessarily deal with finer discriminations than we have made in the general depiction of New Orleans social history.

In this chapter we have traced the origins and development of the wide variety of social forms and cultural meanings that a complex history has made available to the contemporary New Orleans Negro. We have described the organizational structure of the community life, and we have traced some of the levels on which this life is integrated—ethnically for the Creoles, in class terms for the middle and lower class, in occupational terms for the underworld and the entertainment world. Finally, we have showed that these various types of integration are characterized by the expression of differing motivational themes: that they make a difference in the emotional climate of life for individuals located at different points in the general society.

From the standpoint of the individual, we may view all this social heritage as raw material. These are the social inventions, cultural contexts, attitudinal systems, stereotypes, and prejudices from which New Orleans Negroes build their lives. No others are available to them. The pattern of adjustment of each individual must be forged from these materials or from the painful and exhausting process of creative innovation, but it cannot draw on the history and culture of some other, alien milieu. In the next chapter we shall examine what individuals do with the raw material we have described, and how they relate themselves to these complex traditions.

CHAPTER 3

Identification and Identity

Understanding the history of New Orleans society and its present constitution is an important prerequisite to understanding the lives we are here examining, but it is only the first step. We cannot fully comprehend any organism from its environment alone; we must have some conception of its relation to and interaction with that environment. For the human animal the relations between the individual and his setting are fraught with extraordinary complexity and subtlety, and we must turn to this complexity for a deeper understanding of the individuals we are here examining.

We have seen how the society of Negro New Orleans has come to be constituted as a partially distinct, more or less parallel society to that of white New Orleans through the operation of a number of factors centering on the concept of race. Neither at present nor at any time in the past, however, has the cultural meaning of race and the corresponding form of this biracial society been a simple, unitary phenomenon. It differs significantly both in importance and implications from period to period of history, and from group to group within the social system. Thus we have seen a "culture caste" system of colonial Louisiana grow first into a "race caste" system and then beyond it, and we can see in contemporary Louisiana the complex redefinition of "race" that accompanies changes in the varied segments of a highly diversified society.

Not that this complexity is restricted to racial matters. Significant differences of conceptions of society and of men's places in it are widespread in relation to religion, political organization, classes, occupational and professional groupings, and many other dimensions of society. We run the risk of misinterpreting social life as it is perceived and lived by concrete persons if we do not fully face this complexity and deal with its implications.

Within rather broad limits, to be sure, the task of describing a society presents us with no unduly forbidding problems. We can, within such limits, restrict our attention to those social phenomena on which there is general agreement: things that all or most people tend to view in a similar way, where scientifically reliable information is rather accessible, and where there is that necessary degree of consensus upon which all organized social life depends. We have tried to do this in our description of the social development of New Orleans. These limits, however, are confining—even crippling for our present purpose—and we must now essay to transcend them: to describe the important area of social life that lies beyond consensus, and to see social reality as it is seen by people living in the society, their vision always filtered by differential social refraction.

The problems of this endeavor are compounded by the problematic visual distortions of the viewer himself, however scientific his training and detached his interests; it is, therefore, peculiarly necessary to proceed with explicit attention to such methods and arguments as may correct "observer error" in our findings. It is patent that this effort is all the more necessary on a controversial topic engaging the very strongest feelings and deepest loyalties. That the issues centering on race do this for a very broad segment of the American people of all races is perhaps the least debatable of the many important findings of Gunnar Myrdal.[1]

[1] Gunnar Myrdal, *An American Dilemma,* New York and London, Harper, 1944.

The question that confronts us in depicting the segmented social worlds of a broad sample of New Orleans Negroes is primarily a matter of distortion. It is a question of how the individual sees himself in relation to his world, and how he views the denizens of other segments of society. It is a truism that for most people such identifications are multiple, and it may be that no other society in history has provided so many hats per capita as our own. It is perhaps less obvious that they tend to be mutually incompatible or even incomprehensible. The ways in which we as individuals relate to the many overlapping social worlds in which we live may be viewed as a series of patterns of role identification.

Any attempt to describe the patterns of role identification in their full complexity would be shipwrecked at its launching were it not for the constant systematizing efforts of all human beings. This "strain toward consistency," the unending search for principles and order, engages all of us in striving to organize and order our experiences. The crucial effect of this endeavor in turn is to weight some of our roles as of greater importance than others —greater importance, that is, to us. Culturally speaking, then, some patterns of identification may be considered as primary while others are relegated to positions of secondary importance. The process of weighting appears to be a subjective phenomenon, but one which we objectify and communicate in manifold ways, sharing our views with sympathetic peers and protecting them from (or even defending them to) disinterested or unsympathetic outsiders. It is also a problem of biasing, warping, and distorting our view of things into some systematic mold.

The organization of conceptions of self into cultural patterns of identification is, then, a systematization of the first order of importance for understanding the individual in his relation to his society. Its modes are virtually infinite in their variation, and it is easy to become impatient and to insist upon imposing on them an order and logic that they do not in fact possess. There is, in fact, a peculiar danger that scientists, who share a somewhat distinctive conception of *themselves,* may project this image in one or another of its disciplinary guises onto the fluid facts they are endeavoring to illuminate. The danger is not absolute, however, and it is certainly possible, though not necessarily easy, to control a known distortion. It may reasonably be supposed that the limited human ability to confront directly the realities of social experience is not more rare among social scientists than in the population at large.

Furthermore, we have some clues to the nature of cultural identification that aid us in recognizing its concomitants and controlling its resultants. One such clue is the phenomenon of ethnocentrism, which has been all but universally observed but all too often misunderstood. "Ethnocentrism," somewhat like "prejudice," is often loosely used to refer to the shallowness and distortion apparent to us in the viewpoints of other people. It is rarely used to add a somewhat painful insight to our understanding of the same phenomenon in ourselves. More often it is rather casually applied by loose and defensive analogy, as in the statement frequently encountered that the magical and witchcraft beliefs of primitive peoples are "no more unreasonable" than the black cat or ladder superstitions of our own day and age.

Such imprecise analogies often miss the main point. By comfortably comparing one "superstition" we do not believe with another which we also do not believe and which we smugly attribute to the more primitive or ignorant strata of our own society, we shield ourselves from having to question whether our own well-informed and deeply cherished tenets of behavior rest on the same shifting sand. There is far more ethnocentrism in the world than these romantic and deprecatory comparisons would imply; indeed, some of these comparisons may themselves be considered evidence on the point.

It is particularly important to be precise about the nature of ethnocentrism in dealing with our own society. The lack of such precision closes to us one of the main avenues for an understanding of social psychological processes. For ethnocentrism in one of its many guises appears to be a structuring factor in all patterns of primary role identification. Perhaps the greatest source of confusion in interpreting this fact is the temptation to apply the term with narrow etymological clarity. Such a temptation has in the past had a particularly powerful influence in an anthropology overwhelmingly concerned with the cultures of *ethnic* groups. Easily, and at times erroneously, "cultures" have been described as though ethnic identifications are always primary. The implications of class, or caste, or occupation, or sect and so on, have often in such treatment received short shrift. Aztec customs have been compared to American customs and Zuni attitudes to Chinese attitudes as though ethnicity had similar, indeed identical, implications everywhere. The subjective implications of culture are unfortunately not so simple.

The formation of group loyalties implied by ethnocentrism is a process that has long been understood in social science. Over a century ago the famous Count de Gobineau[2] described the process succinctly (albeit not notably more so than Herodotus before him). What is new and relevant about it, however, is not its existence, but rather our painfully and slowly acquired knowledge about its nature and variability. We cannot afford Gobineau's error of equating ethnocentrism with ethnicity or race. Only *some* groups of mankind so conceive themselves. Modern research has added to ethnocentrism the important qualification that its point of departure is cultural: that the reference group in the focusing of primary identifications may be *any culture group.*

Seen in this light, the process of cultural identification may be studied in terms of patterns of self-conception, symbols, and attitudes, always matched by obverse conceptions of the corresponding other. It is to these last (when we study them in other people, at any rate) that we customarily assign the labels "prejudice," "bias," or a range of terms on temporary loan from psychopathology. Such taxonomy has been productive of great heat for obvious

---

[2] Joseph Arthur de Gobineau, *Essai sur l'inégalité des races humaines,* 4th ed., 2 v., Paris, Firmin-Didet, n.d.

reasons, but it is not clear that it has shed a corresponding light on the nature of the process it purports to illuminate. Certainly it contains the danger of being a comfortably pejorative way of dismissing views that most social scientists do not happen to share. And it has the somewhat unfortunate implication of moral condemnation of phenomena on which, *qua* scientists, we are not asked to moralize.

That ethnocentrism is a mechanism of cultural dynamics is a conception of crucial importance for interpreting the cultural context of the lives of individuals. For if culture is a universal aspect of human life, it is nevertheless manifested in a bewildering variety of highly discontinuous segments, separated from each other in space, in time, and in symbolic and social dimensions. It is the particularity of these segments that we must illuminate if we are to understand the diversified social worlds in which we live. An examination of culturally patterned stereotypes of self and others enables us to perceive these worlds somewhat more nearly as they are seen by their inhabitants, with obvious benefit to interpretation and explanation.

Not that ethnocentrism need be construed as the cause of these phenomena. From one perspective, at least, it is man himself who is the cause. For there appears to be little determinancy to the formation of self-conceptions, and a considerable element of creativity may go into them. At any rate we are hardly at present in a position to formulate any stringent laws of social behavior in this area.

In treating American Negro life from this standpoint, it is perhaps the assessment of the cultural distinctiveness of American Negroes *as a whole* that provides us with the most difficult and absorbing problem. The fact that the discrimination of Negroes from whites rests on a quasi-racial basis introduces an element of peculiar subtlety and complexity, and one on which there has been little agreement among observers and interpreters of Negro life. Inevitably, all attempts at explanation must eventually come to grips with race: its physical and social meaning. The question

has often been framed in the form: What is the general meaning
of racial status in a racially conscious society? Or, more specifically: What are the psychological concomitants of an awareness
of socially applied racial distinctions?

At the broadest level of empirical treatment, these are the questions we should like to answer. We regard them, however, as material to the even broader question: How does the individual relate himself psychologically to the society of which he is a part?
Some part of the answer to such a question may be found in an
examination of the explicit ways in which people conceive themselves in relation to society or to specific symbols of it.

There is no lack of theses to be examined in this area. Indeed,
the literature on the American Negro can only be described as
voluminous. Three relatively modern treatments of the problem
seem to merit special attention, however, as they depict with peculiar force and clarity both the problems and some projected solutions: Allison Davis' and John Dollard's *Children of Bondage*,[3]
Gunnar Myrdal's *An American Dilemma*,[4] and Abram Kardiner's
and Lionel Ovesey's *The Mark of Oppression*.[5]

The revised scientific view of the nature of race, fruit of extensive researches in the quarter-century between 1910 and 1935, is
the starting point of Davis' and Dollard's study. The two men initiated their researches in New Orleans after intensive study of the
social life of two different Deep South communities in Mississippi.
They approached the teen-age Negroes of New Orleans with a
high degree of awareness of the complexity of social background,
which illuminates their case studies and interpretations with lucid
insight. Broadly, they were concerned with the social context
in which Negro children learn the culturally patterned behavior
presumably fundamental to their adult life. They found class and
caste to be the dominating factors in structuring this learning,

[3] Allison Davis and John Dollard, *Children of Bondage*, Washington,
American Council on Education, 1940.

[4] Myrdal, *op. cit.*

[5] Abram Kardiner and Lionel Ovesey, *The Mark of Oppression*, New
York, Norton, 1951.

and they emphasized that class was far more important as a formative influence than the standardized frustrations inherent in a system of racial castes. Perhaps the most important of the many significant findings in *Children of Bondage* was the discovery that other factors besides "ethnic" culture—even when this is structured with the peculiar rigidity of caste—may have a crucial influence on how individuals see themselves in relation to others.

For Davis and Dollard the significant "other factor" was social class. And certainly their cases reveal rather clearly the primacy of class over color for many individuals. We may nonetheless question whether the alternatives are exhaustive. Approaching life history materials from a class framework exposes one to the temptation, possibly even the necessity, of reading status striving into every act, and mobility into every conflict. Davis and Dollard are never guilty of naïve error, but their class interpretation seems at times to reach rather a long way for a class angle. It remains subject, too, to the limitations of every class interpretation: the necessity of describing fluid facts in segmental and categoric concepts. This point will be discussed later, but we may question here whether the substitution of "class cultures" for "ethnic cultures" is in fact a radical enough departure for digesting the extraordinarily varied patterns of group identifications that their teen-agers displayed.

In the massive contribution to the study of the American Negro life by Gunnar Myrdal and his associates, the general thesis is proposed and exhaustively explored that the meaning of race cannot be divorced from its relational context in American life. Thus the white American's view of race is seen as an extremely important element in his own self-conception, an element fraught with feelings of guilt and awareness of conflict. Aspects of the Negro's conception of himself are in turn related to this ambivalent white pattern in a complex process of action and reaction. The conflicts of American values are pointed up with peculiar sharpness by Myrdal's analysis, and though the selection of a Swedish scholar to direct the endeavor in order to escape from the American biases on racial matters would seem to have an element of naïveté, it paid off at least in a most insightful discussion of American race relations as seen from the outside. We are left to speculate about the Swedish bias. It seems scarcely possible that Sweden (or Myrdal) has been untouched by the general European racial controversies of the last century or so.

Myrdal's thesis is essentially social-psychological in character, and postulates a conflict between a generic idealistic morality and a series of more particular (and realistic?) "interests":

The "American Dilemma," referred to in the title of this book, is the ever-raging conflict between, on the one hand, the valuations preserved on the general plane which we shall call the "American Creed," where the American thinks, talks, and acts under the influence of high national and Christian precepts, and, on the other hand, the valuations on specific planes of individual group living, where personal and local interests; economic, social and sexual jealousies; considerations of community prestige and conformity; group prejudice against particular persons or types of people; and all sorts of miscellaneous wants, impulses, and habits dominate his outlook.[6]

Possibly the most useful element in this complex assertion for our present purpose is its weighting of a wide range of factors as relevant to the American definition of race. Myrdal points with every justification to the extreme complexity of the elements in American racial conceptions and documents their relevance in admirable detail. Otherwise the interpretations and theories he advances are of eclectic and even bewildering diversity, and we may be permitted a degree of skepticism at an interpretation that relates the generic racial problem to the clash between the ideal and the actual. We can accept Myrdal's distinction between generic Americanism and the more specific role loyalties that often override it without necessarily accepting Myrdal's moral evaluation of them.

Myrdal does significantly broaden the caste-and-class framework of Davis and Dollard, pursuing a more complex theoretical

---

[6] Myrdal, *op. cit.*, p. xlvii.

path also explored by such "institutional" theorists as E. Franklin Frazier, and Drake and Cayton.[7] He follows a modified institutional outline of the problem: economics, politics, justice, social inequality, stratification, leadership, and community, to which he adds an extensive discussion of ethos, demography, and attitudes, and a valuable series of appendixes. There can be no question of Myrdal's monumental achievement. All future investigators of American Negro life will be deeply in his debt. But the very encyclopedic scope of his study confronts us with much undigested fact, and Myrdal's own general conclusions may be seen as fitting into a pattern of developing understanding of "the Negro question." While he has done us a great service by pointing up the relevance of a wide range of social factors in race relations, most of these factors confront us with questions rather than answers.

The complexities of the picture Myrdal paints demand comprehensive simplification. If, as Davis and Dollard argued, the universal experience of caste frustrations cannot be construed as inevitably marking all Negroes with similarly learned psychological responses because class factors intervene, and if, as Myrdal adds, class factors are not the only intervening variables, we are left to conclude that race can have no generic meaning for Negroes: their experiences are too diverse and too diversely perceived.

This argument has recently been countered by a psychiatric attack on the problem in which Kardiner and Ovesey[8] revive the caste thesis in a new and sophisticated form. The authors do not confront directly the degree of variance between their own proposals and those of other writers, but in the context of the pattern we are tracing they may be said to imply that Negroes are unconsciously influenced in similar ways by the generic frustrations of caste even despite the variety of individual personalities and the configuration of other institutionally structured experiences. The argument is persuasive, and the evidence is marshaled in 25

[7] Edward Franklin Frazier, *The Negro in the United States*, New York, Macmillan, 1949; St. Clair Drake and Horace R. Cayton, *Black Metropolis*, New York, Harcourt, Brace, 1945.

[8] *Op. cit.*

detailed case histories of Negroes in New York, representing a variety of social class backgrounds. Evidence is claimed for some degree of unconscious self-hatred in all the subjects, and this is related to the known frustrations inherent in membership in a low-status minority group.

The subtle problems of objectivity in the treatment of patterns of unconscious motivation are well known, and constitute a particular hazard of research of the type Kardiner and Ovesey report. Replication of the study from a fresh point of view is a useful check on the problems of this order that are involved. Among our own cases we find individuals who could be used in evidence to support Kardiner's and Ovesey's thesis, but we also find some who could not. We see the same picture, in fact, in Kardiner's and Ovesey's cases: self-hatred is found in only seven of twenty-five case records; five of these were records of patients in therapy. We are accordingly convinced that the formulation does not do full justice to the range and variety of reactions to racial and caste symbols, nor to the complex evidence available on the social patterning of their genesis and development in the individual.

Interpretation of the supposed impact of caste restrictions upon *all* Negroes may be said to rest on the initial assumptions *that such restrictions will fall with something like equal force upon all, that they will be similarly perceived by all, and that the corresponding psychological reactions will be similar or analogous in all members of the group.* Many aspects of caste obviously do not operate in this way. Differential occupational opportunities necessarily strike men and women with differential force, and often only the special group of those ready to seize these opportunities is disadvantaged. The opportunities for Negro actors are largely irrelevant to the lives of Negro women in domestic work. Even when the caste restriction is generic, as, let us say, in relation to drinking fountains or rest rooms, it may be a source of acute frustration to one individual and of casual inconvenience to another; that is, it may actually be differently perceived. The argument that there are *generic* Negro reactions to caste phenomena must be related to experiences that all Negroes have and that they tend to perceive in similar ways.

These criteria are not impossible to meet, but they do focus our attention on a particular range of experiences, and they remind us afresh of the necessity for precision of analysis. There are few contexts of life in which the individual can be exposed to socially patterned learning free from the impact of prior experiences that would structure his perception and reaction differentially. The Great Depression of 1929–1933 was a massive social fact with something like the weight of a caste system, but it is obvious that it never had and has not now the same meaning for all Americans. Looking closely, we can agree that it could not have. For while it is possible that the depression did nobody any good, the acute frustrations of unemployment, bankruptcy, loss of income, poverty, and attendant ills of the period fell with highly differential impact on Americans of different ages, of different occupations, of different regions, of different sexes, and so forth.

The marginal group status of the Negro and the race-defined restrictions on his behavior are generic objective facts of his life, but our subjects indicate that they may have varying subjective significance. The distinctive castelike aspects of race relations in the South create only a relatively superficial residue of universally or generally accepted attitudes among Negroes. These attitudes are both transient and changeable, though they may occasionally be used as symbolic rallying points. It would be surprising, for example, to find New Orleans Negroes who favored segregation in public transportation or recreational facilities.[9] (The school issue is somewhat more complex for other reasons.) These attitudes may have more dynamic significance at an unconscious level but even then we need not assume a universally similar dynamism.

If we were actively to seek a means of reaching an entire population with an experience capable of producing a similar reaction in all individuals, we should be forced to structure such an ex-

[9] Since this was written, indeed, the public transportation system of New Orleans has been peacefully desegregated.

perience so that it would reach people at an early age, before their view of the world and of their experiences in it has become structured by the knowledge that they have a career in a particular occupation or at a particular class level—before they become aware that life is different for little boys and little girls. For such social roles may indeed affect not only the way we behave in the world and the experiences we are likely to have in it, but also our way of perceiving and therefore of reacting to such experiences.

One context that more or less fulfills these requirements is, of course, early family life. For it is primarily within the family that the child ordinarily encounters his first social experiences, and if there are among Negroes generally shared patterns of family life they should indeed have a general impact upon the psychology of Negroes as a socially defined race-caste. Such experiences as Negroes might share in early family life would have an unique opportunity for universal impact relatively free from the distortions that come with the learning of sex roles, occupations, or associational memberships.

Kardiner's and Ovesey's hypothesis may be said to imply precisely these assumptions. If there is such a thing as "the Negro family," then its customs and traditions would tend to produce similar orientations in all Negroes, some of which might be expected to survive the secondary elaboration of adult experience. Such orientations as had become unconscious would indeed be particularly likely to resist alteration by later experience. How many different types of family systems exist among American Negroes is, however, a researchable question; we have been led gradually to the conclusion that there is certainly more than one, and that there may be as many as four or five.

In a study that compares carefully a range of data on socialization and family life of Negroes and whites, Davis and Havighurst[10] have shown that it is useful to distinguish at least two types of families among Negroes—those of the middle and lower classes.

[10] Allison Davis and Robert J. Havighurst, *Father of the Man,* Boston, Houghton Mifflin, 1947.

In order to explore this further in the New Orleans context, we designed a questionnaire directed toward a selected range of problems in child care. The interviews were presented as a study of adoption attitudes to a random areal sample of 105 Negro women. The results will be found in the Appendix,[11] but it is worth discussing our general conclusions here.

Although we have no white sample with which to compare our data, we do not feel that any of our questions elicited evidence of attitudes specific to Negroes. All the responses that were given by more than 50 percent of the women can be shown either to be so general and platitudinous as to make a cultural interpretation unlikely, or to be related to dimensions of subgroup membership: class, ethnicity, matriarchy, and family stability.

Among the platitudinous expressions are such items as: children's play should be most closely supervised when they are young (63 percent); something should be done when a child gets into a fight (80 percent); if a child is to be left with someone, it should be a relative (58 percent). Other "majority opinions" in our data appear to be a function of the composition of the sample: 60 percent non-Creole; 71 percent lower class; 55 percent Baptist. Most of the women (63 percent) would rather adopt a girl than a boy, but this is a function of whether the woman lives in a matriarchal extended family or not. Most of them (73 percent) agree on avoidance as the best way for a child to deal with aggression, but it is stably married women who hold this attitude, not Negro women at large. Most of them (63 percent) feel that a child should be allowed to go to movies only at certain times, but this is a middle-class attitude rather than a general one. Most of them (58 percent) feel that racial equality should be the dominant motif in teaching their children how to get along with white children, but it is Creoles who express this attitude, rather than all the women. These facts would seem to justify the interpretation that there are differences in significant patterns of child care between Creole and non-Creole families, between stable and unstable

[11] See Appendix 3.

families, between matriarchal and nonmatriarchal families, and between the middle and the lower class.

In their expression of attitudes toward child training, middle-class mothers proved more likely than lower-class mothers to state a preference for adopting a child who has light skin, and who came originally from a "good" (i.e., middle-class) home. They laid more stress on the groups the child might play with, and were concerned over the play group threat of delinquency rather than physical danger to the child. They were more apt to be strict about letting the child go out to movies and specified a preference for having baby sitters in their homes rather than leaving the child in a strange environment. They also preferred a later age for the sexual initiation of girls.

In the same sample, matriarchal mothers were less prone to state a color preference for a hypothetical adopted child than were those not living in matriarchal households. If they did state a color preference, it was more apt to be different from their own. They registered an emphatic preference for a girl rather than a boy and, possibly a related viewpoint, they estimated a later date for the sexual maturity of boys than did the non-matriarchs. The matriarchs also registered a preference for early cleanliness training, and showed less inclination to seek professional aid with their childrens' problems.

The Creole mothers were set apart from the non-Creole ones on only two counts: they are more often Catholic, and they more often express explicit attitudes of racial equality. Similarly, the stably married mothers differed from those who are not in espousing avoidance rather than parental interference when a child has trouble with his peers, and in tending to postpone the period in which the child is permitted to play with other children. All the findings reported are statistically significant ($p < .05$), and this is the complete roster of findings that proved to be so.

From these findings and from more general considerations we conclude that there are no grounds for assuming the operation of general racial stereotypes in the training of Negro children.

Among our subjects, as among the Negro mothers we have interviewed, the indications are that the stereotypes that do exist develop later in the individual's life history. This is not to say that very young children do not develop a high degree of color awareness at what seems to be a precocious age—at least in circumstances favorable to such learning. Goodman's study of a Boston nursery school may be said to have settled this point with admirable clarity.[12] Our data, however, indicate rather considerable variation in the emotional significance of this awareness, a variation doubtless related to the wide variety of learning contexts involved.

None of our New Orleanians remembered being introduced to color at such early ages as Goodman's three-, four-, and five-year-olds in Boston. On the other hand, the folkloristic repetition of stories about the segregation "screen" on New Orleans buses has an apocryphal ring that has led us to the seriously intended psychiatric pun that these are largely screen memories. We conclude that in New Orleans, as in Boston, Negro children experience color awareness much earlier than they will as adults be able to (or care to) recall. The fact remains that there are great differences among our subjects in their reactions to these experiences, just as there seem to have been important differences in the experiences themselves.

From these considerations we find reason to doubt that such a thing as "*a* Negro personality" exists at all. Despite the unquestioned fact that differences of a statistical order between whites as a group and Negroes as a group are well established in a variety of connections, there is no basis for assuming that durable patterns of behavior are related to racial status *as such* even when the emotional implications of the caste system and related stereotyped attitudes or prejudices are included in the social definition of race. Our data confront us with a range of individual reactions to race and color which, if they are culturally patterned at all, are

[12] Mary Ellen Goodman, *Race Awareness in Young Children*, Cambridge, Addison-Wesley Press, 1952.

patterned around a variety of stereotypes rather than a single stereotype for the race. At the same time we need not conclude that the pattern of unconscious reactions to color and caste described by Kardiner and Ovesey does not exist. We do need to question its generality. There undoubtedly are Negroes, possibly even many Negroes, who share a basic personality structure of the type Kardiner and Ovesey describe. They are probably distinct from the Negroes whose adaptations are centered on social class as Davis and Dollard see it. But when we examine the evidence for clues to primary cultural identification, neither pattern seems to explain all the cases, nor do both of them taken together.

If the cultural influences that bear on the Negro individual are not primarily a function of his racial status, it is important to question how they are systematized, and the suggestion that social class is the dominating factor is not to be lightly cast aside. Not all conceptions of social class are equally useful in this connection, and we should make clear that only if social classes can be considered as discontinuous segments of the larger society with differentiated norms and cultures can they be expected to structure individual lives at each class level in a distinctive and identifiable way. Only if individuals of the same class have more in common with each other than with their neighbors of adjacent class rank can we reasonably expect such homogenization of experience and of psychological reactions.

The question of discontinuity between social classes is one of some difficulty. Obviously the existence of some degree of interclass mobility, which is definitionally important to a class system, precludes the possibility of any absolute discontinuity: in any class system there will always be numbers of individuals who are intermediate in social position, presumptively in various stages of transition from one class to another. It is perhaps less obvious, but nonetheless true, that in most dimensions of measurement (and possibly in all of them) the distribution of individuals is so regular and so continuous as to obscure any tendencies towards clustering. The curve of income of individuals or families in most

American communities is a lopsided but simple curve. The distribution of individuals in ranked occupational categories is as continuous as the indefinite subdivision of these necessarily qualitative distinctions permits us to make it. The distribution of education in the population is a smooth curve. Nothing in these data would lead us to suspect the presence of discontinuous cultural entities; rather they seem to confront us with a single complex and continuous ranking system of many intercorrelated descriptive dimensions.

Whatever the level at which we attempt to trace the connections between individuals and their cultures, we may reasonably expect that two relationships will hold: (1) that the cultures in question will tend to be discontinuous from one another at least at some points, and (2) that most individuals will have a primary affiliation with one and only one culture. In order to reëxamine the case for a cultural interpretation of social class, and to explore for other possible dimensions of cultural organization, we have gathered data on one specific aspect of culture that is ordinarily a sensitive indicator of cultural continuity and discontinuity—language. By tape-recording a sampling of the speech of 52 individuals who were asked to read aloud a brief pseudo-test of questions and answers, we obtained a fairly broad sample of the characteristics of New Orleans Negro speech. Transcription and analysis by a linguist reduced this body of data to a check list of 363 selected traits of pronunciation for each subject.

The results of this inquiry are presented in the Appendix,[13] but we may present here our relevant general conclusions. The fact seems to be that there is an enormous amount of free variation in modes of pronunciation, much of it unrelated to other phonetic variations or to variations in social circumstance. We find reason to question our initial assumption that each individual will tend to speak one and only one dialect. There is no individual in our sample who does not have at least some traits of all three of the "dialects" we examined, and there is no individual who has all the

[13] See Appendix 4.

traits of any one of them. For some reason Southeastern dialect
features are associated with light skin color. Non-Southeastern
features are associated with dark skin color and middle-class occupations. These associations are statistically significant ($p < .05$),
and no other relationships were discovered between social variables and speech, though we examined the relevance of age, sex,
religion, residence history, ethnicity, and education.

The New Orleans Negro speech community is neither homogeneous nor clearly segmented. All our subjects have been influenced in at least some degree by the various speech traditions
that have impinged on New Orleans. Most of them speak more
than one "dialect," and a few have some ability to shift consciously
from one to another. There are also hints that alteration of dialect
may take place under stress, a General American pronunciation
being abandoned in favor of a Southeastern one, presumably
learned earlier.

In view of the fluid structure of New Orleans Negro community, these facts do not seem unduly surprising. It may well be
that the geographic dialects we have examined were once far
more self-consistent, but the urban complexity of the city has now
so thoroughly shuffled the families and individuals involved as to
blur this distinctness almost beyond recognition. Out of a welter
of heterogeneous experience, then, the New Orleans Negro must
form his own speech pattern, as he must form his own culture,
from a wide variety of disparate and even conflicting elements.

In our search for the relevant level of integration of the individual's cultural experience, we are led by these data to cling to our
assumptions that cultures are normatively discontinuous entities
to which individuals typically orient themselves segmentally, but
we are forced to reject the assumption that social classes are always cultures in this sense. It would seem more elegant, scientifically, to proceed on the assumption that class cultures do exist,
that they serve as a primary center of the lives of some individuals
and as a force of aspiration for others, but that there are many
individuals for whom the patterns of life associated with these

classes are of distinctly secondary importance or even largely irrelevant.

This point may be clarified with respect to the problems of describing family life, for the cultural significance of class in relation to the individual may be said to rest mainly on the assumption that families tend to belong to one and only one class and that there is a "typical" pattern of family life at each class level. In many aspects this assumption appears to be justifiable. Few observers would confuse the mealtime behavior of a "typical" middle-class family with that of a "typical" lower-class family. Explicit patterns of leisure-time activity, sex role behaviors, general manners, social participation, dress, and consumption spending, and more diffuse patterns in child care, speech, and attitudes can be differentiated to some degree among the different classes. We have described some of the characteristics of the classes of New Orleans Negro society in the preceding chapter. In relating such descriptions to the individual, however, we must note cautiously that some individuals can live in the midst of a class-permeated atmosphere and be relatively insensitive to its existence and uninfluenced by its character. The interpenetration of a series of social worlds differently conceived and differently structured may operate to modify and even negate the influences of one such world through the influences of another.

Repeatedly in the life histories of individuals one sees occasions on which the demands of one role displace those of another, and the dominance of class roles in structuring individual experience and behavior is by no means a foregone conclusion. Class roles do exist in the New Orleans Negro community, but they are fluid and changing, and they encapsulate the primary loyalties of only a part of the population.

It is obvious that just as the diversity of patterns of Negro life in general preclude any tight generalization about general Negro psychology, even so the fluidity of class affiliations and the diversity of individual experiences in relation to them preclude tight generalizations dealing with the psychology of class. It is accordingly appropriate that we delineate the psychological implications not only of the vaguely defined class cultures that may be emergent in New Orleans' social structure, but also of the other cultural entities that serve as reference points in patterns of cultural identification for any substantial number of individuals. If such treatment creates an impression of complexity and flexibility of social milieu it will accord well with the complex and flexible facts.

Our decision to treat the cultural backgrounds of our subjects in terms of their primary role identifications involved us in an analytic effort that proved both exciting and complex. We were forced to innovate to some degree in method, and we have found it difficult in retrospect to summarize our endeavor in a way that will carry the conviction that we think it merits. In the last analysis all we did was to reread our case records, but we did so multiple times, and each time we looked for rather specific things relevant to the identification and ethnocentrism of the individual. Over a period of a few weeks the things we found added up to the picture presented in the following chapters.

We read each case carefully, noting every expression or implication of the given subject's positive social loyalties. We paid particular attention to the groups to which these were referred, and formulated preliminary hypotheses about which of these reference groups might prove to be the primary one for this person. Then we rechecked each case for all expressions of hostility, antipathy, and aggression. In most cases the correspondence and complementarity of these positive and negative dimensions was truly astonishing from the outset. As a further check, however, we arbitrarily composed alternative hypotheses, and for the better part of a month the staff sociologist and anthropologist discussed the cases, one by one, entertaining each available construction of the person's primary role in turn, until we were satisfied that the only viable interpretation was the one selected. At this stage, in fact, we employed a method of explicit advocacy, one of us defending each hypothesis while another attacked it.

The most difficult aspect of this procedure to describe convincingly is the clinching negative evidence. Frequently we read through an entire record (often 200 pages of material or more), looking for something that simply wasn't there. Since we cannot present our full case records on our 20 subjects in much less than 20 volumes, we despair of being able to reproduce for the reader the sense of certainty we sometimes gained from this laborious experience.

When we completed the analysis we found the subjects grouped as they are grouped in the following chapters. The placement of each subject had been carefully considered against all the alternatives there described and several more. We considered separately for each subject the possibility that race, religion, political position, profession, class, sex, age, or intellect might be the dimension of his primary role identification, and we considered a variety of other possibilities in a more cursory way. The affirmation of the subject's present placement, then, rests on the negation of all the alternatives that occurred to us, and each of these was considered separately and at length.

Our resulting conception of the social worlds to which New Orleans Negroes orient their lives may be likened to a complex field of particles in which a number of different forces are operating in a number of dimensions. Most of the particles cluster in organized nuclei of relatively definite structure, while somewhat fewer are scattered broadcast with only a vague attachment to any given nucleus. In this conception, middle-class culture is construed as a nucleus created and maintained by the relatively small group of people who are, so to speak, professionally middle class, rather than as a stratum dependent on the partial or peripheral attention of a much larger group. This conception also frees us to consider the middle class in isolation from the lower class, since the existence of the former need imply nothing about the latter. We are left free to examine each group or each individual for the dimension of social and cultural integration that proves most relevant.

Most individuals do appear to relate themselves primarily to one cultural nucleus—to one social world. In a complex society they do so despite their awareness of the existence of others, often despite rather considerable experience with the alternatives they come to reject. In the simpler context of tribal and ethnic identification, this experience of alternatives is rarer and more limited, and one becomes a Chuckchee or a Hopi almost by default. Our linguistic data indicate rather clearly that differing cultural traditions can be maintained in a complex urban setting only through exercising choice in the face of explicit awareness of competing possibilities. To a degree the choices made by our subjects remain cultural, for they are institutionalized in differing systems of socialization and family life passed on from generation to generation, and they embody differing configurations of roles and differing values.

The structure of these various cultures and their place in the experience of individuals are described in the following chapters. We may anticipate that discussion by outlining the conclusions to which they point as these are relevant to our general method. Briefly, we find that the 20 individuals we have scrutinized most closely fall into five major groups. Four of these are cultures in the sense we have defined, and the fifth is the residual group of the culturally marginal. Each of the first four groups has a distinctive pattern of family life and socialization. We have called them the *Middle Class,* the *Matriarchy,* the *Gang,* and the *Family.* The accompanying diagram (Figure 6) may sharpen further the cultural character of these social worlds. It shows the position of each of our 20 subjects in terms of the character of his parents' family— the number of years he has lived with each parent—together with the character of the family that each has since established by marriage and the influence of that on his oldest child, if any. There is no question of absolute determinism here, but it is striking that there are only two cases of marked acculturation (or mobility) even over two and a half generations.

The patterns of primary role identifications that we are tracing are then patterns of cultural identification, institutionalized in family life and in the manner of training children. We doubt that we have found all these patterns that exist among New Orleans Negroes. We have found enough to conclude that their variability

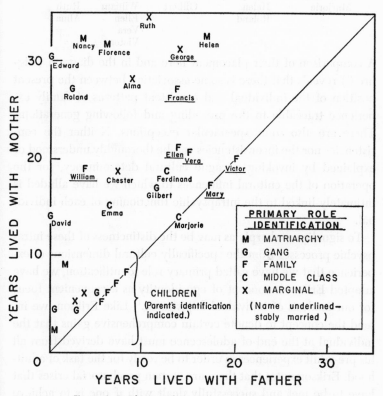

Figure 6. Residence with Parents or Parent-Surrogates.

is sufficient to account for Davis' and Dollard's findings and Kardiner's and Ovesey's, provided no arbitrary claims to completeness or to absolute generality are honored. The enormous cultural complexity of a modern city and the astonishing variety of individual experience impress us with the dangers of pushing on to a premature closure or an overgeneralized synthesis.

The primary role identifications of our 20 subjects may be listed as follows:

Middle Class	Matriarchy	Gang	Family	Marginal
Emma	Florence	Edward	Francis	Chester
Ferdinand	Nancy	David	Mary	George
Marjorie	Helen	Gilbert	William	Ruth
	Roland		Ellen	Alma
			Vera	
			Victor	

A comparison of their placement here and in the diagram (Figure 6) reveals that there is some association between the present position of the individual and consistent patterns of family experience traceable to the preceding and following generations. There are also some spectacular exceptions. Neither the consistencies nor the inconsistencies can be thoroughly understood or explained by invoking a vague cultural determinancy, for the operation of the cultural influences to which we have alluded is intimately linked to the intrapsychic functioning of each individual.

To signalize as sharply as may be the distinctness of these intrapsychic processes from the specifically cultural dimensions of experience that we have called primary role identification, we have adopted Erikson's concept of ego identity as a convenient focus for our analysis of individual adjustment.[14] Like Erikson, we intend the concept to denote certain comprehensive gains that the individual at the end of adolescence must have derived from all his pre-adult experiences in order to be ready for the task of adulthood. Erikson notes that there are certain psychosocial crises that have to be met and successfully dealt with if one is to achieve maturity. These crises are: in infancy, the development of trust vs. mistrust; in early childhood, the development of autonomy vs. shame and doubt; at the play age, the development of initiative vs. guilt; at school age, the development of industry vs. inferiority; at adolescence, the development of ego identity vs. identity

[14] Erik H. Erikson, "The Problem of Ego Identity," *Journal of the American Psychoanalytic Association*, 1956, 4:56–121.

diffusion, and at young adulthood, the development of intimacy vs. isolation. All these developmental periods are intimately inter-related, and defective development at one phase will serve to make the successful negotiation of a subsequent phase more diffi-cult. Alternatively the successful resolution of each crisis enhances the probability that the subsequent one will be successfully met.

One of the most fundamental facts documented in the massive literature on psychological development in the past 50 years is the importance of strategically placed adults in shaping the psycho-logical development of an individual, and the significance of the way such figures are pieced together to form an ego ideal: ". . . The to-be-strived-for but forever not-quite-attainable ideal goals for the self."[15] In this process of evolving an ego ideal, early experiences with older people felt to be psychologically significant define the range within which one can elaborate a personal ideal that has internal self-consistency. The molding of the general de-sign and the embellishment of detail of such an image is a process that goes on through time, and may involve, as it does for some of our subjects, at least the first 30 years of life. But at each of the psychosocial developmental phases there must be an ego ideal figure, an image after which one patterns one's self.

In the subjective but psychologically real world of every in-dividual there is a unifying central core of feelings and attitudes to which the experiences of self definition become consistently re-lated. For one individual the self-defining experiences may be paranoid elaborations. For another they may be a realistic and truly intimate fellowship and expression of emotions in social transactions. In any case the conception of self at any of the stages of psychosocial development represents the intermeshing of con-temporary with antecedent experiences through such processes as condensation, repression, or affect gratification and deprivation.

The development of individual ego identity has a parallel in the role identifications that pattern for each role group, the range of acceptable and unacceptable paths to emotional satisfaction.

[15] *Ibid.*, p. 105.

One's experiences of these roles define for him the aspects of his total social environment that require emotional commitment—delimiting his psychologically significant social world, structuring the way that affect gratifications can be achieved, setting the conditions under which they will be withheld, and creating anticipatory feelings of security or anxiety.

The norms and values in the social worlds of our subjects are revealed in what we have called their primary role identification. The personal residue of the individual's experience in interaction with his society becomes the patterned intrapsychic process that he characteristically utilizes in his transactions with his social world: his mode of psychodynamic functioning. The next five chapters depict the emergence of the primary role identifications of our subjects from their varying patterns of experience, and the development of their psychodynamics in the presence or absence of environing emotional support. Only a full description of these data can do justice to the intricacy and subtlety as well as the intimate interdependence of the social and psychological formation of identifications and of identity.

CHAPTER 4

The Middle Class

The pattern of positive identification of our three middle-class subjects links them to a variety of social roles, but does so in terms of a class conception not dissimilar to that of many social scientists. In fact, some of these people are familiar with the ideas of William Lloyd Warner,[1] and not only use his terms but cite him as their source. Their concensus on the nature of society thus tends to revolve around certain social values, which they believe to be characteristic of a recognizable "middle-class" group of people: achievement, responsibility, respectability, politeness, industry, egalitarianism, and kindred virtues. These tend to be seen as an intelligible and coherent whole, a "way of life," and are thought to be closely associated with and symbolized by a certain range of social statuses in the occupational, educational, and civic spheres. As these quotations from our case records illustrate, our "middle-class" subjects lay great stress on the achievement of these statuses.

Emma: My only concern now—I shouldn't say my only concern —my main concern now is being able to accomplish the thing that I'm trying to do in school.

Psychiatrist: What is that? I don't really know.

Emma: Well, I would like to be an elementary schoolteacher.

[1] W. Lloyd Warner and Paul S. Lunt, *The Social Life of a Modern Community*, New Haven, Yale University Press, 1941.

Marjorie: My race doesn't hold on to property like other people. They tend to get something from their family and let it go. I've made advantage of what I got from my mother and father, but it seems that my husband and other people don't appreciate this.

Ferdinand: These people out at my school are very "country people.". . . It is very difficult for me to lead these people because their thinking and customs are so different from mine.

These people are not only objectively identifiable as belonging to the occupational and educational level usually associated with the middle class (teacher or businesswoman with a college education), they are also subjectively middle class, and point up their status with "accomplishing" an education, "making advantage" of property, and "leading" the community through education. It is obvious that the objective occupancy of a status need not imply this subjective and ethical commitment, and frequently in our cases it does not. In these three cases, however, there is a direct and explicit identification with values seen in class terms.

Adherence to the ethical standards implied by these judgments necessarily structures in a distinctive way these individuals' views of persons who do not share such standards, and if our interpretation is correct it should follow that they will see this out-group in class terms. So, in fact, they do. It is difficult to convey in brief compass the degree to which, in these three cases, all antagonisms are cast in class terms. Emma, for example, has considerable resentment of segregation and discrimination, but this revolves around her own class interests and she even explains the phenomenon of race prejudice in class terms as a lack of manners or of education:

She described in great detail the attitudes of clerks and doctors in the various clinics. She tends to attribute most of the difficulty that Negroes have to the attitude of the clerk. She describes them as being inconsiderate and not very bright.

All three of our middle-class people express sharp antagonism toward the lower class and its unprincipled way of life. For example:

Ferdinand and his brother recently had some quarrels about his sister's conduct with a married man. It seems that she is bringing him to the house at night. Ferdinand feels that this impairs his position in the community, and is not the sort of thing he should do as a public figure of some prominence in the neighborhood. Much to his distress, his brother, who is about a year younger than Ferdinand, took the sister to task for this in such a loud and attacking manner that all the neighbors were able to hear what was going on. Ferdinand feels that the only solution to the problem is for him to leave. . . .

Marjorie, though elsewhere expressing these same sentiments, completes the picture by a fleeting rejection of the upper class as well:

The less people know about you, the better they like you. . . . I like the middle classes; I like the masses. I go to the masses. I don't cater to the upper class. I went to the people whenever I had a problem at the office in any differences between myself, my sisters, or my husband, and the people backed me up.

Expressed piecemeal but emphatically in these cases is a rejection of the criminality, improvidence, uncouthness, ignorance, and dirtiness they feel characterize the lower class. Equally rejected, though seemingly far less important, is the snobbery of the upper class. Our middle-class people, then, see themselves as members of a definite class culture sharing common values and common occupational and educational statuses and they see themselves surrounded by "foreigners" holding different values, different statuses, and different styles of life. They perceive these things as a matter of class and they so explain them to themselves.

Furthermore this view of society is, for these people, dominant over all alternatives. A basically religious, political, or racial identification is made impossible for them because they see class and the symbols of class (occupation and education) as far more im-

portant. In most cases our data present us with at least one instance of explicit choice of emphasis on class over each of the
alternatives mentioned. Thus one subject whose religious orientation is important to her nevertheless makes clear that, in her
theology, God is middle class:

When I was young, I thought God was like Santa Claus: that all you
had to do was pray and He would give you things. Now I realize you
have to work for God.

It is interesting that all three of our middle-class subjects have
been put in the position of choosing between their middle-class
self-conceptions and their loyalties to family. Ferdinand's difficulties with his brother and sister over the etiquette and morality
of class and Marjorie's difficulties with her lower-class husbands
are matched by Emma's complete break with her own family and
successive divorces from two lower-class men, as well as her rejection and denial of her criminal brother. All these people are
church members of sorts, but none of them is really concerned
with religion except as a prop to status or a rationale for middle-
class ethics. None of them could be considered as devout. Occupation and education are important to them, but in an instrumental
and symbolic way. There is no elaboration of a professional identification or of intellectual values for their own sake, and even in
these spheres we can say that it is the class value of these statuses
rather than their intrinsic content that is felt to be important. In
a sense we can even assert that not even sex is as fundamental to
these people as class: all of them are playing atypical sex roles in
which an element of conscious and explicit choice has entered.
This may be fortuitous, but it is consistent with a profoundly middle-class orientation that when necessary, even one's sexual identification may be subordinated.

The impact of a middle-class identification on racial self-conceptions is deserving of special comment. There are marked differences among our three middle-class subjects in awareness of or
attention to racial matters. All of them recognize the existence of

handicaps and discrimination in this connection, but their emphasis on class over color is explicit:

Marjorie said she felt (color) did not have anything to do with the (difficulties she was having in her) marriage . . . (and) went on to state that she felt the more important difference was in background—that she came from a cultured, fairly well-to-do family, whereas he came from a rural, country background and never knew very much about culture.

When I wondered if Ferdinand felt (his being selected for the study) was something that had been on a color basis, since the principal had reputedly been a person prejudiced in favor of light-skinned people, he quickly discarded this as having been important. He went on to say that he felt it was because he was a socially inferior person to the group of students at school. Though he and his family had an adequate amount of money, presumably enough to give him equal status with the other students in this respect, they had no social standing.

Emma, who expresses far more concern with discrimination than the others, rationalizes this to herself as a matter of "intelligence" that cuts across racial lines:

Emma talked of two (white) boys, apparently of late adolescence, who moved when they found they had to sit next to her while filing an application in an employment agency recently. She described this as utterly stupid behavior. She tempered these remarks, however (possibly in an effort not to offend me), with some remarks about the very "intelligent" white people she knew—meaning "intelligence" as disregard of segregation. She said that it was stupid for whites to discriminate in this way, since they came so close to Negroes as domestic servants.

We may conclude that a middle-class conception of yourself does not preclude reacting to other roles, but that there appears to be a tendency for one or another role to become primary and dominate your view of life. A sensitivity to color symbols must be carefully assessed in this context, and in middle-class people the tendency would seem to be to see and interpret color not for what it is but as a status symbol. This would seem to underlie, in turn, the middle-class ambivalence towards color. On the one hand, light skin color is thought to be associated with achievement of an occupational or educational type and comes to share in the value associated with such achievement. On the other hand there is a recognition that skin color in itself is not "achieved," and in statements of an ideal type the middle class expresses emphatically the view that color *shouldn't* matter. The *Louisiana Weekly* phrases this succinctly in its "platform":

The Louisiana Weekly shall work relentlessly for human and civil rights for all citizens and will expose those who appeal to prejudices rather than reason in their approach to problems concerning human relations. The Louisiana Weekly shall strive to mold public opinion in the interest of all things constructive.[2]

Color shouldn't matter but it does. It was a middle-class poet rather than a folk artist who got around to penning a *Segregation Blues:*

> Like Mister Hitler's Jews,
> I got thuh Segregation Blues—
> Got thuh Housing Project,
> Street car,
> Jim-Crow, Segregation Blues.[3]

The middle-class reactions to the paradox of this situation remain varied. Possibly this is the variation in the reactions of most groups of people to the eternal gap between what they believe to be and what they believe ought to be. Middle-class Negroes can hardly see segregation as anything but a threat to their ideology of achievement, equality, and progress, and their common reaction can only be a denial of the evaluation placed upon race and color not only by whites but also by many Negroes. In a transitional period of historic change, however, the denial remains necessary, for the affirmation continues to exist.

It is perhaps this attitude of militant denial of the importance of race that most profoundly characterizes the Negro middle class reaction to its paradoxical position in a segregated society. In-

[2] *Louisiana Weekly,* July 7, 1956, p. 11.
[3] Marcus B. Christian, *Louisiana Weekly,* June 23, 1956, p. 4-b.

creasing numbers of people from the middle-class segment of society are joining groups dedicated to racial progress, talking in terms of being "race right," and subtly shifting their identification to that of the "race man." Such a change may be interpreted in our terms as a rejection of the middle-class self-conception and the substitution of a racial one, but none of our subjects goes all the way along this path. They seem rather to preserve a basic outlook that isolates them from racial issues to some degree and shields them from "too great" a concern with race and color.

If this picture of middle-class identification is valid, the question of how it arises becomes pertinent. We would expect, of course, to find that middle-class people had some common experiences during their developmental years.

All three of our middle-class subjects are college graduates. All of them were teen-age rebels against authority in their struggle to establish an ego identity. Two of them were fortunate in being around adult persons they admired very much, who provided them with emotional support during their psychosocial crisis periods. Emma's ego ideals in fact were two: her favorite aunt, and her "white" grandmother; Marjorie's was her father, and she has become such a successful "businessman" as to be a failure as a mother and wife. Both of them have emerged into young adulthood with coherent ego identities. Ferdinand, on the other hand, has not solved the riddle of his ego identity, and it is worthy of note that the only emotionally supporting mature figure in his life (his grandfather) died when he was 11. Ferdinand feels confused about his sexual identity, inadequate in his occupational world, and fearful of most of the situations that he encounters in life. He employs paranoid elaborations in attempts to make his social world tolerable for himself, and is tottering precariously close to a psychotic breakdown.

Each of our middle-class subjects felt contempt for his parent of like sex, and regarded the parent of opposite sex as the dominant person in the family group. All three have experienced difficulties in establishing stable marital relationships. All of them were indulged by emotionally supporting, significant adults in their first ten years, and they early learned to exploit that indulgence. These adults had in common the achievement of social recognition and status through activities that required the utilization of intellectual qualities, i.e., Ferdinand's grandfather and Marjorie's father both achieved considerable success in business, and Emma's aunt had some success in writing poetry.

All three of these subjects took the initiative in peer group relations in adolescence, and enjoyed prestige and success in the group as a result. The importance of the adolescent rebellion in the working out of their middle-class identifications is not to be glossed over, for the "rebellion" in every case was an attempt to establish their own integrity as an individual. Even though only one of our middle-class subjects came from a middle-class family, this paradigm of rebelliousness seems to hold for all of them. Only such a rebellion could give rise to the highly individual emphasis on personal achievement, autonomy, independence, competition, and atomism that are the essence of middle-class virtue:

Marjorie opposes all family traditions and is very radical. She feels that the family keeps her too close, and prefers to associate with "poorer" people.

Eventually Marjorie's opposition to her family resulted in her outdoing them in entrepreneurial achievement. Emma and Ferdinand moved successfully from lower-class origins to a middle-class identification and level of achievement precisely through rejection of their families.

The range of attitudes towards race to which these people were exposed as children is strikingly broad. Marjorie's mother's attitudes are not reported, but:

Marjorie's father always said you can't solve a problem by running. Negroes should stay South and fight.

Marjorie says of her father:

People have a joke on my father. They say he was twenty-one years old before he knew he was a Negro. They say when he woke up and saw he was a Negro he has been *mad* ever since. He just hated he was a Negro, but after he knew he was a Negro he decided to make the best of it he could. He just decided to go on and be a *good* Negro.

Ferdinand's mother and father both tried in vain to teach him to be a "good Negro" in the more classical Southern sense; his father reports:

Now, when I speak to those white boys, I say "Mr." and "yes, sir" and "yes, ma'am" to them. I try to tell that to Ferdinand, but he can't see it like that.

Ferdinand says of his mother:

She says it don't make no difference if people be standing up all over the street car, I don't have no business doing nothing. If some white people don't move I don't have nothing to do with it. But not me. I just go on and sit in front when I know they see me. I don't tell them anything.

Ferdinand's father explains perceptively the source of his son's refusal to "see it like that":

Ferdinand got so smart as to tell me they didn't teach that in school. He says they tell him in school to say "yes" and "no" to white people, but you see I know when you got to work for white people you can't do to suit yourself.

Emma's mother does not report how she instructed Emma on racial matters, but her attitude seems to express the same fearful accommodation:

White people sure are funny. They'll treat you all right as long as you act dumb or never get to be more than them. But once you try to be superior to them they sure are going not to like you. They don't want to see a Negro get ahead of them. They think all Negroes are dumb, and if they don't act dumb they get mad with them and try to kill them.

Emma's aunt, however, expresses something closer to the class ideology that has since become Emma's own:

Yes, Negroes ought to learn how to act. They don't know how to act. That's why they don't get as much as they can. . . . I think if the Negro could become more interested in doing the right thing, in being more moral, I think they'd get along much better.

The life of Emma Fisk exemplifies a broad range of the processes and problems peculiar to a middle-class adaptation and to class mobility. At the same time it points up the flexibility of these patterns and the subtlety and variety of their manifestations in individual experience.

EMMA FISK: MOST LIKELY TO SUCCEED

Emma Fisk is a sociological phenomenon and a fascinating personality. How this pleasant, poised young woman of bright normal intelligence has survived and overcome the severe handicaps of an unequivocally lower-class origin is a dramatic success story in the great American middle-class tradition. Emma exemplifies a driving, aggressive, restless segment of the younger part of New Orleans Negro society, and embodies in many ways the useful and constructive ethnocentric trend of her generation, even though she has pushed mainly to make things better for herself and with only a hazy awareness of altruism. The problem in studying Emma is to understand from both the cultural and intrapsychic viewpoints what motivates her ambition.

Emma is now in her early thirties. She was born in 1922, the youngest of three children in a lower-class family. Her father had been variously employed as a porter and musician, and at times also gambled for a living. Emma has a brother about five years older than she and a sister one year older. Her family remained intact through the first six or seven years of her life, and when her parents separated Emma remained with her mother and siblings until about 1937. She was married briefly at 15, interrupting her high school education. She was remarried several years later, and held a number of jobs both in New Orleans and midwestern cities before she finally returned to high school in the mid-1940's. From that point on, her efforts have been aimed at securing a college degree so that she could become a school teacher. Both her first and her second husband were musicians. Her third marriage, to a stably employed auto mechanic, was contracted shortly before the beginning of the present restudy of her life.

Emma described her mother's mother as an entirely white Irish girl who was rejected by her own family when she married a dark Negro. Emma has never openly admitted that this was not the case, but occasional discrepancies prompted careful investigation of the matter. The truth seems to be that Emma's grandmother and her siblings (Emma's maternal great-uncles and great-aunts) were reared as Negroes, though they were light-skinned and had little difficulty passing for white. All of them except Emma's grandmother married white persons and reared their children as white. There is a legend that the seven great-uncles threatened to kill Emma's grandfather, but evidently this did not happen. Emma's cousins knew about their Negro ancestry and one of them was rejected by her white husband when he discovered that she was part Negro. Emma saw some of them at least once at a family funeral. Her evasiveness concerning the ancestry of her maternal grandmother would appear to be quite deliberate, but she may have managed to deceive herself about it in order to remain a little closer to the prestige and status that white descent carries for her. Even apart from her racial affiliations, Emma's maternal grandmother is a figure of great importance to her. After Emma's grandfather died, her grandmother married a second time, again to a Negro, but she had no children by Emma's step-grandfather, and he is now deceased. Emma remembers him as having a French name. The maternal side of Emma's family lived in a section of New Orleans in which there were a great many Creole Negroes but she had no Creole forebears. "Creoleness" is of importance to Emma, probably because it, too, implies "whiteness." Her considerable emphasis on her white ancestry contrasts with the attitudes of the majority of the subjects we have contacted, and even with Emma's own adolescent views.

Emma's mother married a very dark-skinned musician. The marriage was in direct opposition to Emma's grandmother's

wishes, in a striking parallel to the grandmother's own marriage.
Emma's first marriage was also to a very dark musician, and was
contracted with the strong disapproval of her mother. There is no
evidence that Emma's mother was a very talented person, but she
is reported to have met her husband while she was a teen-ager
performing in a vaudeville troupe in New York. He was one of the
musicians with the troupe, sixteen years older than his wife, and
had not been married before. His employment as a musician was
undoubtedly sporadic in his later years.

Emma's mother and maternal aunts have lived fairly close to
her grandmother during most of their lives, and her grandfather
has been in the same locality as far back as Emma can remember.
Emma's parents separated when she was six. Her father survived
until she was about 13. As nearly as can be determined, Emma's
parents' family life was stable during the time they lived together.
Her father worked at times as a common porter. Allegedly he also
engaged in lottery vending and gambling. It is reported that he
gave his wife about $60 every two weeks after their separation.
Considering that this occurred during the depression, he appears
to have been a fairly competent wage earner, and he certainly
felt a significant degree of responsibility for his family. His attitude toward Emma during the years following separation from
his wife was one of affection and indulgence: she was clearly his
favorite child.

Emma's mother is light-skinned but not light enough to pass.
She behaved toward her husband as a spoiled child would to an
indulgent father. They had been married about 12 years when
they separated with mutual accusations of infidelity. Emma's
adolescent account of the circumstances of the separation may be
a screen memory, but in this version Emma relegated all the responsibility for the break to her mother. She said her mother had
all the furniture and clothing removed from the house after her
father left for work, and she left without telling him, taking her
three children to friends and relatives, and allowing her husband
to come home to the shock of a completely empty and deserted

house. Emma sympathized with the sadness, pain, and shock that she believed her father must have felt. It is likely nonetheless that her father had more responsibility for the separation than Emma admits.

Following the break, Emma's mother led the family's fortunes steadily down hill. She began to go out with men a great deal, and left the care of the children to friends or relatives. Emma has described this period with great bitterness, blaming her mother both for her father's departure and for the deprivation and instability of her life throughout her grade school years. There is a significant relationship between this traumatic period and Emma's strong need to compete, to be at odds with the opposite sex, to disparage others, and to indulge in almost malevolent attacks on men.

Emma's mother has now remarried although she has had no further children. Following her separation, her means of support were certainly obscure, and it appears that she may have relied mainly on money given her by a series of common law husbands. At times she was employed as a seamstress. Some ambiguous information suggests that she was a casual prostitute. Emma still sees her frequently, but irregularly, and expresses great contempt for her.

Emma and her older sister have never gotten along well and have little to do with each other. This sister tried to assume a controlling, maternal role in the family during Emma's early adolescence, and Emma resented this a great deal. Her sister was married the year Emma's father died. She was pregnant at the time, and her marriage was most unhappy and violent. For a while following the marriage her sister and brother-in-law lived with Emma and her mother, but within a year, Emma herself married, at the age of 15.

The oldest child in Emma's family, her brother, has been more or less continuously in trouble with the law since childhood. In 1937, several years after he had left home, he was described by his mother as "probably dead." This was an open and conscious deception, since he was at that time in prison, and his mother and sisters were terribly ashamed of him. He has continued to be a petty thief, and is continuously in and out of prison. He is a source of great concern to Emma. She feels that if anyone should find out she has a brother with a criminal record it would be very damaging to her own reputation. She attempted to hide this information at first during her current interviews, just as her mother had attempted to hide it some years ago from the original interviewer.

As their vaudeville experience would imply, both of Emma's parents were musically inclined. Emma's mother, particularly, tried to teach all the children to play and sing. Her son was forced to play the violin, which he resented bitterly. Emma remembers with some amusement that her mother tried to make her brother behave like "Little Lord Fauntleroy."

Emma credits her interest in education to the influence of her father's sister. Emma was very close to her and spent a great deal of time in her home from about the age of ten on. She describes her as being self-educated, very intelligent, and acquainted with many classical works of literature, which the old lady still reads frequently. This aunt is a definitely positive influence in Emma's life and Emma has a great deal of fondness for her.

Emma's mother was punitive to her children when they were of early grade school age. Emma remembers her mother as stingy, suspicious, demanding, and controlling. She was very strict about Emma's choice of friends until Emma reached puberty. As young adolescents Emma and her older sister joined forces to foil their mother's restrictions, although mistrust and suspicion were otherwise the dominant feelings between them. The relative stability of Emma's earlier childhood up to age six is demonstrable in purely material ways. There was enough money and food then, and the family routines were consistent. The circumstances emanating from the breakup of her parents' marriage changed all this and it was during this later period that Emma's brother established his reputation as a petty criminal. Correspondingly, Emma became an accomplished rebel at school. When she first began the current series of psychiatric interviews, she identified herself as a disciplinary problem and indicated her belief that she had originally been selected for study on that basis.

Emma's mother felt that Emma's infancy was normal. She was both breast and bottle fed and there were no difficulties involving eating or toilet training. Occasional enuresis occurred until the age of nine. There were no outstanding illnesses. Her mother felt that she was essentially a good child and "easy to control" until she reached puberty at about the age of 12, when she became unruly and had many quarrels with her teachers. She was expelled from school several times and always turned to her father to get herself back in. She also enlisted her father's aid against teachers she believed were unfair, and she would go to her father for indulgences such as candy and spending money. In the midst of all of this turmoil of near delinquency, rebellion, and probably sexual experimentation, however, Emma began to demonstrate one of her notably constructive and useful adaptive techniques: she was a leader. This amounted to "gang" leadership in part, but it was responsible leadership in many respects. At first it was confined to her own sex—girls' sports, girls' clubs, etc.—but a social and heterosexual note quickly emerged. She loved dancing, and still does.

Both in 1938 and in the current study Emma denied any heterosexual experience prior to her first marriage. A Negro psychiatrist, however, secured admissions of her first such experiences by aggressive questioning. These occurred when she was 14. The first was described as literally a rape, which was painful and frightening. Her second sexual experience (with her husband to be) occurred not too long afterward. She says it, too, was a painful and unpleasant experience. Only after several months of marriage, she says, did she find any pleasure whatsoever in sexual intercourse. Emma's mother was sure that Emma was sexually promiscuous when she was in high school, and was openly accusatory and suspicious about it, which Emma bitterly resented.

While Emma was in grade school and high school she was close to her group of friends and very prominent in their club activities, but feelings of jealousy and rivalry also entered the picture to some extent. There was apparently a good deal of fighting for power and domination among this group, and Emma usually ended up on top. There is some evidence that she got along much better with boys than with girls but this may represent a personal prejudice of the 1938 interviewer. She managed to get by in school, but without distinguishing herself scholastically. Her capacities for profiting from her school experience were obviously limited by her hostility toward teachers. She felt that she was discriminated against and probably she was, since she provoked such treatment. She is most sensitive still to any implication of personal discrimination of any sort, whether on the basis of color, social background, or jealousy of her achievements, her ambitions or her physical appearance.

In typical early adolescent fashion, Emma had little conscious thought of the future and there was certainly almost nothing to indicate her later interest in becoming a teacher. The only hint we have of influences in this direction was her closeness to her literarily inclined paternal aunt. Emma's ideal conception of a woman or mother appears as a condensation of elements in the personalities of this particular aunt and her maternal grandmother. She deeply appreciated the superior position her white grandmother held in her social relationships with other members of the family.

As an adult Emma remembers how she always determined that she would be the very best player at any game she undertook. She has always been apt to explode in times of tension, and she describes her own worst trait as being a tendency to push determination into stubbornness: "I think a lot of my disappointment lies in the fact that I expect too much, and that I want everything just right. My greatest strength is also my greatest weakness. My strong determination cripples me when it becomes stubbornness."

Emma met her first husband through one of the adolescent social clubs to which she belonged. Her mother's objections to the relationship served only to spur on Emma's interest in the boy. In the heat of her conflict with her mother, she impulsively ran off to marry him. The entire experience was precipitous. She was 15 at the time and he was in his twenties. She and her mother "did not speak" for some time thereafter, a characteristic occurrence with Emma when she is at odds with anyone. Her husband rented an apartment for them in New Orleans but left town soon afterward. He was a musician and had an engagement with a band in Ohio. She joined him there, her first venture out of the segregated South.

Emma's husband apparently treated her in an indulgent way, much as her father had done. He gave her money and made few demands upon her. She had some enjoyment of her sexual relationship with him, though she did not establish a mature marital relationship. She finally allowed her mother to coerce her into leaving him, and the two women went to Chicago, where Emma worked in several places on defense jobs or running an elevator. She was never fired from any of these jobs, but she says, "On several occasions I should have been." In other words, she continued to act as a rebellious early adolescent.

Emma's mother succeeded in her efforts to break up this marriage by exploiting Emma's suspicion and distrust of others. Emma suspected that her husband was still attached to a previous fiancée who had reportedly had an illegitimate child by him. Although they did manage to effect some sort of adjustment, it was based on his leaving her alone and allowing her to do what she wished. Her husband's income fell off rapidly, and their standard of living became increasingly unsatisfactory to Emma. She was unable to get enough money from him to spend all day in the movies. There was little to their relationship other than this sort of exchange. At first she described their separation as being of her own volition. Later she blamed her mother, but her mother must have had an easy time of it in view of Emma's rebellious impulsiveness. In any case, Emma bitterly resented her mother's interference in her marriage, and still feels that it might eventually have been a success. The amount of hostility invested in this distortion is directly referable to Emma's feeling about her own father's defection when she was six. Her marriage occurred less than two years after her father's death.

Among the dreams Emma reported in 1938 was one of particular interest, which reveals some of her feelings about this. Emma dreamed she saw her father's face superimposed upon her mother's while both were in bed. She woke from the dream feeling frightened. We have several possible interpretations of the dream to consider. It indicates a great deal of confusion in Emma's mind about her own sexuality. She does have a durable pattern of relating to men as maternal figures, which persists even in her third marriage. It may be that this attitude is a purely manipulative and exploitative one with implications of class and caste determination, but it would be more reasonable to see the heterosexual patterns of her life as stemming from her mother's ambivalence.

From a more developmental point of view, one can consider the dream as a rather direct reference to the primal scene, with corresponding oedipal implications. Her mother revealed in 1938 that it was certain Emma had witnessed parental intercourse because it occurred while the child was in the same bed with them. The affect of fright associated with the dream is consistent with a primal scene theme. Another association was that Emma felt menstruation was "the worst thing that could happen." Violent misconceptions of the sexual act and fears of penetration have been implied in some of her productions.

Another significant experience had occurred when Emma was 13. She was visiting her father while he was sick. She stayed over night and woke in the morning to find him looking "in a pitiful state," and staring at her. She thought that he had intended attacking her. She was very frightened and got another man living in the same building to intervene. Her father was suffering at the time from heart trouble, which shortly resulted in his death. Emma has always spoken of a great deal of attachment to her father, and describes him as the only giving and warm person of her family. She denies any complicity on his part for the failure of her parents' marriage, and refuses to see any significance to the fact that her father was the one who literally left the family.

It is difficult to see how Emma, as she appeared at the age of 13 or 14, could possibly have succeeded in mobilizing her resources and making the dramatic social advances now visible. At that time she appeared to be well on her way to a life of repeated marriage and stormy interpersonal relationships within the lower-class level of society. The "blind" psychiatric analysis of Emma's 1938 record uncovered no indication that she might achieve even a minor degree of success in any area of life. The psychiatrist predicted disturbed interpersonal relationships throughout her life, numerous marriages, a need to exploit men, and no particular capacity for mothering. He implied that she might engage in some variety of prostitution, that she would never finish high school, and that she would be unable to do any but unskilled work. It also appeared to him that she would attempt to control and dominate her friends. Many of the traits predicted do persist in her adult life, but the fact is that she has become a fairly responsible member of society, and the malevolent or antisocial overtones to her activity as an adolescent have now been almost completely attenuated, and relegated to specific and personal areas of her life.

With Emma's first marriage and break-away from her mother there began a series of events that had considerable influence in channelizing her aggression and determination along the lines that we see in adulthood. It seems in retrospect that this extended experience, a period of at least four years, was a "second latency period," or "psychosocial moratorium,"[4] a time during which the individual may freely experiment in order to find a niche in some section of society that is firmly defined and yet seems to be uniquely made for him. In such a period, there is a diminution of all the overt and unstable qualities of early adolescence and a return to some of the mutual satisfactions between mother and child. After her marriage Emma continued through many stormy

[4] E. H. Erikson, "The Problem of Ego Identity," *Journal of the American Psychoanalytic Association*, January, 1956, 4:56–121.

years to work toward the achievement of a personal integration. Much of the ominously antisocial tone of her earlier years is gone as she approaches her early twenties, and begins to form a sense of identity rather than simply identifying with one individual or another. What finally emerged from the fusion of Emma's personality was a person to whom society began to respond positively rather than negatively.

In retrospect, too, there must have been some basis in the earliest period of her life for the remarkable security that Emma now manifests. Over and over again she has demonstrated her enduring trust in the possibility of satisfactory relationships with others. She has been able to recuperate from narcissistic blows and to expand her adaptive techniques steadily as a result of some good early interpersonal experience. The benign account that Emma's mother once gave of Emma's infancy also suggests this. Another significant point about Emma's mother, perhaps, is that her oldest son was bad. Possibly this boy served as a scapegoat for her conflict with males, and diverted from Emma and her sister the worst of their mother's ambivalent feelings. Emma's mother did permit her to enter school with some capacity to utilize her opportunities for learning competitive techniques, and Emma made the most of them.

Emma remembered the jobs she had in Chicago as evidence that white people can be fair to Negroes, although she was cognizant of the fact that there was racial discrimination in the North as well as in the South. This geographical factor appears to have had little influence, however, on her selection of a place to live. She and her husband made one brief attempt at a reconciliation while she was in Chicago, but it did not succeed. Her life with her mother was on a much better basis in Chicago than it had ever been previously. This must have been related to Emma's increasing responsibility for her own support and a marked diminution in her need for constant rebellious conflict with her mother.

Toward the end of World War II Emma returned to New Orleans. Her first marriage had finally been annulled. She still made no effort to resume her high school education; and her mode of life, her associates, and her jobs through these years still did not give the slightest hint of the future. After she returned to New Orleans, she married for a second time, again to a musician, and some of the difficulties that had interfered with her first marriage promptly cropped up again. She lived at first with her husband and his family but found herself antagonistic to the women with whom she was thrown. Although they attempted to maintain some superficial amicability at first, she mistrusted these in-laws, and felt that they were using her to their own advantage, a theme that appeared in Emma's thinking more and more as she grew older. She had had some training in beauty culture during the interval between her two marriages, and now she felt that her mother-in-law wanted her around mainly to take care of her hair.

This interlude was cut short by her husband's departure to enroll in a Negro college in a distant state. He stayed there only one semester and was then drafted into the Army. When he left for college Emma was unable to go with him, and remained with her female in-laws. This was distasteful to her, and the marriage really began to disintegrate over this separation. The fact that her second husband was interested in a college education seems to have been an important element in Emma's subsequent determination to educate herself. She has not said this in so many words but has emphasized the fact that she really became aware of this possibility for herself through his interest. It may also be pertinent that she was attracted to another man at this time who had something of a bent toward education. Like her previous efforts to train herself for a definite occupation as a beautician, Emma's intimations of educational ambition hint that some direction was beginning to emerge from the previous chaos of her life.

Probably the most important element in clarifying this developing sense of direction was the frustration of Emma's desire for children. Two necessary but mutilating operations, performed as emergency procedures during her second marriage, left her sterile. Unable to pursue the ideal of motherhood and fulfilled femininity in the biological sense, she had to undertake an important psychic readjustment, or substitution, to maintain a clear integration of her competitive needs and her restless drive to achieve security and freedom from anxiety. Appropriately, and in accord with the opportunities available to her, she turned to education. She has sublimated a frustrated need to function as a specifically biological mother, if you will, by becoming a specialized social one.

The internal conflicts that she experienced in her second marriage suggest those that one would find in a person attempting to effect some kind of satisfactory relationship with his mother. With her husband, Emma consistently put herself in the position of a child attempting to secure both revenge upon and affection (or approval) from mother. After her husband was drafted she got a job as a clerk in a department store, and with considerable emotional cost to herself and others eventually managed to get away from her in-laws and her own family to live more or less on her own. Significantly, she did make a mother figure out of her landlady after she managed to get away.

When her husband returned from the Army they made several attempts to continue together. It was a very stormy time and ultimately resulted in a violent break between them. They separated permanently after two and a half years, and were soon divorced. She had gone to a social agency in New Orleans for help regarding her marriage about a year before, which was in itself evidence of her need to succeed in it. She continued contact with this agency for about two years. An abstract of the record kept of her visits during that time indicated that she occupied herself mostly in complaining about the inconsiderate and excessive demands of her husband. There were many complaints of a somatic nature, and she expressed a great deal of distaste for sexual life, though much of this seems to have been directed toward gaining the sympathy and appreciation of her case worker.

Quarrels with her mother paralleled the marital ones. She treated her mother and her husband in much the same way, being critical and hostile toward them yet coming to them repeatedly for sympathy and help. Any real threats of dissolution of either relationship aroused a great deal of anxiety in her.

Very much in the center of the conflict with her husband was her inability to have a child. When her husband went away to college, she says that he did not write and she did not write him. When he came home, they quarreled openly. She began to quarrel more violently with his mother and sister. It was at this time that she first became pregnant. It developed that her pregnancy was tubal, and she underwent emergency surgery when it began to rupture. Prior to the operation she was suspicious of the doctor and consented to the surgery only when she was told it was a matter of life and death. She still expresses disbelief of the diagnosis and of the necessity for surgery. Her strong emotion about this is determined by the resultant feeling that she is an incomplete woman.

Her recovery was uneventful, and within a few months another pregnancy occurred. At this time she was even more at odds with her husband, though she was continuing to live with him. She was visiting her husband's relatives in the northern part of the state when the second obstetrical emergency arose. She had another tubal pregnancy which ruptured and she was again hospitalized for surgery. This time she raised no objection, probably because she was a good deal sicker than on the first occasion. When she left the hospital she went to the home of her husband's relatives, none of whom she knew well. She was very lonely, and felt her husband was annoyed and disappointed in her. She now describes this as "the real beginning of the end" of her second marriage. Her recovery from the second operation left her again feeling suspicious of the surgeon's motives.

There was a subtle and striking contrast in Emma's presentation of herself and her two operations to the two psychiatrists who interviewed her, one Negro and one white. To the white psychiatrist she outlined the sequence of events that led to her sterility in a way that seemed to distort the attitude of the white doctors.

She intimated that one was molesting her in the performance of his medical duties and implied that there were overtones of sexual motives. To the Negro psychiatrist she described the same sort of motives but directed the distortion toward her second husband rather than the white doctor because "he must have given the doctor permission to operate." In both instances she ignored or belittled the fact that the operations were emergency life-saving procedures. The latent content of the divergent versions of the operations refers to Emma's need to do two things, economically combined by the defensive operation of her ego: to please the interviewer; and to revenge herself for damage to her narcissistic self-conception. She acted as though the white interviewer would not tolerate sexual interest from her by a distortion assigning erotic wishes to the white surgeon. For the benefit of the Negro interviewer she accuses her Negro husband whom she had already identified as a person of great sexual interest to her. (She had also admitted to some speculation as to the sexual capacities of the Negro psychiatrist.) In both instances the unconscious and implicit request to the psychiatrist is to accept her evaluation of him as a strong sexual figure. The validity of this interpretation is documented repeatedly in the anamnesis both in her wish for a dominant father and in her disappointment with her father for his repeated failure to cope with her dominant mother, who represents to Emma her own poorly controlled destructive wishes. Hostility toward both interviewers is obvious.

The transference noted has to do with Emma's unique relationship with her father rather than with color per se. Her image of her father is the image of the strong man who is a sexually attractive attacker. She used the same historical material in talking to both Negro and white psychiatrists but slanted and distorted it in a way that was definitely influenced by the color of the person to whom she was talking. She wished to see the white doctor as the good mother, or as her good self. The good mother is personified for Emma by her "white" maternal grandmother. The Negro doctor was equated more explicitly with her Negro father.

In her initial interviews Emma had concurrent contact with a Negro interviewer and a white interviewer, and there, too, a perceptible transference was observable with the same color relationship, the white being mother and the Negro being father. The later emphasis on sexual material in her interviews with the Negro psychiatrist was also a transference of her feeling for her father. There is nothing hidden about her hostile and aggressive use of sex in social situations. However, in the interviewing situation, with clear transference implications, she assigns sexual functions to the interviewer. To the white psychiatrist, she says in effect that Negroes are bad and that the white interviewer is a big nice man to take care of her. To the Negro psychiatrist she emphasizes that white doctors have sterilized her, that therefore they are no good, and that it is up to the Negro to take care of her.

Following her second operation, Emma returned to New Orleans, still convalescent. Her husband had become attached to another woman, and there were many quarrels, threats of lawsuits, violent recrimination, and physical fights before their final separation. Emma's description of her attitude at that time is quite revealing. She says that she knew her husband could not tolerate the idea of a wife who couldn't bear children, and since she was rejected on this basis, she was determined to gain revenge by holding on to him as long as she could. She talked to him as little as possible, and would not allow him to have sex with her if she could avoid it, but she continued to live in the same house with him. Yet part of the reason for her visits to a social agency just before this had been her hope of adopting a child in order to preserve the marriage. In spite of her ambivalence, some glimmer of her old determination to make a success of it shines through. Emma still feels inferior because of her sterility and seldom talks of it without breaking into tears. When they quarrel, her mother is apt to inform Emma that she cannot have children because this is the way God wants to punish her for having been bad.

During the latter part of her second marriage, Emma had returned to high school and graduated. Within a few months after her second separation she registered as a freshman in college. At this point in her life her ambition had become clearly channeled towards teaching as a profession. She obtained money for tuition for her first year in college from a boy friend who appeared on the scene after her separation, but she was also working at night to support herself. In spite of all the emotional turmoil involved in her life during this period, she was more and more focused in working out her conception of herself and of the direction of her life. In this connection her need to revenge herself may have worked to her advantage. She hated her husband for rejecting her, and it was in keeping with her personality to show him up by succeeding where he had failed—in securing a college degree.

The more destructive aspect of her revenge revealed itself in Emma's attempt to jail her husband for beating her during the last turbulent days of their marriage. The judge threw out the case because of lack of evidence. Emma claims now that her chief witness, her landlady, refused to live up to an initial promise to testify on her behalf. This landlady was another in the succession of women that Emma attempted to establish in a maternal role, and the event exemplifies Emma's need to distrust any person upon whom she must depend. She had many wishes for revenge on the allegedly unfaithful landlady and satisfied these by a rather typical device. When she married for the third time, about a year following her second divorce, Emma did not tell the landlady of her remarriage, allowing her to think she was living out of wedlock with the man. She felt that the landlady and others would feel like fools when they discovered that she had actually been married to him all along.

Since her first year of college, Emma's life has assumed a much more stable and definitive pattern. Her third husband is exactly her own age and had been married once before. He has no family of his own in New Orleans. She claims that he has no interest in having children and is most affectionate toward her. She has represented this as the best of her three marriages. Her present husband holds a steady job as a mechanic's assistant, and is evidently interested in getting ahead in the world to some modest degree. Emma reports that he is well thought of on the job and she herself maintains a lively interest in his welfare and becomes concerned and helpful whenever he runs into difficulties at work.

Nonetheless, there has been some discord in the marriage. Emma has tended to distort information about her sexual life, one way or the other, particularly if she felt it was to her advantage in her relationship with the interviewer, and this tendency emerged in her account of her marriage. She presented it in quite acceptable terms on the first occasion, but later, to a Negro psychiatrist, she revealed a great deal of information about her extramarital flirtations. It is true, however, that Emma leads a fairly quiet life with her husband. There is relatively little of the overt disturbance that dominated the two previous marriages. The old atmosphere of mutual suspicion and distrust lives on, but it is less maliciously expressed. The pattern of provocativeness toward her husband is much the same sort that she indulged in with her previous husbands and with her mother. She is determined to achieve acceptance by her mother, or by any person she puts in this parental position, and she holds tenaciously to important emotional relationships with other people with immature techniques and considerable self-sabotage. The predominant neurotic pattern in her relationship with her husband is her need to gain control in a power struggle, and yet retain the feeling of being cared for. She does this by withholding sexual favors and by picking quarrels with him for not being neat and well dressed. He responds to her criticisms and demands by being deliberately slovenly; then when she stops pressuring him, he spontaneously resumes the neatness that she originally requested. During the interviewing she came to see her part in all this, but cheerfully remarked that the satisfaction of provoking him was more important than having him dress well. Even though this is her best marriage to date, there is some question of its survival if it continues in this vein.

Emma still has some financial difficulties, but they are hardly serious compared to those of the past. Her husband is steadily employed and helps her a great deal. In addition, she works part-time as a clerk in a small department store patronized chiefly by Negroes and owned by a white man. Her college record was consistent and good but not outstanding. The pattern of leadership in extracurricular activities that she established as an adolescent reappeared in college, where she was a full participant in such things as student-teacher organizations and singing groups. Her social life was like that of a college girl living with her father. She got her husband to take her to dances and school functions, but he did not participate, and left her to enjoy herself with the other students while he stayed in the background, regarding her with fondness, indulgence, and affection. She went out a great deal by herself and said petulantly that her husband grumbled but did not prevent her from doing it. When she goes to bars or night clubs with groups of her friends, she tends to be teasingly flirtatious with men, and she has made several men extremely angry with her for enticing them into making advances and then refusing them.

Emma's attention to appearance and personal grooming are obvious and speak for a considerable degree of self-respect, not so much in themselves as in relation to other evidences of ego integration: her careful speech, interest in accomplishments, steady work records in recent years, and considered plans for the future. Her face in repose tends to look depressed, though she smiles readily and appropriately.

The fact that Emma is suffering from a considerable degree of chronic depression is consistent with an interpretation of an unconscious self-hatred. The main sustaining relationships in her life stem from her family background, especially on the maternal side. Her maternal grandmother continues to be a very important figure and is highly idealized in Emma's mind. She regards her grandmother as white, and the maternal side as the "white" side of her family. She ascribes almost all the "badness" in her family to darker members. For Emma black is bad and male; white is good and maternal. Her brother is the outstanding illustration of this. During her current interviews she brought up only one dream: it was about him, and it was "horrible." In it she saw her brother lying on the ground in front of a large supermarket where she shops. She felt that someone was with her in the dream but she could not identify the person. Her brother looked "sort of dead— like spoiled meat—a tainted look, purplish—he tried to talk to me but his eyes didn't open." During the preceding session she had been talking of matters relating to Negro-white relationships, and during the session in which the dream was presented, she devoted most of her thoughts to the disadvantages of being Negro.

When we last saw Emma she had just graduated from college. She was pessimistic about getting employment as a teacher following graduation,[5] and apprehensive about the integration of the schools because she felt that the surplus of white teachers may be a factor in forcing Negro teachers from their jobs. She desires integration and feels that she will have to bear it if it costs her some delay in pursuing her profession.

Emma's explicit opinions about race are expressed almost entirely in terms of stereotyped situations, excluding to the greatest possible degree any reference to her own personality. Furthermore, her opinions are carefully geared to her conception of the person to whom she is speaking. Consequently, throughout her contacts with four different interviewers in the current study, one finds slight but significant variations in both the content and emotional emphasis of her color reactions. Emma likes to refer to prejudice as being undignified and stupid. She calls street car segregation "stupid" because of the acceptability of close contact in other white-Negro relationships, such as between a white employer and a Negro domestic servant or nurse.

Emma's antiwhite prejudice tends to be brought into play whenever something threatens her self-esteem by suggesting a fall in social status. Her attempt to reëstablish her opinion of herself is

[5] She did get employment by the fall term and is apparently well adjusted.

couched in terms of intellectual justification or superiority. She likes to tell stories of street car conductors or other whites who are pat symbols of the racial oppressor in which they are made to look ridiculous. It is also characteristic for Emma to picture the Negroes or herself as stereotyped objects of pity. When she saw a bus conductor threaten to have a woman on the bus move because she was sitting in front of the screen, Emma was very pleased when the policeman who appeared on the scene refused to support the bus conductor's threats. Emma's satisfaction was in picturing the white conductor as ridiculous and frustrated. One of Emma's professors in college gives this appraisal: "It has always been my feeling that if she had any prejudice where white people were concerned . . . it was certainly on a very deep level, and I think that most of her attitudes toward whites are a result of attitudes she has come in contact with through her associations. Now, she knows the correct thing to say. For instance, if she was presented with a Negro-white conflict, she knows to identify with Negroes. She knows that this is culturally expected. But if you let her talk, and she does talk a great deal, she deliberately avoids, it seems to me, bringing up any question of color where she must identify with Negroes voluntarily."

Emma expresses no particular interest in her place of residence in the city, but she openly resents the fact that Negro schools are not as good as white schools. She denies having been discriminated against in her jobs, but she avoids jobs where she might be. She has carefully adhered to activities and associations that are entirely compatible with segregation. She has associated herself in no direct or participant way with formal groups devoted to alteration of anti-Negro social practices. She does not belong to the NAACP or similar organizations, probably because she does not see this as a way of furthering her own future, her own personal security, and her position in society. She does not allow her objection to public segregation to be rigidly restricting. She will defiantly assert that she will never go to a segregated movie, but then if a good picture is showing and she really wants to see it, she does.

Emma's lack of rebellion against racial discrimination does not represent disappearance of her adolescent conflict with authority, but rather reflects her useful sublimation of aggressive drive (successful competition). She substitutes acceptable behavior (college) for unacceptable behavior (being a disciplinary problem). Her erotic and maternal needs or strivings are also satisfied. For her need to have a child, she has substituted a need to help children in a classroom. As with most people, the sublimation is only partially successful. The "left-over" ungratified needs are probably relieved by such processes as dreams, or mild neurotic symptoms. Her patterns of life reveal no gross areas of phobic avoidance. Rather she tends to ignore unpleasant situations, as in her apparent indifference to crowded and inferior housing.

The treatment that developed in the interviewing situation is secondary to the main purpose of the study, but it, too, brought out some serious questions relating to color-caste and its influence on a therapeutic relationship. The interviewing psychiatrist felt that as the relationship developed the color factor loomed larger and larger as a possible deterrent to significant dynamic ego changes. Considerable support and improved ego functioning did result from psychotherapy, but the anxiety Emma presented about color and its personal implications made it doubtful that a therapeutic relationship could gain sufficient stability and strength to survive the transference remobilization of her rage and frustration toward her mother. Fearing her own hostile impulses, Emma tended to see the analyst as a highly idealized person who could not tolerate her hostility, placing him in the role of her own conscience. No marked degree of self-sabotage occurred in the therapy. Perhaps the white-Negro aspect of the relationship in itself prevented this from coming out in transference form.

Emma's tendency to distrust people from whom she craves warmth and affection is constantly recurrent, and her dependency needs are clear in her description of these relationships. She has never done more than very remotely imply that such feelings carried over to her visits to the psychiatrist. Nonetheless, her strong dependency needs underlie a self-sabotaging need for a mother. Much of her conflict with her mother throughout her life has centered on her need to have her mother accept her as a woman, too. Loss of her reproductive power was a severe and genuine blow to Emma and had a very strong determining influence in her subsequent life. Compensation for frustration seems to characterize her shift in interest from marriage to education. Something of her driven determination must stem from this underlying depreciation of herself because of her sterility, although the social prestige of teachers in the Negro community and the availability of this opportunity for upward mobility are certainly realistic determinants also.

She rationalizes her wish to teach children of junior high school age on the basis that they would be more satisfying and less difficult to handle than younger children. This attitude is a reflection of the painful aspect of the same period in her own childhood. Significantly she turns to an age group that approximates the age at which she experienced some of her more notable conflicts with her mother and finally found a way of mobilizing her own defenses.

Emma's need to care for others refers historically to her relationships with her mother and grandmother. She depreciates her mother and older sister because of their failure to care for her grandmother, and thus can see herself as the only one of them who has any real interest in helping her. This has basis in fact, too. When her grandmother broke her hip, it was Emma who took care of her. Nonetheless Emma can remember very well how she was rejected because she was darker than the other children in the family, and there is a direct connection between this and her need for the approval of white authority. She attempts to regain grandma's approval to compensate for the fact that she is darker-skinned than the others. The mechanism here is akin to reaction formation, for the rejection must have caused anger and hurt. Her resentment does break through occasionally, as when she describes caring for her grandmother while her brother, who did not even express any liking for her, basked in her affection and sponged money from her shamelessly. Emma's identification with her grandmother is confirmed when she, too, later gives her brother money and looks after him.

Emma feels guilty about the rebellious impulses she feels toward her mother, yet she must act on the premise that that is what her mother wishes her to do. Her first marriage in particular was an attempt to do what she felt her mother unconsciously wanted, but her mother was not too happy about it. She had repeatedly stated to Emma that she was not going to allow her to run away from home and get married as her older sister had, but these expressed fears actually amounted to an accusation before the fact, in which the parent's accusation is unconsciously interpreted by the child as a request to do what is prohibited.[6] Thus, her mother's repressed conflict and wish to rebel against her own mother make their appearance here in her relationship with Emma. Receiving her mother's admonition as a suggestion to carry out a forbidden activity, Emma feels forced to maintain her relationship with her mother by giving her some vicarious gratification. She is then in the terrible dilemma of being forced to carry out antisocial activity in order to maintain gratification of her own dependency needs, but is also additionally burdened with her mother's guilt. One can look beyond what seems to be sexually demanding behavior, and find that Emma has really attempted to work out her relationship with her mother on this basis. Her relationships with men never achieved the faintest trappings of maturity until her third marriage, and even then there is ample evidence of poor integration.

Emma has had a major problem in dealing with her own rage, which has been turned mainly toward the men that she felt have

[6] Adelaide M. Johnson and S. A. Szurek, "The Genesis of Antisocial Acting Out in Children and Adults," *Psychoanalytic Quarterly*, 1952, 21:323–343.

failed her. Her father, after all, had failed her by dying, and by his inability to control her mother's aggressive and sexual impulses. Emma's unreasonable need to defend her father, and her refusal to believe his shortcomings, is evidence of her unconscious conflict in this area. She has lived out some of her rage against him in the person of all three of her husbands, yet all of them have functioned as maternal figures in her life. Perhaps the point of conjunction is that all the significant men in her life have failed to be really masculine in the sense she wishes—as reliable authorities. A part of her feeling of shame about her brother stems from her conviction that he should have been more to her than he was.

Somatization of her needs has appeared in recent years, especially since the sterilizing operations. Her symptoms are primarily gastrointestinal. She complains of chronic constipation and suffers from mild dysmenorrhea. Frequent visits to doctors fail to bring relief, and she has little understanding of the role her symptoms play in her emotional life. More than likely, their continued existence serves to both "justify" and to expiate guilt for various "bad" impulses or acts, and they clearly constitute a self-deception. Though psychopathological, these somatic complaints are minor elements in her total life.

The psychological tests Emma took bear comment at this point. On the Wechsler-Bellevue she earned a full scale score of 113, which would place her in the high average range of ability. Although her verbal scale score was 116, there was a good deal of scatter within this section of the test; she earned a weighted score of 7 on the arithmetic section and then a rating of 17 on the comprehension questions. Her general fund of knowledge was not as good as might be expected, but her failures tended to fall in history and geography, subjects she has had little to do with since grammar school days.

Emma's Rorschach presented the picture of an individual who has built up neurotic defenses, many of them of a compulsive type. She tried to be very systematic in her approach to situations;

she is careful in the use of detail, and her concern for detail points up a need to operate on the periphery. Her concern for minutiae offers her an opportunity to express her dissatisfactions through an overly critical attitude toward her environment rather than by other, more blatantly hostile patterns. She has by no means succeeded in establishing the rigid defense system associated with the typical compulsive. There is a tremendous amount of emotional feeling expressed in the record. Her repeated expressions of anxiety on the heavily shaded cards suggest that this finds expression whenever Emma is subjected to emotional pressures. She gives the impression that she is well aware of her many anxieties, and that she spends a lot of time in attempting to understand and dispel them. Though her efforts are not really effective, her constant concern serves to keep her occupied with minor difficulties, and thus, by intellectualizing her problems, keeps more threatening ideas from emerging. One would anticipate that Emma would be impulsive, from the manner in which she responds to the cards. She makes efforts to control herself, but her impulses are strong, and often when she is under pressure she becomes erratic. The records suggest that she would be capable of temper tantrums, for example, and there are indications that at times she expresses conflicts by physical aches and pains. She has good intellectual endowment, but her need to deal with things very carefully reduces her capacity for creative thinking. She saw very few people on the cards, and explained those she did see as vague concepts. She described women as having many masculine characteristics. Feelings of suspicion were expressed by considerable interest in eyes, seen on all the cards.

The TAT was of interest also. A repetitive figure of an unhappy female appeared in her stories: a young girl having a baby and being subjected to the ridicule of her peers; a woman deserted by a man whose feelings for her were never sincere; or a woman made anxious by unpleasant advances from men. All these individuals were young and she seemed to be talking about herself. A few stories involved older women, whom she designated as mothers, who had meaningful relationships with their children. A feeling of dejection and depression would come to the foreground very often when she was talking of the trials and tribulations to which women were subjected. She implied that all males are tied to their mothers yet are free to do as they please and to enjoy their freedom.

The enormous complexity of personality, and especially of ego functions and security operations, is revealed by the switch from one self identity to another or the automatic assumption of roles to enable rapid and facile integration or resolution of relationships with other people. Emma's skill in appropriate and constructive use of a variety of roles is a measure of her emotional health, just as her persistently repeated failures are a measure of her lack of maturity. The failures consistently recur in areas of her life that involve intimate relationships with others.

A conception of Emma's personality may support an interpretation of self-hatred. Yet even in the early history of Emma's life we see that when her childish self-esteem was lowered by unfavorable comparison with her light-colored siblings, she evolved a way of compensating. Color is the central issue and is the bad or unacceptable part of herself, which must be denied by a variety and succession of methods. As one follows the developmental ills in her life one can see that resentment and aggression were followed by identifications, which in turn were followed by some partial sublimation of her needs. That her success in her endeavors to find a final sense of personal identity is only partial is evidenced by the fact that she really functions as a mature individual in only one area of her life, her pursuit of academic success or professional status. Yet if we compare Emma's striving with that of such other subjects as Chester Olivier[7] or Francis Gregory,[8] the differences are genuinely striking. Emma's endeavor to achieve status through education is almost entirely devoid of self-sabotage, a characteristic of genuine sublimation. Indeed her personal

[7] See Chapter 8.
[8] See Chapter 7.

feelings of insecurity or inferiority have evidently lent some impetus to her impressive effort to rise professionally, while Chester and Francis have been caught firmly in a neurotic pattern of using education in their intrapsychic and interracial struggles. Many Negroes will deny segregation and discrimination to some extent, as Emma has, because the denial is necessary for security. They dwell upon the evidence of their acceptability to others in order to maintain self-esteem.

In a study of Negroes' personalities, there is some temptation to argue that it is pathological for a Negro not to make an issue of racial problems. We find that Emma stays clear of trouble by ignoring areas of race conflict because she feels that she cannot get anything but trouble out of them. Through her interest in the disciplinary problems of the children that she will teach we find that she sublimates her rebellious and anti-authority impulses. Her difficulties do come out in other areas, in personal emotional relationships and in a continuing failure in marital adjustment. Davis and Dollard[9] accepted the proposition that the caste barrier frustrated Negroes, and that consequently all Negroes would be aggressive to white people. There are many levels or kinds of reaction to frustration, however, and a better integrated personality is apt to find and use the most constructive ones. Emma, in contrast to other subjects, has managed to continue in the direction of true maturity in some major aspects of her life and thus makes good use of opportunities as she can find them even within the limitations of racial discrimination.

[9] Allison Davis and John Dollard, *Children of Bondage,* Washington, American Council on Education, 1940.

CHAPTER 5

The Matriarchy

In three of our cases we find a pattern of identification with the matriarchal family in dramatic contrast to the class orientations we have been discussing. Florence, Helen, and Nancy are lower-class women, to be sure, but their view of the world is not a class view. Rather, they see the difference between the sexes as the most basic of social categories, and they align themselves psychologically with their mothers in a solidary phalanx against men. Emma, our middle-class schoolteacher, expresses this succinctly in relation to her own matriarchal upbringing:

. . . she went on to discuss something of her own and her mother's relationships with men. She brought in her sister somewhat, and began to see how similar their attitudes were in this respect. Mainly it amounted to her noticing how her mother, her sister and herself tended to regard men as undependable, and how much this attitude has carried over from generation to generation.

The matriarchal family of the Negro lower class is only faintly matrilineal, because it provides almost no place for men at all. It does place strong emphasis on the solidarity of mother and daughter against all comers—specifically those of the male sex. The emphasis is expressed imaginatively by Florence, a domestic worker:

Florence commented some time during the interview that she would never marry again, and, pointing to her mother, "That's the only husband I'll ever have."

This identification of mother with daughter is fraught with strong moral overtones. Witness the outraged sentiment of one lower-class mother whose daughter had moved out to live with her husband:

Mrs. Jackson explained that the Henrys had moved to an apartment of their own . . . (and) that this was the reason for her not feeling very well on this day. She did not want her daughter to move from her home, but Mrs. Henry had explained that her husband wanted her "in a place of her own," so that there was nothing for her to do but move. Mrs. Jackson described this as having been "a terrible setback for me that I shouldn't have had."

And the choice of mother over husband, characteristic of the matriarchy, is explicit in the life of Nancy, an employee at a hospital:

Her main reason for staying in New Orleans (while her husband is living elsewhere) is her mother. She said that her mother needed her, and that her mother, being a semi-invalid, had to depend entirely upon her because there are no other children.
She expressed a strong sense of loyalty and obligation to her mother, who is ill, and has a conviction that it is her duty to remain with her mother. She told her present husband that she would do this before agreeing to marry him. Both her first and second husband wanted her mother to live with them outside of New Orleans, but her mother refused to leave. Mrs. Hodge became very aggressive when it was pointed out that she had chosen her mother over her first husband.

Our subjects who center their identification on the matriarchy are unanimous in seeing their mothers as the center of their lives and the primary source of security. This is not a solidarity of one kin group against another in the manner of the matrilineal clan, but rather of one sex against another. It is this antagonism of the sexes that seems to lie at the heart of the matriarchal family, and in its positive manifestation it appears as a mother-daughter solidarity against the world. The pattern, in fact, is as much Amazonian as matriarchal.

It is natural that people who see themselves primarily in terms of a sexual identification should view their group enemies in sexual terms, and there can be no question but that men receive the unanimous disapproval of the matriarchs:

> Louise, Florence, and Mrs. Lewis began a discussion of Louise's husband. They were quite vindictive towards men in general, commenting that they were all "dogs," and that they could not understand how they could be so mean to innocent little children as to not take care of them.
>
> Mrs. Jackson then said something to the effect that her daughter was more interested in David than she was in her, and that she could not understand how her daughter could go with her husband and forget children and mama and all.

Men are beasts. That is the constant theme of these women. It follows that men are not to be trusted in or out of wedlock, and that you should have nothing to do with them except when it is clearly to your own advantage:

> Mrs. Lewis has rather mixed emotions about Florence's affair. On the one hand she is resentful of Florence's sexual relationship with this man, and on the other hand she is giving Florence advice as to how to exploit the man better.
>
> Helen continued that she knows that her husband "has been ratting on me," but that she feels that all men are going to "rat on their wives anyway" so she doesn't worry about it. Then her friend supplied this information: she said that her mother always told her that when a man is jealous of his wife that means that the man is "ratting on his wife." Helen seemed to have agreed with this statement, and added that some women are "fool enough to believe that their husbands don't rat on them," but she said that she would never be that much of a fool.

The matriarchal view of the male sex is that it is irresponsible, exploitative, sexually aggressive, fickle, and brutal, if not downright depraved. Florence thinks men are dogs; Helen's husband is a rat; Nancy, with delicate sentiment, named her dog after her first husband. On the other hand the matriarchs see in men exploitative possibilities that may make the difference between survival and dissolution of the matriarchal family, and they are willing to trade sex for security if the terms are favorable.

The primacy of sexual identification in the matriarchy is congruent with the matriarchal viewpoint that men are the source of all evil. Thus other social factors tend to be seen mainly as they are obliquely reflected in sexual institutions. Though these women are usually lower class, they do not think and react in class terms, nor are they particularly sensitive to color, religion, educational symbols, occupational status or political loyalties. They firmly believe that "men are all alike," and this fact for them overrides the minor distinctions of creed, class and color; Florence says:

Men are all alike. Men with six and seven kids at home, sitting at the bar fooling around, spending money. I don't have anything to do with men like that. I like to sit there and watch them. I have no sympathy for them.

The conversation turned to men, and both Helen and her friend seemed to have a very low estimate of men—and they included me in their statement that "even though you are a professional man and belong to the higher society, you are still human." Helen said that her husband was not only human but he was a "rat."

It seems congruent with this attitude that when these women do have any affiliations beyond the limits of the matriarchal family they tend to be sisterly in character: a "girls'" bridge club, a ladies' religious society, or an informal group of "girl friends."

Despite their lack of sensitivity to class as such, all three of our young "matriarchs" are aware of the advantages of occupational preferment and educational advancement. It appears to be the case that they view these in terms of the same dynamic of security and exploitation that colors their other relationships; certainly there is no elaboration of any attitudes suggesting a "calling" or profession in their relation to their work, and education is seen somewhat vaguely as a practical and useful endeavor relating to more secure economic placement. Intellectualization of these values is minimal. Achievement motives have no place. These three women see their somewhat spotty educational efforts—Florence's night school efforts to learn shorthand, Nancy's abortive nurse's training, and Helen's boasted high school diploma—purely in instrumental terms as leading to more money and hence to greater security. Their aspirations in these fields, then, are vague and limited. It seems clear that the mobility motivations which suffice to drive people to the attempt to get out of the lower class are by no means identical with those that will admit them to middle-class society. This is dramatically illustrated in the case of Nancy, whose marriage to a gambler and consequent achievement of financial security (at least until the Kefauver investigation) was all that Florence or Helen might have dreamed of, but whose unchanging commitment to the matriarchy and rejection of middle-class values have left her culturally unaffected by the experience. None of these women is devoutly religious, though all of them have had some brush with piety. It seems possible, however, that both the hysterical possession and the promises of eternal rest and security that figure largely in lower-class religious cults may be closely related to the circumstances of matriarchal life.

The conditions of life in the matriarchy seem to make values centering around racial issues rather less important than they are for middle-class people. There is no ideology of achievement to be frustrated, no sensitivity to equality to be aroused. There is, however, a lively sense of exploitation and an explicit attitude that insecurity is related to racial matters, and the matriarchs tend to see this in sexual terms. Nancy focuses it specifically as a matter of sexual exploitation; Florence feels that "people" think they can take advantage of her, and she specifically mentions white men in this connection, but she feels that she is not the easy mark they think she is; Helen, who manifests more concern with class symbols, complains in economic terms:

I asked the subject if she would like to be white. She answered that, "It is hard to be colored. It is awfully inconvenient to be black. But I was born colored and I am perfectly satisfied with my race—but you know how it is. Many times you just can't get anything to do if you are colored. Sometimes I wish I was white enough at least to pass, so that I could get the kind of job that I want."

A firmly held and deeply felt belief in the immutability of the male character clearly dominates the view these women have of race: white men are, after all, men:

Florence commented, "I don't see no girl going with any white man and getting anything out of it (but) his making a fool of her."

An emphasis on sexual exploitation in relation to race appears to be specifically matriarchal. Nancy finally agreed to be interviewed by a psychiatrist providing he was a Negro. As she explained it:

I don't say I hate them, but I have learned that most white people simply want to use Negro people. Furthermore, most white people already believe that Negro women are prostitutes, and they refuse to realize that all people if they are normal have normal sexual desires and will express these desires in the same way. Instead, they prefer to believe that Negro women are prostitutes, and if I would tell them something about my sex life this would only be one more piece of evidence which they would have to prove their point.

The middle-class emphasis on achievement and striving in relation to color is definitely replaced here by an axis of security and exploitation. These women do exploit men for security when they can, yet they see themselves rather as the victims of exploitation —an exploitation more sexual than racial or economic. In at least one case, this view of the world extends to a kind of kinship with white women in a neatly projective matriarchal theory of society:

Mrs. Lewis said that it is all right for one to have a man on the side as long as one is discreet about this. She commented that white women always have more than just their husband.

The norms of Florence's, Nancy's, and Helen's world are definitely distinct from those of the middle class, and there is little mystery to how these are perpetuated. All of them tell us explicitly that they learned about men (which is for them equivalent to learning about the world) from mother. And mother's teaching on the point is, as some of the passages quoted illustrate, emphatic and to the point. The emphasis on motherhood, filial duty, family solidarity and security that lies at the core of matriarchal ethics is not only institutionalized in a distinctive family structure, but also internalized and endowed with deep emotion. Any breach of the code arouses strong feelings of guilt:

Her mother is also very demanding and curious about her activities— wants to know who calls her, where she's going, how much she's earn- ing, and so forth. Florence gets very angry at this, but at the same time feels guilty, although she couldn't quite verbalize it as explicitly as this, and feels that she's not really being a good girl for she's not living up to her mother's demands.

Mrs. Jackson replied with a great deal of feeling that she was indeed keeping (her daughter's) children, and that if "they" took those chil- dren from her "it would kill me."

Though the continuity of family structure tends to facilitate the growing identification of daughter with mother, the vicissitudes of matriarchal life and the genuine lack of security in its lower- class setting make the process far from smooth. A truly moving account of the emergence of a matriarchal self-conception is given in Ethel Waters' autobiography, where she describes the moment of realization in relation to her playing the part of a mother in *Mamba's Daughters:*

I was Hagar that night. Hagar and Momweeze (her mother) and all of us. . . . "Elida, if I died here and now," I told her, "it would be all right. For this is the pinnacle, and there will never be anything better or higher or bigger for me. I have fulfillment, Elida. At last, I have fulfill- ment." And I burst into sobbing as I humbly thanked my God. Because even if no one else knew it, I had been no actress that night. I had only been remembering and all I had done was to carry out His orders. And I had shown them all what it is to be a colored woman, dumb, igno- rant, all boxed up and feeling everything with such intenseness that she is half crazy.[1]

[1] From: *His Eye is on the Sparrow* by Ethel Waters and Charles Samuel. Copyright 1950, 1951 by Ethel Waters and Charles Samuel. Reprinted by permission of Doubleday & Co., Inc.

Special exception must be made of Nancy in relation to matriarchal upbringing. Born to a stable middle-class family, and class-conscious to the point of snobbery in adolescence, Nancy appears to have reached a matriarchal identification for reasons that are accidental and possibly idiosyncratic. Her father's early death and her mother's critical illness are undoubtedly factors in this, as is the fact of her being an only child. However, the effect of these and other factors is that Nancy has been, in class terms, downwardly mobile. In cultural terms she has identified herself with the values of the matriarchal family and has explicitly chosen these values over those of class at many points. Increasingly she is placing herself in the position of making her own living and depending on "boy friends" for money, as her tie to her husband is loosened and the necessity for totally supporting her mother becomes more stringent.

The matriarchal family backgrounds of Florence and Helen are more consistent and explicit on the inculcation of the cultural values peculiar to the matriarchal family. Florence's mother states the case with vigor:

Mrs. Lewis: I was took up with this baby's daddy then. He was a sweetheart man. I was just doing that so as to git good for these here other children, and I ain't done nothing but got me more mouths to feed. But now I'm through with all that stuff. No sweethearting; no nothing.

Interviewer: Did you love him?

Mrs. Lewis: What's love? Ain't no sech thing as love. I love this here (pointing to the baby). I love what's part of me—what come out of me. But love a man? Ain't no sech thing. I tell my girls: don't hear what no man say, but see how much he got.

Helen, who was an only child, describes quite unselfconsciously to an incredulous middle-class interviewer an almost pathological dependence on her mother in early adolescence: even at age 14 she was often on her mother's lap or in her mother's comforting arms, and it is obvious that she was so sure of

the matriarchal nature of the world that she couldn't be bull-
dozed out of it:

Interviewer: Why don't you join some of the clubs for girls your age
at the Y and learn how to play?

Helen: I wouldn't want to, lessen my mother could come too.
School is about the onliest place I come without her.
That's why I don't like school much.

Interviewer: Well, what are you going to do when you get married?

Helen: I can live with my mother.

Interviewer: But suppose your husband doesn't want that? Where
does your cousin live now?

Helen: He live with his wife's mamma. . . .

The genesis of matriarchal attitudes toward race tends to be
focused in mother's attitudes too. In 1938 Florence's mother expressed a classic view:

Shucks! Ain't but one way to be white, and that's have a white
mamma and daddy, 'n' if you ain't got that, no matter how white you
be, you nigger right on. And niggers know they can't have what white
folks got. They just ought to be grateful for whatever they kin get.
They learning. They got schools. What they worrying what de school
looks like fer?

And while Helen's concern with economic discrimination may
be her own, her lively sense of exploitation obviously comes from
her mother, who comforted her after a scrape with the school
authorities by saying:

Honey, your mother loves you. You know you're Mother's best friend,
and just because you're black, she's not going to let all these people be
picking on you all the time.

Nancy, on the other hand, was raised as a color snob, and re-
solves racial problems by dissociating herself from them. When
asked about her attitudes toward lynching, she declared, "The
Negroes they lynch aren't like me." Of the matriarchs, Florence
may be most typical of the Negro women of little education and
limited experience whose lives center on domestic work and the
care of their families, and while Helen and Nancy have much in

common with her, their own positions are somewhat more influenced by class considerations and mobility aspirations. This is consistent with their somewhat wider experience.

Women identified with the matriarchy work out their life patterns in a relatively uncomplicated frame of reference. It is built around two values to which they were exposed from earliest infancy: mothers are all-powerful in doling out or withholding gratifications; men are to be mistrusted, exploited, and used, and one should never relax one's vigilance toward them.

The psychological implications of this pattern are fairly straightforward. Daughters in matriarchal families accept thankfully the gratifications their mothers give. They inhibit or repress all feelings of hostility toward them, thus welding a strong bond of dependency on their mothers. Deprived of any experiences with men in which positive feelings could be established, they are instead taught that males are threats to themselves, and they have introjected this attitude. The lack of meaningful contacts with males together with these introjected feelings of menace prevent such women from developing any semblance of mature heterosexual relationships. Early experiences of mistrust and doubt and the fixation of the daughter's dependency on mother disrupt any orderly psychosocial development. Failure to resolve the earlier psychosocial crises prevents the evolution of an independent ego identity, and creates instead a dependent self: "I am my mother's daughter." The possessive use of mother in this statement has psychological as well as grammatical significance.

The restriction and deprivation that these women have experienced in their emotional life result in a feeling of depression, a dependence on magical thought processes, and the development of the shallowest type of interpersonal relationships. At the same time, it will be apparent that there are sources of psychological strength as well as weakness in the matriarchal tradition. Its continuity and stability rest on a distinctive family system that has proved to have remarkable tenacity and viability in the lower-class Negro environment. It is culturally viable in that it provides for the maintenance of a coherent value system in a chaotic world. It is psychologically viable in that it creates a measure of real security for the matriarchs and their daughters and their daughters' daughters. The strong mutual dependency of mothers and daughters becomes, in fact, almost a physical bond. At age 30, Florence comforts herself when she has nightmares by climbing into her mother's empty bed! In a sense, that is the story of her life.

Florence Lewis: Best of the First Batch

Florence Lewis is a domestic worker. Her life centers in a family controlled and dominated by her exceedingly powerful mother. In such a family the father's influence is relatively negligible since he usually leaves the family and retains only a passive interest in its welfare. Florence's life shows further how one generation follows the pattern of the preceding one, establishing the same type of family organization with closely similar transactional patterns.

When she was interviewed in 1938, Florence was a slight, brown-skinned 13-year-old. Her hair was kinky and unruly, unlike the "good" hair of her two half-sisters, and she was "forever complaining" about it. She was quiet, largely uncommunicative, and generally subdued, and she thought of herself as very obedient, concerned about her mother, and very helpful in chores about the house. This was not the picture that her mother presented to the interviewer. Mrs. Lewis complained that Florence was disobedient, unruly, and forever fighting and quarreling with her sisters:

Dat black girl, she ain't no mo' help than this baby. Florence, she don't do nothing 'less I beat her. She won't wash a dish. She don't iron even her own clothes, and all those children puts on clean dresses every afternoon. And Florence, she don't take no care of what she got. I don't know what's da matter wid dat girl.

Obedience to mother is the essential theme in Florence's life.

During her current interviews (1953–1955), Florence was about 30 years old. There is something childlike in her face and attitude so that one might easily suppose her to be eight or nine years younger. She is of medium height, has a nice figure, and is usually attractively and tastefully dressed. Her skin color is dark brown and her dark hair is arranged in soft curls around her face. Her features are regular and pleasant, and on the whole she is attractive. She usually looks worried, with a slight frown on her face. When she does break into a smile it is often a somewhat embarrassed smile, although it has definite warmth in it. She speaks earnestly, sincerely, and often very rapidly, so that at times it is difficult to distinguish what she is saying. In addition to slurring her words because of a slight speech impediment she often will jump from one thought to another without making clear to the interviewer the link between the thoughts. She occasionally mixes up past and present events as if they were concurrent happenings.

Florence's general attitude indicates a desire to please. She is compliant and submissive but never sickeningly ingratiating. She knows how to be pleasant and agreeable, but she can also be very stubborn and defiant, like a pouting child. She is evasive at times, but if the interviewer is sympathetic and persistent she invariably discusses whatever she is attempting to hide. When her self-esteem is too threatened she cannot talk about what is troubling her, and then she skips her appointments. This happened particularly when she had been leading a promiscuous sexual life and had been ashamed of it, and when she had been depressed because of her rejection by a lover. Running away is one of her most frequent methods of dealing with troublesome things.

Generally she reacted to her interviewers as if they were parents to whom she could reach out for support, although she regarded the Negro psychiatric social worker more as a friend and equal. She felt more comfortable with a Negro than with a white psychiatrist, but her orientation to them was essentially the same: "I am a child and helpless to deal with my difficulties. I would like some help."

Florence was born into an unstable lower-class family, the

eighth of 13 children. The instability arose from her mother's numerous lovers, her father's desertion when she was six, and continuing economic privation, particularly during the depression years when she and some of her siblings actually had to beg for food. Florence's mother ascribed her children to two different fathers, and the two youngest girls, her "second batch," were notably lighter than the other children and clearly their mother's favorites. A social caseworker visited the family in 1932 when they first applied for help. Florence was then seven. The worker described the family as living in a condition of extreme poverty and untidiness. The plaster was broken and crumbling and the home was sparsely furnished. A baby was lying on a dirty mattress with a piece of soiled cheesecloth thrown over her face. Flies crawled on the baby and the cheesecloth and were thick on the walls and on furniture. Florence's mother yelled constantly at the children and insisted that they show the social worker that they wore no panties. She raised her own dress to show the social worker that she "had no drawers to go to Heaven in." The worker reported that Mrs. Lewis was not actually married to Mr. Lewis but that when he started living with her she was actually married to a man named Buddy George.

In 1938 the family was still living in unbelievable squalor. The rooms they occupied were always dirty, with peeling wallpaper and plaster. They used wooden crates and boxes for seats and tin cans for cups and dishes. Flies were everywhere, and the children were dirty and unkempt. Florence's mother was an untidy, toothless woman smoking a pipe and rocking in a rocking chair. In these physical surroundings the family's main preoccupation was survival, and its primary technique was the manipulation of welfare and other governmental agencies. The family has been on relief throughout Florence's life until the very recent past.

Throughout her childhood, Florence seemed more infantile than her siblings. She had a number of childhood phobias, particularly toward insects, which often symbolize younger siblings. Information regarding her early training is lacking, but we do know something of the emotional and physical climate in which she grew up. The family has always been poverty-stricken and has frequently lacked even the barest essentials of life. The children had a steady diet of beans and rice from infancy, occasionally supplemented by surplus foods obtained from the relief agency. Toilet training and weaning were haphazard and grossly inconsistent matters, with whippings based more on the mother's frustration than on the child's performance.

Florence was a bedwetter until she was 14½ years old; for one year after her marriage at age 13. She was teased and ridiculed a great deal about this, and finally stopped only because one night after "passing over" (her term for having sexual relations with) her husband she wet him. His ridicule "cured" her, and she never wet the bed again. Prior to this accident she wet the bed regularly, "putting it on him." Although she tried to pass herself off as a very good, obedient 13-year-old who was "mother's little helper," Florence was very much concerned with violence, voodoo deaths and poisonings, and fears of sexual attack. She told one interviewer: "I can't sleep on account of I'm afraid of dreaming about cutting and slashing all the time." Again, "I don't want no old nasty boy talking dirty talk to me. When they come talkin' nasty to me I just bust them in the face. I'll have 'em when it's time." Her talk was replete with descriptions of the violence around her. She said of her parents: "So when he came home she start fussin' with him, an' he take a hatchet an' hit her in the head an' she hit him back wid a hammer, an' they both went to the hospital." She made frequent reference to voodoo, mysterious poisonings, and decapitations: "My sister had six children, three dead. One of them, the baby, it was sick and kept getting sicker. So she called in a voodoo woman and when the woman came she say something over the baby and the baby sat up and began to cry, and the voodoo woman smacked the baby in the mouth. She had poison on her hand and the baby gits some of it and so he dies."

Florence made constant references to her feelings of obligation to her mother, despite the fact that her mother seemed to favor her two younger half-sisters: "But my ma, she have a hard time. She ain't got nobody to help her. My poppa don't give her nothing. Any of us got any money we got to help her." Mrs. Lewis worked explicitly at instilling these feelings of obligation and of guilt, for she remarked to the 1938 interviewer, "But I'm telling you, I believe if a child treats his mother good then he'll get good, and if he treats her bad then he don't get nothing but bad."

Even at 13 Florence shared her mother's view of men as necessary but dirty and untrustworthy beasts. They both expressed marked outspoken hostility toward men, and although they recognized that men were necessary in order to obtain money, food, or clothing, they regarded them as dangerous objects of exploitation, certainly not of love. It was Florence's mother who said, "Don't hear what no man say but see how much he got."

Florence went only as far as the sixth grade in school and was an indifferent student. Most of her siblings were also somewhat retarded. Florence was forced to leave school and marry after her mother found out that her future husband had seduced her. Florence had met him at a dance and on their second date she had intercourse with him. Feeling guilty, she wrote him a letter that was intercepted by her mother. She and her husband were both forced into the marriage unwillingly. Florence's mother wanted to get her daughters married off as quickly as possible in order to rid herself of responsibility for them. There wasn't even a question of pregnancy.

Florence's husband turned out to be a probable schizophrenic who could not earn a living and who was unwilling to support his wife and the two children who soon came along. This, and her husband's bizarre and chaotic sexual life, which included promiscuity, attacks on small girls, and perverse sexual behavior, soon led to a separation. Many attempts at reconciliation failed, and though he would still like Florence to return to him, she still refuses to accept him back. At present he is paying her $40 a month for the support of his children, though previously his failure to support her was itself a major cause of marital discord. The sexual difficulties between them seem to have been as important as the financial ones, for Florence herself has many sexual problems.

Her first child, Junior, was born in 1942, a little over two years after her marriage. Florence was 16. During her pregnancy she had an affair with a white man who owned a bar where she was working. She was afraid her husband would find out and was also afraid the relationship with the white man would modify the physical characteristics of her unborn child, making him look like a white person. She felt very guilty about this relationship. She continued to work as a barmaid, however, and was widely promiscuous. During this time there were many separations and reconciliations with her husband. He had gone into the Army on two occasions, but without any change in his personality or in their relationship. Their second child, Louis, was born in 1944.

In 1947 Florence became ill with tuberculosis, and she was eventually hospitalized in January of 1948. After five months she deserted the hospital because two of her best friends among the patients died suddenly in a way frightening to her. She describes these incidents as if there were an evil spirit connected with them. In the same year her father finally moved out of the house permanently and remarried. He had been in and out of the house all through this period but had played a minor role in Florence's life. The diagnosis of her illness and her father's final desertion through remarriage produced a sort of "conversion experience," and must have convinced her of the error of her ways, since she interpreted these events as retaliation for her sins. Upon her father's urging she returned to church and was baptized, and she has been a regular church-goer ever since. She goes as often to the Catholic as to the Baptist Church, although the latter is the family's church. For a time her promiscuity, drinking, and general instability of life decreased markedly, although they never completely disappeared. She still goes to bars to drink, but she is somewhat less promiscuous and more interested in church activities. Her primary interest, however, is in rearing her two children. She lives with her mother and has continued to work both as a domestic and as a barmaid in order to supplement relief payments which the family has been receiving. She has had to do this work surreptitiously, since the relief checks would be cut off if she were known to be working. For some time she has really made the largest contribution to the family's support, and in terms of providing the food she has certainly done more than her two half-sisters.

She works hard, getting up at 5:30 or 6:00 in the morning to cook breakfast, and going to work at about 7:30. She works as a domestic from 8:00 until 6:00. Until recently she had been working three nights a week in a barroom but has stopped because it was too hard for her. She has dates at night, and not infrequently the men sleep in her house on the sofa downstairs. She has little recreation other than meeting men at bars. Occasionally she watches television with her children. She is often depressed, cries a good deal, buries herself in her room, or goes for long walks alone. Her only stable relationships are with her children and her mother.

In 1938 Mrs. Lewis made a point of demonstrating her misery to the interviewer in every possible way. Even though it was devastating to her own self-respect, she literally made herself a beggar in order to elicit some sympathy or material reward. At that time Mrs. Lewis manifested a good deal of affection for the infant in arms but was much more hostile, though not completely rejecting, toward the older children. She showed a great deal of direct resentment toward Florence for not helping her sufficiently. Mrs. Lewis expressed her wish to rear the children decently, and hoped that they would all grow up to get married, but this seemingly real interest was mostly selfish, as she hoped that then they would be able to support her: "I'm trying to raise 'em decent until they get married; after that they can be big whores if they want. It won't be none of my worry. I'll have did my best." In the meantime she was sending her children out to beg for food.

Mrs. Lewis referred to herself rather vaguely as "Creole," though she was neither Catholic nor French-speaking. She came from the country. She was illiterate, and learned to sign her name only when taught by one of her daughters. Florence's father was an illiterate porter, who was described by Mrs. Lewis as "that no 'count nigger from Mississippi." Although never responsible for the family, he was not totally devoid of feeling for his children. He took in two of the children when they had trouble with their mother and was helpful to Florence at various times. From time to time he gave her some financial help with her children.

Between 1938 and 1953, Florence's siblings married and moved out, and by 1953 the household came to include Mrs. Lewis, Florence, her two half-sisters, and Florence's two boys. Florence's married sisters were constantly in and out of the house. Florence was very envious of her unmarried half-sisters. They worked, and were able to buy pretty clothes, but according to Florence they didn't help her mother as much as she did. Though she regards Florence as "the best of that first batch of children," Mrs. Lewis shows an open preference for Florence's lighter half-sisters, based on her expectation that they will marry better than Florence had. (Florence's youngest sister has recently married the son of a wealthy undertaker.) Her rivalry with her half-sisters gives Florence a constant feeling of resentment and injustice. They quarrel frequently about who is doing the most for their mother and over the sharing of the family's limited resources. Her sisters react to Florence's hostility by "pouring salt on open wounds." Secure in their expectations of mobility, they are contemptuous of the "trash" Florence brings home. One of her sisters makes Florence pick her up at night as though she were a respectable girl, while Florence can walk the dark

streets alone because it doesn't matter. These two girls are the
only members of the family who are socially mobile, and Mrs.
Lewis has favored them all along, encouraging their educational
achievements to a far greater extent than she had those of the
other children. Of course, their native endowment may be a
factor, and there have been considerably more educational opportunities for Negro children a decade younger than Florence.
In any case both of the younger girls have finished high school
and obtained good jobs.

There has been a great increase in material possessions in
the Lewis family since they were first visited. The kitchen is
furnished with a chrome and plastic dinette set and a washing
machine. The bedrooms are adequately furnished. Florence has
a double bed, a rollaway bed, a large chifforobe, and a dressing
table and bench in her room.

Despite this economic improvement the family is still lower
class. Florence herself is contemptuous of her older sisters, their
large families, their husbands who desert them and are therefore
sent to jail, and their inability to keep themselves, their children,
or their houses clean. One of Florence's married sisters lives in a
housing project and is the mother of four children. She is less attractive than Florence and generally wears soiled clothing and a
harassed expression. Another married sister is the mother of
seven children and is likewise generally unkempt. She and the
children visit Mrs. Lewis weekly and strong family ties are
maintained. On one such visit the children were noticeably dirty
even though it was an early morning hour. This did not seem to
bother their mother, who bragged that she had also left the breakfast dishes unwashed, since her husband, "a Creole," was more
interested in cleanliness than she was and would undoubtedly
wash the dishes and cook the dinner when he returned from
work in the evening. Another sister lives in the neighborhood
with her 22 children in a two-room tarpaper shack.

Florence's full brother has a police record for drunken driving
and theft. His 12-year-old son has been arrested for stealing

and is now at a correctional school. This brother and his wife are described as alcoholics and have been in difficulty with the authorities for serious neglect of their children. Another of Florence's sisters is described by the family as an alcoholic who often neglects her children, while one final sister, unlike the others, rarely visits the family and is described as a hard-working woman who takes in washing and ironing and tries to live and rear her children respectably.

Florence feels that she functions best as a mother. Perhaps the key to her performance in this area lies in her complete identification with the boys as another child who is able to live her life through them. Indeed, Florence is at least relatively successful as a mother. She cares for her boys economically, and she gives unqualified approval to their educational achievements. She speaks with deep feeling and authority when she says, "I tell Junior that if he finishes school and wants to go on, I'll see to it that he has what he needs." The children are adequately clothed and fed and have bicycles and a television set. These purchases required a great deal of hard work, sacrifice, juggling of pennies, and meeting of time payment deadlines. Florence is in communication with the schoolteachers, and although she occasionally permits the boys to stay home from school without censure, she also brags about their achievements and their school attendance. The oldest boy, Junior, received all E's (for excellent) on his final report card; and although Louis' grades were less satisfactory, both boys were promoted.

The boys share a bedroom with their mother and the indications are that sex is no mystery to them. Conversations about intercourse are held in their presence. Junior is a quiet, reserved 12-year-old. He is brown-skinned, with regular features, straight teeth and a warm smile. Generally he is sober and reflective, spending a great deal of time at home reading funny books, drawing, or watching television. He engages in neighborhood baseball games and handles himself well. Although he probably prefers to be passive, he has nonetheless learned to protect himself adequately. When angry or aroused he engages in heated fist fights, and he cries bitterly if stopped by his mother or grandmother before the fight is successfully completed. He reads well and apparently extensively, for his knowledge of grammar is far superior to his home and neighborhood associations.

Junior was born when his mother was 16 years old, two years after her marriage to his father. Florence did not plan for his arrival nor did she take steps to prevent it. She accepted pregnancy as something over which one has no control. Her pregnancy was normal and free of symptoms. Florence's husband neither looked forward to nor regretted his paternity. It simply made no difference to him. There was little talk about the expected child and no strong preference as to its sex. Junior was breast-fed until he was three years of age. He learned to drink from a cup at six months of age, receiving both breast and cup until he was three. Florence breast-fed him throughout her pregnancy with Louis on the grounds that "people say it makes them strong if you breast-feed them a long time." His bowel training was begun when he was nine months of age and was completed in a few months. At three years he was able to remain dry during the day, but he continues to be enuretic at night. Feeble efforts have been made to "cure him." Florence has not been consistent or particularly vigorous about this, perhaps because of her own problem in this area, though she was serious about the other aspects of training and care.

Junior walked at 13 months of age and talked at about two and one-half years. He was cared for exclusively by his mother except for baby-sitting, which was done by various maternal relatives, particularly Mrs. Lewis. When Florence was hospitalized in 1948, Junior was six years old. His grandmother then cared for him full time for the two years of his mother's illness and convalescence. Though Mrs. Lewis was frequently verbally rejecting, she made many real sacrifices to keep the children with her. For a period of about four months she received no financial assistance for their support, yet fed and clothed them from her own very meager welfare grant, with occasional help from Florence's father and father-in-law. Because he is an obedient, pliable child, Junior was her favorite among the grandchildren and received considerable approval.

Ten-year-old Louis is a handsome youngster of somewhat slighter build than his brother. His animated smile is pleasant. He is restless, "on the go," and very self-willed. He is more frequently the subject of his grandmother's verbal tirades because he "does not listen." He refuses to run errands or do housework, and "gets away with it" because his mother tells the chagrined older brother, "You are the oldest and should clean up whether Louis helps or not." Louis was bottle-fed until six months of age and then was completely weaned to the cup. There was some breast-feeding in the first month, but since he had to share mother's breast with Junior he grew to rely almost completely on the bottle. According to Florence, Louis did not wet the bed at all after he was two or three months of age! His bowel training began at nine months of age and was an accomplished fact soon after. Discipline for both children is mild and consists mostly of "hollering at them." Occasionally they have been whipped by their grandmother. Attempts are made to "shame them" or they may be deprived of movie privileges. Florence says, "I like to talk to them and show them where they are wrong. Nobody likes to be beat on." Louis sleeps in a double bed with his mother because Junior wets the bed.

One of the most significant factors in the boys' development is a consistent lack of a father figure with whom to identify. Their father has been absent from their home and, indeed, from the city for long periods of time and has otherwise been an object of their mother's and grandmother's scorn. Their other male relatives are unstable and given to frequent desertion and irresponsibility. They have had no male companionship and no man has assumed any responsibility for their growth. Their contact with their father has been inconsistent and infrequent, and what little there has been was traumatic. They have witnessed terrible battles between their parents over their father's sexual behavior and financial nonsupport, and the impotence of his role in their growth and development is a repetition of the pattern that existed in Florence's own family.

The absence of significant male figures in the lives of Florence's sons and the resulting internalization of matriarchal values by both boys is revealed, strikingly, in their test protocols. They were ten and 12 years old when tested, and both of them exhibited many neurotic patterns (as did their mother). Despite the restriction due to these patterns, both had Stanford Binet IQs of over 100. Louis' Rorschach protocol contained suggestions of schizophrenic development, but there was not sufficient evidence to make such a diagnosis definite. (His mother's Rorschach protocol was that of a schizophrenic with paranoid traits). On both the Rorschach and TAT tests the most outstanding characteristic was the ease with which the boys talked about the relationships between children and their mothers and the total absence of "fathers." The adult females were the obviously strong individuals in their stories. They made the decisions and did the punishing of males, who were generally engaging in "bad" activities— stealing, killing, getting drunk, and not working.

The cohesiveness of the Lewis family has been achieved through its need for survival. They have had to stick together in order to secure the bare necessities of life. To this end they have had to agree on a certain code of behavior, involving varying degrees of deceit in dealing with governmental agencies dispensing money (and, during the depression years, food). They have become adept at this and coöperate effectively in achieving these ends. Sometimes, however, they attempt to blackmail one another, holding over each others' heads the threat of revealing something to the "committee" that will reduce their welfare grant. In this family the mother reigns supreme. She has done the manipulation over the years and continues to wield the power, make decisions, and dispense rewards.

The weakness of Florence's family stems from an intense competition. Relationships are seen not on the basis of shared affection but on a competitive striving for the bare necessities of life. When there isn't enough to go around, the family members fight with each other for food and clothing and money for entertainment. They are extremely jealous of presents or favors that any one member of the family bestows on another. Siblings fight constantly with each other and try to use their mother as a pawn in their battles, while she manipulates one child against another in order to retain her own favored position. Her dependency relationships are complex and, in some ways, even reversed. She is an earner only by virtue of welfare money and she depends on her daughters for support even though she owns most of the furniture in the house. This role-reversal further confuses the self-identification of the children.

Let us see how the family patterns affect Florence. She was born to the lower class, educated to the lower class, and made a lower-class marriage. She is still lower class. Despite her mother's "Creole" affiliation, the family does not even bother to assert claims to respectability but eagerly produces proof of the poverty in which it lives. There is an aura of petty criminality to Florence's life. Her brother and his son and at least one brother-in-law have been jailed, apparently all for theft, although this is the one crime Mrs. Lewis denies in her children.

Though lacking in respectability, Florence's family is not devoid of standards or stability. Its values are stably lower class. Florence has no great faith in marriage and is a believer in discreet sexual promiscuity on a *quid pro quo* basis. She is not ambitious, although at one time she wanted to be a stenographer, and she is only vaguely ambitious for her children, even though eager to provide for them. Despite financial and personal difficulties, the family has held together relatively well. It is difficult to evaluate Florence's personal contribution to this result, but it appears to have been considerable.

Florence has strongly ambivalent feelings toward her mother.

There is often intense rage, sometimes expressed, more often displaced to her two younger sisters, and often suppressed, making Florence feel very guilty about not living up to her mother's demands. She feels these demands are unjustified, but she continues to feel guilty and fearful of some kind of retaliation. Evil spirits will get her and she will be sick. Her mother is able to manipulate her easily by holding over her the threat of abandonment. She continuously holds up to Florence how much she has done for her and plays upon her guilty fears.

Florence feels tremendous rage toward her husband, and at times, strong fear of him. She is resentful of his excessive and perverse sexual demands and of his lack of trustworthiness in giving financial support. She is angry at his lack of concern over the rearing of the children. She is afraid of his repeated violent assaults. Shortly after they were married, he and a friend of his got drunk and raped her, her husband holding Florence while his friend "passed over" her. He has also demanded such perverse sexual activities as sucking his backside and sucking between his toes. These sexual assaults have only increased her sexual fears and inhibitions, which have existed since early childhood. She described a number of traumatic incidents. Once when she was begging on the streets, a man tried to entice her into his automobile. More significantly, these sexual fears probably stem from frequently witnessing her mother having intercourse with the various men in her life and misconstruing this as violence. There have been a number of incidents in her current life in which she has been assaulted. The indications are that she complied passively with most of these sexual threats, although sometimes she has responded to her husband's threats with equal threats of her own such as picking up a butcher knife to throw at him, or hitting him over the head with a chair. At other times she is unable to do this and breaks down and cries.

In addition to the difficulties that the world has imposed upon Florence, she has some internal ones. Her test IQ is only 79, putting her in the borderline group, although clinically she impresses one as being somewhat brighter than this. Nonetheless, there are certain defects in her thinking processes that are obvious clinically as well as on psychological testing. There is a scattering of thought processes, a jumping from one thought to another, sometimes mixing up past and present in a chaotic fashion. This often makes it difficult for the interviewer to know exactly what she is talking about. She is unable to be concise and to the point. Her thinking is fuzzy. It is no wonder that her reality testing shows some marked distortion at times. The most striking evidence for this is her attributing her tuberculosis to evil spirits, her fear that an evil spirit is causing the claustrophobic nightmares of which she complains, and her frequent references to voodoo magic. We may regard Florence's spirit beliefs as a genuine cultural survival, but such beliefs are now so rare that they may typically imply personal meaning too.

Florence's perception of the outside world is that it is a very threatening place. She constantly expects to be hurt, particularly by people in authority, and sometimes she seems to provoke such damage. When she gets too upset she acts out by promiscuity or drinking and winds up losing money and pride and feeling further humiliated and disgraced. On at least one occasion she has been robbed of her savings while drunk. She seems unable to find a man who is willing to take any responsibility toward her and toward the children.

Florence's sexual adaptation is fearful and full of conflict. She is a frigid, hysterical girl who, though not overtly seductive, is subtly so. She uses sex as a bargaining point in order to gain material rewards or some show of affection. She doesn't seem to enjoy sex for its own sake. There are times when she seems to allow herself to be used sexually because of her fear of losing the support of some powerful man. A number of white employers have either seduced her or attempted to. Her structured symptoms in this area revolve around her fear of elevators and her claustrophobic reactions, and her associations to these phobias indicate a fear of penetration. Sex and violence are intimately associated in her mind and the tender aspects of love have been dissociated from the sexual act.

Florence's main goal in life remains security for herself and her children. She perceives her world primarily in terms of money problems, and if she could be financially secure she would take her chances on emotional security. She said she would accept a man who would bring home his pay check and generally support his family, even if he cheated. In this she expresses the goal of a whole family unit. She wants someone to care for her, and to love her, but these goals are secondary to the primary one of economic security. Her fears of going hungry have been marked ever since she was a beggar child and had to struggle to find enough money for groceries. Her present satisfactions are very few. The most lasting ones are related to her children's academic success, particularly Junior's. Her other activities seeking fun and release of tension bring very fleeting gratification and generally create feelings of guilt, which she expiates by going to church.

She sees herself as a kind of martyr who sacrifices herself for her children and her mother. She feels that through this martyrdom she should be taken care of magically as if to say: "If I do for others, they must do for me." There is a certain fatalistic, pessimistic quality to her, for she has by and large accepted defeat. Most of the time she feels it is completely unlikely that she will find a husband who will take care of her and she is resigned to a constant hand-to-mouth struggle for existence. She has some hope, just as her mother had, that her children will take care of her when she is older. At times she has a stubborn, rebellious, defiant attitude toward the world, but this is infrequent compared to her resignation and acquiescence in defeat.

There was considerable evidence on the Rorschach Test that Florence has marked paranoid characteristics, and the clinician diagnosed her as a paranoid schizophrenic. Clinically, her use of projection is marked, and her use of fantasy in place of reality is suggestive of that diagnosis. Her method of relating a particular incident, jumping from one thing to another as if the interviewer knew all about it in advance, is also typically paranoid. Nonetheless, she does not present the usual feelings of persecution and of rage. If she is paranoid, she is a beaten-down paranoid. Her rage does flare up, but it has never been seen by any of the interviewers, with whom she is passive and submissive. It is difficult to tell how much of her attitudes are paranoid on a uniquely personal basis and how much of her attitudes are culturally induced and would be found very frequently among her peers. We believe that we cannot use the usual criteria for evaluating these reactions. A better term to use may be "pseudo-paranoid."[2]

Florence's primary defenses are repression, avoidance, denial, pain-dependency, and use of rituals. She sleeps with a Bible under her pillow and says prayers before she goes to bed. If she has a nightmare, she gets up and says the Lord's Prayer. She has a good deal of unconscious guilty fear, which is expiated through going to church and through the rituals mentioned above. Her control of her rage is generally fairly adequate, except when she is drunk. She has become assaultive at times, though this is rare. Her dominant emotion is guilty fear. In short, Florence sees herself as a child who has been picked on, discriminated against, unfairly accused throughout her life, and unable to share in the good things of life. She thinks of herself as a good mother for her children and this elevates her self-esteem considerably. She has a defeatist attitude toward life and only occasionally has fleeting feelings of hope. Her main techniques have been those of exploitation with those people whom she might be able to manipulate, usually in terms of ingratiation. She rarely uses coercive rage.

In 1938, Florence mentioned her desire to look like her "bright" sisters and her desire to pass. She stated that white people were more decent than Negroes, that white people had more things, and that therefore she would like to be white. This envy of whites

[2] Many of the characteristics of paranoid symptoms are necessities for survival in the lower class, e.g., being suspicious of "strangers"—such as bill collectors—from the middle-class stratum of society.

was in conflict with the teaching of her mother, which was very definite: "The niggers know they can't have what white folks got. They just oughta be grateful for whatever they kin git."

Apparently Mother's teaching prevailed. Instead of attempting to deny her color and to identify with the whites, Florence is excessively assertive about her colored status. On an application blank she gratuitously signed her name "Florence Lewis, colored." She has worked out a pattern of obsequiousness and ingratiation with authorities that is somewhat more exaggerated with white than with nonwhite authorities, although not strikingly so. Her attitude of obsequiousness toward the Negro psychiatrist was similar to her attitude toward the white psychiatrist. This pattern is modified by a strong stand of defiance whenever she feels she is being treated unfairly. She can speak up and assert herself when necessary. She resisted undue demands on her time and energy by a white housewife and by the white boss for whom she worked. On one occasion when the daughter of her employer came home drunk and vomited, she made the daughter clean it up herself.

She has had both good and bad experiences with whites. She has been helped by white physicians. She had a white mother-substitute who took care of her briefly when she was 12. At the same time, white employers have unjustly accused her of stealing on at least three occasions, and some white employers have attempted to seduce her and apparently have succeeded. This creates ambivalent feelings toward whites. On one hand she sees that they have the power and can help her, a viewpoint strongly augmented by the fact that white social workers have given more aid to the family than have Negro social workers. At the same time, these powerful whites are in a position to hurt her. Accordingly Florence runs away when threatened, or stands up to authority when pushed too far.

Despite her ambivalent feelings toward whites there is no evidence that Florence rejects her own identity as a Negro or that there is self-hatred from this fact. Her jealousy of her half-sisters is primarily based on the mother's preference for them: it is not strictly color-oriented. If she had identified with whites the chances are that she would have accepted the opportunity of living in her white employer's home, an opportunity that has been offered her a number of times. She feels it necessary to maintain her independence.

It should be mentioned in this connection that it is very difficult to demonstrate a one-to-one relationship between color attitudes and particular bits of behavior. For example, her defiant attitude toward white employers is also based on a protection against a deep-seated passivity and submissiveness. This submissiveness is very frightening to her. She has claustrophobic "incubus" dreams in which she struggles against it, experiencing it as a fear of being pressed down by a weight on her chest.

One of the important indications that Florence does not reject her own color to identify with whites is that she had a much more marked positive response to the Negro psychiatrist than to the white psychiatrist, writing him a letter after the end of the interviews in which she expressed her gratitude toward him, and a wish to see him again. If there had been an identification with whites, this reaction should have been to the white rather than to the Negro. Florence actually identified with the Negro psychiatrist who interviewed her in the sense that her ego ideal was apparently modified by her contacts with him. Another indication of her positive identification with her own race was her denunciation of a recent white-supremacy candidate for governor who continuously derogates Negroes and who had called the mayor of New Orleans a "nigger lover." Florence stated that she thought the whole business of segregation was silly and inconsistent, and mentioned that when traveling with her white boss, for example, she was always able to get accommodations at hotels in the South.

The stability of Florence's adaptation is pointed up by the predictions the psychiatrist made in 1955 after examining *only* the 1938 data on her life. He felt that Florence was making a less effective adaptation than her contemporaries or siblings. Her character traits appeared to him infantile or inappropriate, notably her enuresis, lying, and quietness. He noted her phobias, presumably used as a defense against her own rage, and on this basis anticipated an adult use of phobic and counterphobic defenses. He saw the presence of nocturnal enuresis in a 13-year-old girl as a clear indication of a very strong passive-dependent quality of character, which would certainly extend to adult life. Accordingly he expected that Florence would do housework or nursemaid work with frequent changes of job and with rather marked dependence on white employers' largesse. The permanence and cohesiveness in Florence's family group and the absence of any appreciable antisocial behavior led him to expect that Florence would not gravitate toward a life of prostitution or become involved directly in other criminal activities. Noting evidence of projective techniques employed by Florence, especially in regard to such authoritative figures as doctors, he expected that some rather paranoid traits would appear in Florence's adult personality, but found no evidence that this would lead to ego disintegration. Though she appeared to be identified in her femininity at the age of 13, her heterosexual attitudes and behavior seemed to the psychiatrist to be unstable and mainly extractive in character. He further expected that she would become narcissistic in her attitudes toward children, as her mother seemed to have been, and noted that Florence definitely had some interest in children, which might well afford some basis for future occupational adjustment.

The accuracy of these predictions is clear and demonstrates the stability of patterns of behavior and ego mechanisms over time. Florence is still a subdued, obsequious, submissive girl who once in a while reacts to her submissiveness by an excess of defiance, rebelliousness, and coercive rage. She is still operating generally under the assumption that the good, obedient girl will be rewarded, although her lack of trust in others makes it necessary for her to supplement this behavior by direct extractive and exploitive techniques. Her ego defenses are essentially the same as in adolescence: denial, repression, the substitution of fantasy for reality, projection, and expiatory behavior in atoning for her guilty fears. Guilty fear was a dominant emotion then; it still is today.

In two important respects Florence has changed. She is much more responsible now than she was as an adolescent. Apparently this is an attempt to gain gratification through her children, seeing them as extensions of herself. Another important change is in her attitude toward color. In adolescence she was openly envious of whites, even expressing a wish to pass. She since has rejected identification with whites in favor of a modified "Uncle Tomism." She has the feeling that she will gain the things she wants not only despite the fact that she is a Negro, but perhaps because she is Negro. She has accepted this particular interracial role and is devising techniques to reap maximum benefits from it. Her real lack of aspirations toward upward mobility may be a vital factor in her acceptance of her color role. She assigns no definite, positive value to her color; her attitude is rather a passive acceptance of it, and more generally, of her lot in life. Florence has accepted a degree of defeat. She looks for security only to her mother, and for hope only to her children.

The matriarchy, described and illustrated by Florence's life, is a form of family embodying strongly held, emotionally toned values differing from those of other parts of society. It has its own frame of reference, its own ego ideals, its own culture, and these are intimately related to the affective life of the individuals in it. Even for a woman, the matriarchy leaves its emotional scars. It is difficult to see how a boy who has been exposed to the day-by-day expression of the negative value placed on men in the matriarchy can still establish a healthy, mature self-concept. Our next chapter considers this problem in the lives of men born within the matriarchy.

CHAPTER 6

The Gang

The culture of the matriarchy is so emphatic in its exclusion of men that a corresponding male culture would have to be invented if it did not exist. The male culture, however, does exist, and its impact on a large number of men, especially in the lower class, is dramatic and profound. This is the culture of the gang, a fraternal clique group of protean structure involving elements of age-grouping, neighborhood solidarity, occupational determination, and perhaps others.[1] Many gangs involve criminal activity, and most of them center on an ideology of at least technical illegality and immorality. Accordingly it is difficult to get explicit first-hand information about gang life: a passive but deeply protective secrecy surrounds it, and even nonparticipants preserve an air of impenetrable ignorance about other people's affairs in the social strata touched by the gang.

The gang identity is highly individualistic rather than communal; each member of the gang is expected to make his own way and to gain that position in the group to which his abilities and fists entitle him. This ideology is most often expressed in sexual terms as a definition of what makes a man different from a woman: Gilbert puts it succinctly: "I or any man like independence." Gilbert speaks more wisely than he knows. The inde-

[1] Albert K. Cohen, *Delinquent Boys: The Culture of the Gang*, Glencoe, Illinois, The Free Press, 1955.

pendence of the gang member is not simply, as Gilbert fervently believes, independence from one's mother-in-law, but independence from all responsibility—independence from mother, wife, and children. To be a person in the gang you must be a man. A classic, if romanticized, picture of the ideal gang member is painted by Louis Armstrong in his autobiography:

> When I was in my teens Benny was about twenty-six, a handsome fellow with smooth black skin, a strong body and a warm heart. He would not bother anyone, but God help the guy who tried to put anything over on him. . . . The gang love both Benny and Nice. . . . The cops knew Benny well, and they like him so much they never beat him up the way they did the other guys they arrested. When Benny was serving time in jail the captain of the Parish Prison would let him out to play at funerals with our brass band. When the funeral was over he went back to prison just as though nothing had happened. This went on for years, but Benny never served more than thirty days at a stretch. He was never in jail for stealing. It was always for some minor offense such as disturbing the peace, fighting or beating the hell out of his old lady Nelly. When he was not in jail for fighting, he would be in the hospital recovering from a carving she had given him.[2]

It seems likely that women are not the primary out-group for the gang members; their ultimate wrath and scorn are preserved rather for anyone who represents or symbolizes effeminate culture, most particularly effeminate men. Gilbert's description of gang initiation is typical in pointing up the sharp dichotomy between the bully and the sissy:

He said that many of the boys had been forced into homosexual acts, and had been forced to do many other quite indecent things. He said that the only way you could live in that neighborhood was either to be trampled upon by these bullies or to become a bully yourself. He said if you were not a bully, the boys would laugh at you and call you sissy, would take your lunch money from you, and if you had any baseballs or bats, they would take that from you, and make you get down on the ground and kiss the ground at their feet.

[2] From *Satchmo: My Life in New Orleans,* by Louis Armstrong. © 1954 by Louis Armstrong. Published by Prentice-Hall, Inc., Englewood Cliffs, N.J.

While it is manhood that constitutes the basis of the gang identification, we can see that it is manhood in a somewhat special sense. The psychic economy of the gang demands aggressive independence, a touchy and exaggerated virility, and a deep, protective secrecy. Acceptance by the gang provides almost the only source of security for its members, but such acceptance is conditional upon continual proof that it is merited, and this proof can only be furnished through physical aggressiveness, a restless demonstration of sexual prowess, and a symbolic execution of those illegal deeds that a "sissy" would not perform. These activities victimize women, but it would seem that they are not specifically directed toward women. Rather the enemy of the gang is the world of people (especially men) too unmanly for survival in what has often been described as a social jungle.

The he-man self-conception of the gang appears to exercise the same dominance over other patterns of social identification as we have found elsewhere for other self-conceptions. It minimizes class solidarity, since it is difficult to found any broad fellowship of feeling on the insistent independence of achievement that gang activity involves. It scorns religion and occupational and educational achievement as effeminate. Most of the highly organized social institutions fall only within the peripheral ken of the gang and are thus little known and generally disregarded. Only the more rigorous sports, law enforcement agencies, and perhaps the armed forces have the virility to be taken seriously. While the matriarchy and the gang agree that sex is the most important of all social categories, it is clear that sex is seen in quite different terms by the two groups. What is for the woman a matter of preserving family solidarity becomes for the man a question of individual assertive virility.

The impact of a gang orientation on color attitudes may be said to result in a rebellious touchiness that flares up despite the hopelessness of the gang members' power position. David told his white boss during an argument:

Don't holler to me. Just talk to me like I'm people, because I don't need to be hollered at.

Edward disregards even the special discipline of "the hole" (solitary confinement) at the penitentiary and the attendant loss of "good time" (credit towards reduction of sentence), when his feelings get to be too strong:

> Edward: . . . You don't win nothing: if you're right, you're wrong; if you're wrong, you're wrong any way it goes. It don't make too much difference one way or the other.
> Psychiatrist: So you just keep it under your hat if you can?
> Edward: . . . If you feel they're doing you something wrong, you just tell 'em about it and go in the hole. If they take your time, you just lose the time.

Nor is there any "cottonhead" or "Uncle Tom" taint to Gilbert's reaction to his job:

> He said that unlike the other Negroes who work with him, he does not "play" with (the white men over him). . . . The white men on the job seem to joke with the Negro men. . . . They pretend that they are going to hit them or kick them, or tell jokes at their expense, but he said that he noticed that they do not "play" with him, because they know he does not "stand for that stuff."

The genesis of gang attitudes is a complicated problem. Typically, of course, the little boys who are recruited into gangs come out of matriarchal families. Often they have little or no contact with their fathers. It does not appear that they get markedly different maternal treatment from that accorded to little girls, but it seems clear that vesting all parental authority in a woman would have rather different consequences for boys and girls, and the spirit of rebellion against authority so prominent in the gang is mainly derived from this source. The matriarchs make no bones about their preference for little girls, and while they often manifest real affection for their boy children, they are clearly convinced that all little boys must inexorably and deplorably become men, with all the pathologies of that sex. The matriarchal mother usually projects the blame for this result on the bad boys that lead her own little angel astray, and not infrequently attempts to counteract such influences with harsh if erratic punishments, but these frequently mask her own unconscious expectations of her son, and may do a great deal toward shaping him in the image of men she knows and approves or fears and represses. Whether the child actually contacts these men or not, such personifications have profound implications for his developing personality, especially in the first years of life. Whatever the influence of these aspects of the matriarchal climate, boys cannot learn to be men in a manless family, and we may assert unequivocally that this learning is institutionalized in the gang for most Negro boys of the lower class.

As a socialization context, the gang is highly structured. The clarity of differentiation of the roles of the bully and the sissy, the explicit establishment of a definite pecking order through a constant round of fights in which few rules are recognized, the inculcation of the code of secrecy through punishment for "squeaking," and the remarkable displays of verbal aggression called "playing the dozens" all contribute to this structure. The pressures for conformity to gang standards are severe; enforcement is physical and violent, and the gang viewpoint is deeply and traumatically inculcated. "Playing the dozens" probes for a boy's sensitive spot and brings it out for group attention in a manner not altogether dissimilar from some "brainwashing" techniques. Even a leader in gang life does not soon forget this hazing, though memory may kindly shade the more painful aspects of it. Years later Edward, who was cruelly tormented for not knowing who his father was, still remembered this initiation though his memory distorted the details:

In his early school years he remembers very well being teased because of the deep dimples in his cheeks. He was called fruity names. This caused him to fight back, and he finally convinced his schoolmates to stop teasing him.

Gang life begins early, more or less contemporaneously with the first years of schooling, and for many men lasts until death. Sometimes the gang's nucleus is a school grade; sometimes it is a neighborhood; sometimes it is an eclectic group of friends. Often a particular group will maintain its identity for many years, though a certain amount of instability seems more typical, and most men will move from one gang to another throughout life. Although each gang is a somewhat distinct group, all of them appear to have a common structure expressing and reinforcing the gang ideology. Thus an organizational form that springs from the little boy's search for a masculinity he cannot find at home becomes first a protest against femininity and then an assertion of hypervirility. On the way it acquires a structuring in which the aspirations and goals of the matriarchy or the middle class are seen as soft, effeminate, and despicable. The gang ideology of masculine independence is formed from these perceptions, and the gang then sees its common enemy not as a class, nor even perhaps as a sex, but as the "feminine principle" in society. The gang member rejects this femininity in every form, and he sees it in women and in effeminate men, in laws and morals and religion, in schools and occupational striving.

In relation to color, it is likely that most gang members are initially exposed to the accommodative attitudes we have already found in the matriarchy. David is an example:

He doesn't remember his mother's ever teaching him anything about white people except that when he would go out to perform she would tell him how not to get in trouble and how to ask people for money without insulting them.

It is apparent, however, that even the most humble may be pushed too far. David's mother reports:

One time, another place we was living, I sent my little girl to the door to tell the landlord I was out. I had the front door locked, and I was up there listening. My little girl was on the front steps. She tell him, "Mama ain't here today." He hollered at her and try to make her say where I was. My little girl just keep on saying she don't know. Then he say, "Get out of the way, you lying nigger." He come all the way through the alley and come in the back door. Then he walked all the way up to the front of my house. He looked at me standing behind the front door. Said to me, "You dirty slouch." I spit right in his face.

While the general tone of color training in the family seems to be focused on "staying out of trouble" with whites, the gang places the accent elsewhere. There is much talk of gang warfare, and with some frequency this is a matter of Negro boys against white boys, yet such experiences do not appear to be universal. Gilbert's remarks are typical:

He said his little brother, who is six, is very hot tempered, and that he will fight if anybody calls him a "nigger." . . . He said he himself takes after his father and mother, who are very peaceable, and will not fight unless meddled for a long time.

Thus it seems likely that the distinctive touchiness of color feelings in gang members is due less to specific color training than to the general ideology of not letting anyone take advantage of you. Although the "breaking point" may be differently placed by different people, self respect seems to demand that one rebel when others "go too far."

Despite the clarity of structure of the gang, we meet here again something of the variability we have already encountered in the matriarchy and the middle class. Edward, a fatherless boy of the lower lower class, has pursued the classical gang career in crime. After taking a leading role in the theft of Dollard's fan in 1937[3] he has gone on to drug addiction, dope peddling, and more significant thefts, and is now in prison. David, on the other hand, from an almost identical background (he was serving his third sentence in the boys' home when interviewed in 1938) has absolutely no police record, a real career in entertainment, and a family life with intimations of respectability and stability.

The importance of a clear ego ideal is strikingly revealed in the contrast between David and Edward. The ego ideal that David picked was a white jazz musician, a trumpet player who had his own band. This musician took David off the streets and gave him an opportunity to dance with his band. He has continued to help and encourage him down to the present time.

[3] Allison Davis and John Dollard, *Children of Bondage,* Washington, American Council on Education, 1940, pp. 68–70.

David is now married, and while he continues his gang associations and is far more frequently with men than with women, he had sufficient family feeling to force his wife to leave the matriarchal home in which she had been reared and take up separate residence with him. His self identity now is strong, and he is completely absorbed in his dancing and his career. In talking about his adolescent and childhood struggles (usually we caught him at some bar between shows), he frequently became emotionally upset by some of the memories to the point that he was unable to talk. He would then communicate by dropping a nickel in the juke box and dancing. Twice he corrected the interviewer for calling him by his legal name, and insisted on the stage name, "Little Bit." Edward, on the other hand, had no analogous opportunity for selecting a male ego ideal. He simply had no contact with adult men who might have given him emotional support during his identity crisis period. He has grown up to be a criminal with only a hazy and confused sense of where he has been or where he is going.

Gilbert, once a peripheral member of Edward's gang, compares himself favorably with the members of the gang who "turned out bad," and is proud of having finished high school. He even talks, somewhat vaguely, of going to college. But Gilbert's unstable marital life presents a classic picture of the gang problem, and his behavior reflects the hedonism and "independence" of gang ideals. While the consequences of gang life are similar in all these cases, it seems apparent that there is no strict determinancy to this affiliation. Each of our gang members has come to his position by a distinctive route and with his own reactions to the structure of his world.

It might be assumed that the gang is only the masculine phase of the matriarchal culture of the lower class, and certainly the two bear an intimate and partly complementary relationship to one another. They have usually, indeed, been described as aspects of "lower-class culture," and most gang members do in fact come from matriarchal families of the lower class. Roland, however, illuminates the situation further by demonstrating that there is such an anomaly as a male matriarch!

Roland lived with his mother all her life, and devoted himself completely to caring for her. Her sudden death, when he was 27, was the tragedy of his life. He had not lived with his father since he was three, and he has remained in the apartment he had shared with his mother, his "bachelor apartment," and he takes a womanly pride in the furnishings and their care, and in the genteel entertaining he does there. He does not cook, but this seems to be primarily because his brother and sister-in-law are next door and he finds it easier to board with them.

Roland is compulsive, fearful, and not given to self-revelation. However, the sociologist who interviewed him noted at the first contact that:

The subject seemed most interested when he was talking about his mother, which he did almost enthusiastically.

The enthusiasm is remarkable because he is still easily brought to tears by thoughts of her death (four years before these interviews), yet he talks of it on the slightest pretext in great detail.

Roland also displays considerable sensitivity to symbols of class prestige, and he talks about entertaining friends in his apartment with the absorbed attention to preparation and detail of a good hostess. The class pretensions are somewhat feeble, however: there is much name-dropping but no real intimacy, and there is very little genuine participation with the middle-class acquaintances he claims. Almost all the people described in his interviews are women, and there is no evidence of a strong peer group or gang orientation either in early life or later. The suggestion is strong that Roland is psychologically and even sociologically female.

Roland's psychological test responses indicate much confusion over his sex role, confirming the impression gained from the home interviews. His passive messenger job is just fine with him, and he has no ambitions, though at one time he wanted to be an embalmer. He appears to spend most of his time with his brother's family, and he is an enthusiastic uncle to his brother's children. The general pattern of his life would seem to be the paradoxical one of carrying on his mother's role in a family already partly dissolved.

Psychodynamically, gang members are characterized by deep-seated feelings of dependency and inadequacy. The feeling of dependency on mother is the same as that established in girls reared in the matriarchy. "Little Bit" provided a neat dramatization of this when he invited an interviewer into his home to see his new television set. He was obviously proud of it and described its many features enthusiastically. Ushering the interviewer into his living room, where the set was located, he then called his wife to come in and operate the set, explaining with some show of pride that he didn't know how to work "all those dials and everything."

The feelings of inadequacy of the gang member are specifically related to sexual confusion. Extensive homosexuality is institutionally part of gang life, and the subsequent insistent masculinity protests too much to be anything other than a necessary reassurance against self-doubts. Such feelings date from a childhood in which being a male in a matriarchal home is equated with being unworthy. The emotional intensity of this feeling is indicated by "Little Bit's" description of his visit to a German war orphan camp to entertain the children. After his performance he stayed at the camp for two days, visiting and entertaining the children. He wept as he explained that he did this because he knew what it was to be a small child and not have a man around that loved you.

The gang is a necessary institution, but it is at best a second-rate substitute for the security and stability of life in a family. Doubtless the self-doubts and insecurity of the gang member would be even stronger and more crippling than they are if they were not pooled and shared by gangs of frightened and confused little boys and the tough but embattled "mama's men" they grow into. But while the gang furnishes male role models, it is neither stable enough nor emotionally secure enough to be a satisfying substitute for a family. The life of Edward Dodge depicts the painful subtleties of this dilemma and the many faces of ambivalence in a human maze that seems to have no solution.

EDWARD DODGE: NAMELESS CON

Born and reared in the slums of New Orleans, Edward Dodge is the illegitimate son of a migrant tenant farm woman. He is currently serving a ten-year prison term for peddling dope. Edward is the "Nameless Boy" of *Children of Bondage*.[4] He has grown up to be a nameless man, and a convicted criminal.

Davis and Dollard felt that the environment in which he grew up was so full of "conniving, fighting, violence, and crime" that the choice for him was between cutting "all ties with his neighborhood to become inconspicuous; or . . . (finding) anonymity by allying himself with the criminal world where fewer questions are asked."[5] The blind psychiatric analysis of our data on Edward's classically delinquent adolescence led to substantially the same prediction. The psychiatrist felt Edward's career in crime to be virtually inevitable, and further expected his personal relationships to be narcissistic and intensely hostile. He predicted sporadic unstable liaisons with women and doubted that Edward would even be able to effect any very useful pattern of homosexual activity, though he noted that Edward's familiarity with casual homosexuality should predispose him to resort to this outlet for his sexual feelings in any limiting environment, "such as in a prison situation."

The predictions are accurate. Davis' and Dollard's framing of the alternatives fits the pattern of Edward's life so well that it is tempting to believe that Edward read them, though the evidence is strong that he did not. In any event, he tried the first alterna-

[4] *Ibid.*, Chapter 4, pp. 68–96.
[5] *Ibid.*, p. 96.

tive and left New Orleans for New York. When that failed, he returned and took up a life of crime.

Except for one visit to the psychiatrist's office, Edward was interviewed in prison. He is a stocky, muscular man of medium height, with dark skin and kinky hair. He has several small scars on his face and one of his rare smiles reveals a few prominent gold teeth. A tattoo of a bosomy girl is prominently displayed on his chest and he sports a rather unkempt Van Dyke beard and a poorly trimmed mustache. He is usually sullen and displays little emotion in his facial expressions. A flatness of affect pervades his low, monotonous voice, though there are muted overtones of hate and bitterness, of hopelessness and resignation. He was suspicious of the interviewer's motives. When one interview was tape-recorded, he was acutely concerned about what was going to be done with the record. In general, he coöperated only if he could strike a bargain for favors in his behalf, an extractive tendency also noted in 1938, when he consented to be interviewed only on being promised sodas or passes to the movies. This time he wanted a promise that we would raise money for his bail bond. This attitude is to a large extent determined by Edward's experiences of gang life, and is shared by his peers. He holds no hope of reward for good behavior. In taking the Wechsler-Bellevue intelligence test, Edward was asked to tell the manner in which praise and punishment were similar. He replied: "You suffer both ways. If you are punished you suffer. If you are praised you could suffer. If you are praised, people could get even with you by not talking to you."

This somewhat obscure conviction encapsulates the central problem to understanding Edward: his criminality. His own attitudes and those of his mother and his childhood associates repeatedly and obscurely confound the double standard of ethics and morality to which Edward has been exposed but which he cannot quite resolve. Praise and punishment, guilt and innocence, good and bad are profoundly disturbing dilemmas in his life, and he is deeply ambivalent and confused about them. In some respects they symbolize the other deep dichotomy in his life: male and female, or more precisely, gang and mother.

In 1938, Edward was described as "a slim, strong boy of 13. He has brown skin with a coppery underglow, kinky hair and Negroid features. His clothes seem to consist of odds and ends of apparel."[6] His home was "a 'two-room apartment' which is reached by walking down a long alley between two ramshackle houses. . . . The unscreened windows of the house were an invitation to flocks of mosquitoes. But the place was clean and pleasant smelling. Edward and his mother and her boy friend, when he was there, lived in the one room and kitchen. There was no telephone, bath tub, running water, or electric light in the house. There was a fenced-in toilet in the yard and a tap for running water near it. Edward's mother, Mrs. Martin, paid $1.75 per week as rent for two rooms, a lower-lower-class rental."[7]

Before he was sent to prison, Edward was living with his mother in an upstairs apartment of a four-family wooden house. This was an improvement over their 1938 housing. Most of the time he used his mother's house for changing clothes and entertaining his girl friends. He slept out often, presumably at his current girl friend's apartment. Edward never had a separate home except for a few brief months right after he was married. When he and his wife separated, she and their baby daughter went to live with her mother. His mistress was a frequent visitor to his mother's house. Pictures of Edward are prominently displayed around the house, together with photographs of his many girl friends.

His mother is now Mrs. Burton, since she recently "married" her sixth husband, a Sanctified preacher. During most of the period of our interviews, Mr. Burton was in another city, preaching. Edward has no use for his new step-father. He told his mother, "If I ever come home and find that nigger here, I'll take some-

---

[6] *Ibid.*, p. 70.
[7] *Ibid.*, p. 72.

thing and run him out." Mrs. Burton was very much amused as she related this to the interviewer. She evidently sides completely with Edward, and shares his contempt for her husband. Edward addressed a letter from prison to his mother as "Mrs. Martin" rather than "Mrs. Burton."

Mrs. Burton blames Edward's trouble on bad company and women, explaining that he had to obtain lots of money to be able to entertain his girl friends. She thinks of herself as an exceptionally fine mother, and claims to be proud of her son, but her pride is inconsistent. She praises Edward's accomplishments as a swimmer and boxer, as well as his abilities at outwitting the police, but almost in the same breath she comments that "jail is just what he needs to straighten him out." She expressed the same feeling in 1938 when she placed him in a reformatory. Similarly, she feels called on to exaggerate his skills. She says he was a pilot in the Air Corps during the war. In fact, he was an unskilled member of a ground crew that dismantled damaged or obsolete planes. Despite her conviction that women are the cause of Edward's troubles, his mother is exceedingly proud of his prowess as a lover, and delights in pointing out the number of good-looking girls he has had.

Though she claims to be a Baptist, Mrs. Burton's church-going is sporadic and relatively insignificant in her life: "I go when I have a good meeting." Just as in 1938, her club is the nearest beer parlor. She describes in high glee how she rebels against her preacher husband's demands, and drinks, smokes, and eats pork, in violation of the strict taboos of the Sanctified church.

Mrs. Burton much prefers Edward's current girl friend to his wife, openly condoning the illicit relationship and attacking Edward's legal wife at every opportunity. In view of her own multiple "husbands," some of whom were living with her concurrently, her attacks on her daughter-in-law and the simultaneous accusations of infidelity she levels against her husband seem almost ludicrous. Mrs. Burton got very angry with Edward's wife when she asked for help in raising $400 for the lawyer who had promised to get Edward out of jail in a year instead of the ten to which he was sentenced.

Despite her approval of Edward's criminal successes, Mrs. Burton is deeply ashamed of her son's being in prison. She tells ·her friends that he is in Chicago. Although there can be little doubt that her basic identification is with the criminal element, this reaction reveals her ambivalence and her submerged sensitivity to standards of right and wrong. Otherwise, 90 percent of her conversation is about crime and criminal activities, and particularly about the "rackets" in the law enforcement machinery: the shyster lawyers, the gouging bondsmen, the crooked judges, and brutal and discriminatory police. While there is probably some truth to her allegations, they are greatly exaggerated. In describing the escape of a prisoner from the prison in which Edward is jailed, Mrs. Burton left no doubt that when it comes to cops and robbers, she roots for the robbers.

When we tried to relocate Edward after a lapse of 15 years, it was all but impossible to find him. Neighbors guessed vaguely that "he lives somewhere on Ninth Street," or "he hangs out at a bar around the corner." In spite of inquiries proved later to have been made within two blocks of his home on at least five occasions, we could find no one to direct us to him. In the slums one's business is his own, and the first and fundamental commandment that *Thou Shalt Not Squeal* protects the guilty and innocent alike with an all but impenetrable cloak of anonymity and secrecy. Slum dwellers are close-mouthed about themselves as well, and neither Edward nor his mother proved willing to give us any complete picture of his associates and friends. Though we tried, we were never able to talk to Edward's wife or his girl friend.

Edward's wife works as a nurse. She is a year younger than he and appears to be genuinely attached to him. She regularly puts pressure on him to get a steady job and go straight. While he was awaiting trial she did her best to raise money for his bond and for his defense, despite the fact that he had apparently not been living with her regularly for six years. Edward expressed a vague dependency on his wife and he has some pride in her. Although his relation with her is completely obscure, Edward leaves us with the impression that it is emphatically onesided. She has been living with her mother and he with his "because of lack of space," Edward explains. He denies that they are separated.

His relation to his current girl friend is similarly structured, and similarly obscure. She also is a nurse, and also proved loyal to him when he was jailed. To some extent, in fact, this girl was able to enlist the coöperation of both Edward's wife and mother in her efforts on his behalf, and remarkably she and his wife shared his attention on visiting days at the jail more or less amicably. Edward expressed no emotion about this girl in any of his interviews, and indicated that he had no expectation that she would be faithful to him during his prison term. Yet he clearly has some genuine success with women. An even more casual girl friend who worked as a barmaid near his mother's home also tried to help raise money to get him out on bail before his trial.

Edward's other relatives in New Orleans mean nothing to him. For a while he lived with an aunt in New York, but they were never close. Aside from his mother and his girl friends, his most significant associates are vaguely described as "friends." Lonesomeness for these New Orleans friends, he says, was his chief motivation for returning to New Orleans, and certainly Edward's success as a dope "handler" implies some network of "pushers" who retailed the narcotics he was able to obtain. For obvious reasons, Edward says as little as possible about the members of his gang. Only eight people are mentioned, in fact, in his recent interviews: his mother, wife, daughter, step-father, and girl friend, a policeman, his lawyer, and his bondsman.

Even in adolescence Edward was enveloped in the anonymity of the slums, and his associates of that period are spectral figures, known only by their ephemeral nicknames: Meatball, Steamboat, the Greek, Weed, Little Joe, Tennessee, and Sonny Boy. These were all real people, however, and many of them were interviewed in 1938. Edward is most reluctant to discuss their counterparts in his current circle, and we can only assume their existence and their importance to him. Sonny Boy, recently released after serving an extended prison sentence for rape, is still a part of Edward's gang world, the only point of contact between his adolescence and the present besides his mother! The vagueness of Edward's gang is probably typical. His secretiveness about it is almost certainly so. In the dog-eat-dog individualism of the gang world, it is perhaps not surprising that Edward is not driven by feelings of solidarity and fellowship to discussions of his "friends," but his criminal success, psychological makeup, and rare but significant hints in his conversation all point to their importance to him.

Edward was born in 1925 in New Orleans. His mother was a young girl, 18, fresh from the country, where her parents had been tenant farmers. Her mother had owned a little land at one point, but lost it. The identity of Edward's father is completely in doubt. At one point, in an interview with Dollard, Edward's mother identified a casual lover named Thornton as his father. To another interviewer she said that Dodge was Edward's father, and described him as a "Creole" from the bayou country. The obscurity and inconsistency of the subject does not end there, for both Edward and his mother describe Dodge, a pullman porter, as an important childhood memory of Edward's, yet Little Joe Martin, Edward's step-father in 1938, claims to remember Edward's weaning at the age of two. Mrs. Martin compounded confusion by registering Edward at school as "Edward Phillips," her maiden name, and Edward ultimately decided on the basis of personal liking to call himself Edward Dodge. When we found him again, he had changed his mind, and variously identified himself as Edward Martin or Edwin Marsden. He is nameless still.

As far as we know, his development was "uneventful." There are no indications that he was delayed in walking, talking, sphincter control, or other early skills. It is clear that in his formative years his mother was very inconsistent toward him. Since she was working as a maid, Edward was frequently cared for by a neighbor, who was paid for this service. One of his mother's sisters lived with them at least some of the time, and there is a meager hint that her death, when Edward was five, may have been a shock to him. It seems almost an understatement to call Edward a neglected child.

By the time he was ten, Edward had been thoroughly initiated into the gang. Playing the dozens, the "game" that has come to be an almost ritual initiation into gang life and consists in informal taunts and insults designed to provoke the victim of the moment to fight, made a deep impression on him. He was "jived" or teased frequently about his bastardy and fatherlessness, and he was called "fruity names." Doubtless there were the usual insults to his mother as well, but it was the lack of a father and being called a sissy that stung him most. Stronger saplings than Edward have bent under such pressure, and he readily became devoted to the athletic interests, petty thievery, and defiance of school and playground authorities that gained him gang prestige. At 13 he was having sexual relations "often" with little girls at school. He started "doing it," he says, when he was eight.

Edward was an indifferent student, and by 1938 he had reached the fifth grade. He worked as a delivery boy, and later at shining shoes. He was active and successful in the activities of his gang, sometimes exercising a degree of leadership. Surprisingly, he went to Sunday School more or less regularly, if unenthusiastically, at a Baptist church. This is probably the explanation of the sanctimonious (and comical) horror Edward sometimes expressed to Dollard about the immorality of his associates, and of his attempt to present himself on occasion as a "good boy." He and his friends were active participants in sports at the "Center" and avid fans of gangster movies during this period. All of them were graduates of the juvenile delinquents' Home, to which Edward was committed at his mother's request shortly after he was interviewed.

Edward left school in the seventh grade in 1940 for "financial reasons." He continued to work at odd jobs, and was very active in athletics, notably swimming, football, and boxing. In boxing he was particularly successful, fighting as a lightweight and winning "almost everything" in New Orleans. He stopped fighting and declined to turn pro, he says, because he was overmatched. Actually, he got too heavy for his class and he bitterly resented being forced to face stiffer competition. When he was 16 to 18, delinquent gang activities became his major preoccupation. He was arrested six times and served one short jail sentence. At 18 he was inducted into the Army. He was given a "can't do duty" discharge a year later when he admitted having smoked marijuana, and went to New York, where he worked for about six months as a porter in a theater.

In New York he lived with his mother's sister and ran around with a fast gang. He was lonely and depressed. Though he had had some experience with marijuana, it was at this time, he says, that he started taking dope. He took heroin, and got a "fairly big habit." He was familiar with cocaine, too, but once remarked that he didn't see how it was possible to get "hooked" on cocaine. Both in New York and in New Orleans he was able to get heroin at five dollars a cap. He shot it directly into his veins, and at one time was taking 150 milligrams a day, a big dose. Driven by lonesomeness for his New Orleans friends, Edward says, he returned to New Orleans. Another factor may well have been his assessment of his financial opportunities and the expense of the narcotics he was using.

Back in New Orleans Edward worked for two months as a shipping clerk for one firm and for six months on the production line for another. His relationship to his white co-workers on these jobs was tense and hostile. He was apparently active in narcotics peddling on the side, presumably as a pusher. Within the year he was married. He was 21. His wife was 20. The fact that his wife and his most recent "steady" girl friend are both nurses may bear some relationship to Edward's narcotic habit, but we are unable to confirm or deny this. For a few months he and his wife set up a separate household together. Then they lived together for a time in Edward's mother's house. Edward's mother and his wife never got along, and eventually his wife moved out, returning to live with her own mother. They do not admit to "separation," and apparently he continues to see her and visit her often when he is free. Edward's wife is very anxious for him to give up his criminal activities and get a steady job, but he has never worked at anything for long. After his war job folded up he worked summers as a life guard, but held no other steady employment. About 1949 his daughter was born. He has never manifested any interest in the child, and has never lived with her.

With time Edward was able to become a considerable criminal success. He never "ratted" to us about his source of narcotics, but he was able to come by considerable quantities of drugs, and became a "handler," with a number of other people peddling for him. He made a lot of money and lived flashily. It is likely that this was the period of his biggest consumption of narcotics, too. He comments that a handler has the opportunity to get a much bigger habit than a pusher. His own drug habit may have cost him $15 or more a day at this time, although he probably had his ups and downs. He ran around with a number of women, and what they added to his overhead can only be surmised. In 1950 the police arrested him with "only one marijuana stick" in his possession.

He was indicted, convicted, and sent to a federal hospital for cure. Immediate deprivation of drugs caused him no withdrawal symptoms and he was discharged as cured and transferred to a federal prison for the remainder of his sentence. He was in prison less than two years. On his return to New Orleans he immediately resumed his flourishing narcotics business and was frequently arrested. He and his mother both feel strongly that the police persecuted him, arresting him on suspicion for every crime that was committed. While the harassment of these brushes with the law undoubtedly cramped Edward's style, they clearly did not drive him toward reform. He interpreted each event as a malicious and personal persecution. Somewhat feebly he advances the claim that he was going straight and curing himself of the drug habit, and that he could have made a go of it if the police had left him alone. Although he claims to have cut down his heroin dosage to a third of what it had been, there is little indication that he was even able to convince himself that he was going straight.

In any event, he was again arrested on a narcotics charge in 1954. The women in his life went his bail bond, and he was freed until his trial. He freely admits that he was using and selling narcotics, but again felt bitter and misused by the police over what he felt to be technical irregularities in his arrest and conviction. He was sentenced to ten years and is now in prison.

Edward's current life consists of three phases: his gang, his numerous girl friends, and the law. His daily routine outside prison can only be reconstructed from incomplete evidence. He appears to have engaged in his criminal and amatory life most of the night, coming home to his mother's house after she had left for work as a domestic. After sleeping through the morning and early afternoon, he dressed in the freshly laundered clothes his mother laid out the night before, ate the food she left for him, and sallied out in search of his underworld companions. He described his role as leader of a gang of dope runners with pride and satisfaction.

The extent of his promiscuous activities can be gauged by the frequent references made to them by his mother and by the pictures of numerous girls in his mother's house. His expensive shirts and suits were proudly displayed to one interviewer by Mrs. Burton, and Edward himself once came to the door in silk pajamas and a fancy bathrobe. It is obvious that he does need money to dress so expensively and to entertain his girl friends so lavishly.

His encounters with the police, federal agents, wardens, guards, fellow prisoners, lawyers, bondsmen, and judges fill a substanial part of Edward's history. He has been arrested many times (six times between the ages of 16 and 18 alone), often on suspicion. His angry, bitter comments on the frequency of these arrests "on suspicion" are probably justified. According to him, he could be picked up any time on sight, often when he was with a girl. The girl would often be kept in jail over night, while he would be locked up for three days and subjected to endless questioning and physical beatings. On the occasion of one arrest he is reported by his mother to have hit a policeman back and broken his teeth; he was released from jail with a swollen jaw. He used the frequency of these jailings as his excuse for not going straight, for every time he started at a legitimate job he was soon picked up by the police and lost the job. There is probably some truth to this, but it has been greatly magnified in Edward's mind.

Edward stoutly maintains his innocence of the charges against him in his most recent trial: that he was in possession of a hypodermic syringe at the time of his arrest. The syringe was buried in his back yard and not actually "in his possession." This difference, absurd as it is, assumed such importance to Edward that he refused to coöperate with his lawyer, who wanted him to plead guilty, despite the lawyer's assurance that if he would do so the District Attorney would ask for a two-year sentence instead of the maximum penalty of ten years. Such was Edward's perception of guilt and innocence that he felt he *was* innocent, and that he should be set free. He refused to "cop out." In consequence, he was given the ten-year sentence. As a clue to his perception of right and wrong and to the nature of his conscience, his reply to another question on the intelligence test he took is most revealing. Asked why laws are necessary, Edward said, "Because if we didn't have laws, you wouldn't know right from wrong, you would just do what you want. There would be no right or wrong." With this viewpoint, one can see why he felt he was innocent; the strictest interpretation of the law defines what is right or wrong. This didn't prevent his breaking the law, but interpreted strictly, the law could be used to maintain his innocence. Right or wrong to Edward is something external that someone else regulates and that can be manipulated to fit the occasion.

Though he felt his white bondsman was gouging him in usurious notes, he gladly complied with the bondsman's request that he get him a Negro woman for sexual purposes. Edward had no hesitation at pimping, despite the fact that pimps are looked down upon by many denizens of the underworld. He did his bondsman a favor, and he expected a better financial arrangement in return.

Edward feels himself to be the victim of a brutal world in which he is the constant object of harsh and unfair treatment. He has always been deprived, particularly of love and affection, and he sees himself unconsciously as weak and defenseless. He never admits this to himself; rather he idealizes himself as a powerful but misunderstood and mistreated man. He thinks he is a great lover, and even a proper family man, and he maintains this rationalization despite overwhelming evidence to the contrary.

Edward's basic patterns of behavior are exploitative, extractive, and manipulative. He seeks by fair means or foul to obtain from his environment everything he can in the way of material rewards or gratification. He has no feeling that he can obtain these things by legal effort. His entire training has led him to believe that it is only through cleverness or power that a man can get what he wants. His underlying inability to relate positively to other people and his lack of any warm feelings, even insincere ones, makes it exceedingly difficult for him to attain his ends by ingratiation. Accordingly, he relies primarily on the hit-and-grab technique, the power struggle of the gutter or the alleyway. He sees relationships purely in terms of power, and maladaptive and primitive attempts to secure power underlie his boxing, promiscuity, and narcotics-running. Convinced that security can only be achieved through power, Edward uses people rather than relating to them. He has exploited his mother, his wife, his mistress, and presumably many others. He attempted to exploit the interviewing psychiatrist in the same way. Possibly because of his inability to express or even to feel any positive emotions, and perhaps because of his limited intelligence, Edward's efforts are ineffectual when dealing with masculine authority. Apparently they have been more effective with the women in his life, and with his gang peers.

To some extent this power struggle has been sexualized. Edward has fears about his manliness that seem to be altogether unconscious. Crude defensive methods, such as his beard and the tatoo of a girl's bosom on his chest, are evidences of his conflict about this. The most intense emotions that he expressed during the interviews centered on the brutality of the police, being called sissy by his gang, and the taunts he received about his father. In adulthood it was the "sissy" charge that he remembered, and it still rankled.

One of the most striking characteristics of Edward in adolescence was his deep emotional involvement in the fact that he had no father. Early in the 1938 interviewing he broke down and cried when questioned about his real father. In a later 1938 interview he was asked why the inquiry about his real father had caused him to cry. The interviewer noted: "He sat silent and depressed for a few moments; then he said, 'The boys kid me about it.'" Edward himself was highly adept at playing the dozens, so the interviewer felt moved to ask, "Well, maybe that is the way they put you in the dozens—by talking about the fact that your real father has left?" Edward agreed.

In subsequent years Edward was never able to recover from the trauma that there was no significant male adult in his formative years with whom he could relate. This was the crucial deficit he experienced, and it offers a key to an understanding of his adjustment in later life. The males with any significance in Edward's early experience were his seniors in the gang. The oldest of these boys were graduates of the juvenile home who regaled the younger boys with stories of the sadistic punishments administered there, and who were already embarked on a life of crime, promiscuity, and violence that Edward was later to emulate. Edward was the only member of his gang who had not been sent to the Home at the time he was first interviewed, and before the study ended his mother had him committed. The seriousness of Edward's deficit is suggested by the circumstance that no less than four of the members of his juvenile gang "turned out well." Three of them are on the police force! The indications are that while these boys resembled Edward in matriarchal upbringing, they were able to find "fathers"—an uncle, a step-father, in one case a white band leader. Edward never did.

It is only partly true that Edward is unable to cope with problems of authority. It just happened that in his life the only psychologically real authority was that exercised by women: his mother, his wife, and his girl friend, and he apparently became very adept at dealing with them. As a matter of fact, his adaptive skills for handling his mother's restrictions may well explain his ability to maintain simultaneously the attachments to his wife and his sweetheart.

The central role of the confusion of sex and power in Edward's makeup is brought into sharp relief by some of his psychological tests. His drawings of a woman and a man suggested that his acceptance of himself and other males would permit him some meaningful relation with his own sex but that he had never had a warm relationship with a mother figure. He was concerned over aggression in both men and women, and his drawing of a man, apparently a self-portrait, suggests virility strivings in such details as broad shoulders, profusion of hair, and the addition of a beard. In his TAT stories his indecision over what was taking place in cards where men were being aggressive points up again his inability to cope with hostility, while he often described women as large, powerful, and freely aggressive.

Edward's Rorschach was meager, and conduces to the interpretation that he is schizophrenic. Periods of anxiety and depression were indicated by his classification of some of the achromatic cards as "black spots of dirt" or "a map." He reacted erratically to the colored cards, though his usual pattern of response seemed more passive than aggressive. He blocked on card seven, the most important in eliciting "maternal" imagery, then described it as two mountains held apart by steel bars, pointing up his fear of women and his view of them as unyielding and powerful. The tests suggested that masculine authority would be difficult for Edward to handle, and that his own masculinity was of prime importance to him. Edward's test IQ in 1938 was 71. In 1955 it was 83. Although some of his responses to other tests indicate a striving toward intellectual accomplishments, he exerts no real drive in that direction, and his intellectual functioning is clearly impaired and restricted to a dull-normal level.

Edward's basic conflicts relate to the fear of detection and punishment. His conscience is certainly underdeveloped, with few if any inner regulating devices. His morality is external. If he can get away with it, he does it. He is a hedonistic, impulsive man in conflict with a depriving world. He does not understand why this world should not grant him his infantile wishes for a stable of women, a fancy car, and a hundred suits.

It is clear that Edward's behavior is not antisocial so much as it is dyssocial. He has grown up in an environment that has manifest disregard for the usual social codes. He has lived all his life in this abnormal moral atmosphere and he has adhered to the values of his own predatory and criminal group. He was deprived of any real love in his childhood. His mother was working most of the time, so that he was actually separated from her, and their relationship, such as it was, vacilated between extremes of punishment and indulgence. The boy must have acted out many of his mother's unconscious wishes. He had no real, meaningful father figure with whom he could identify, since the men in his mother's life participated in the same abnormal environment, and his main relationships came to be with members of his gang. The importance of their acceptance to his self-esteem is all the more significant when we consider that he was never exposed with any intensity to any other way of life. The result of this pathological rearing is that Edward has only a stunted capacity for joy, love, or hope.

It is evident that Edward is not accepted by the larger community. The degree of his acceptance by his own gang is unknown. We have only the evidence of the loyalty of the women in his life. It is likely that his position in his gang was never very secure; probably it couldn't be, by the very nature of things. It is doubtful that he feels much inner comfort or acceptance, either, since chronic depression is one of his recognizable personality characteristics. Underneath, he must feel himself to be a failure, even in terms of his own social values and moral code.

For a while, however, Edward was something of a success. No doubt he was envied by many of the young people in his community. Reared as a ragged, dirty, and sometimes hungry child, he has had money to throw around in his adolescence and adulthood. The collection of photographs in his mother's home attests to his conspicuous consumption. He wore clothes that were usually sporty, and always flashy, though he could be semi-conservative on occasion and sometimes appeared in full dress. In a sense Edward has always belonged to a leisure class. His work record has been more experimental than a serious attempt to earn a living. The several jobs to which he aspired in childhood are almost forgotten now that he is an adult. When he was asked recently what kind of work he was prepared to do, he was at a loss to answer. Strictly speaking, he has never worked. While the large majority of slum people labor to make enough for their food, Edward's mother assures us that he has spent vast sums on whiskey and dope and good times. She is very proud of the fact that he was greatly sought after by the young men and women in his community. Men thought of him as a leader; women were proud to be seen with him. For a while at least Edward was a real gang success. He has been well socialized into the culture he has known.

Perhaps some individuals who achieve criminal successes are happy. Edward is not. If his only standards were those of the dope ring and the teen-age delinquency that led him to it, possibly he might have been. But Edward's mother was all too much aware of the standards of the larger community, and all too inconsistent in her reactions to them. She encouraged his delinquency and then put him into the juvenile home; she approved his sudden wealth, but she figured that jail is just what he needs to straighten him out. Despite his bravado and assertive masculinity, Edward has never been able to leave his mother, and he has long since internalized her ambivalence towards crime.

Edward has been continuously exposed to an environment of immorality and antisocial activities. He is hedonistic, has a poorly developed conscience, and lacks the judgment or ability to learn from experience or from punishment. He is manipulative and extortionistic, and continually uses the presocial technique of hit and grab. He has violent emotions and lacks ability to form lasting ties with other people. His lack of a father figure has led him to seek his identification in the gang. His social world did not sublimate or otherwise direct his gang activities in adolescence. He tried isolation and found he could not tolerate it. Crime was the only alternative. In his heart of hearts, Edward knows himself to be a failure—weak, nameless, and criminal, and he is unhappy.

The Family

For six of our subjects life appears to revolve primarily or even exclusively around the family. All of them are in upper lower or lower middle-class occupations: postmen, maintenance workers, service station operators, janitors, mail clerks. All of them have been stably married for many years, and though they express a rather wide diversity of other social attitudes they are emphatic in the value they place on family life. William, whose ambition is to build a 14-room house to accommodate his large family, is typical:

He said that he is afraid that when his children grow up they will forget about him, and he said that he wanted very much to rear them in such a way that when they grow older and get married that they and their children and wives would always remember him, and that he would always be near them.

Francis' feelings toward his family are no less strong:

(He has) a keen sense of isolation, revealed by his intense interest in his family, and his initial need to present them as a very cohesive group. His use of the pronoun "we" was frequent in his references to his family.

Victor's first thought is also of his family:

He said that when the doctor told him . . . that it would be at least two months and perhaps more before he could return to work . . . he became very concerned and very anxious about what he was going to do about supporting his family, being off work for so long. . . .

And Vera makes it explicit that cohesiveness is the heart of the matter:

She referred to members of her family as "the fighting Hills." I asked her why she called them "the fighting Hills" and she said, "Because we fight like cats and dogs together, but when one of us gets in trouble all of the others share the trouble."

For these men and women family life is the most important part of all life, and family solidarity the most important value. Such an emphasis places a special stress on the responsibility of parenthood, reliable and steady employment, and family support, and to a remarkable degree this is an all-embracing passion for these people. Most of them have no involvement whatsoever in outside social groups of any kind: they do not join clubs; they do not "go out" even to visit friends; they do not become involved in organized church activities or political movements. Their lives revolve around job and family, and they conceive the job as a means to family ends in a clear system of priorities.

Family loyalty of the absolute kind these people feel involves considerable suspicion and mistrust of the agencies and forces of the "world outside." The ethnocentrism of family is therefore structured by the dichotomy between the little world of domesticity and all the rest of society. Our "family types" appear to have no general agreement on a single arch-foe of their common identity, but they reflect diffusely all outside influences. Ellen says of her job:

At my job—I'm an exchange adjuster, by phone—it's all on the telephone, so I feel comfortable. I don't ever meet these people. . . . It's a waste of time, not a career or profession like teaching.

William, who is almost never critical of his fellow man, nonetheless disapproved of his neighbors' purchase of fancy cars:

He seemed to have spent a great deal of time thinking about this, because his criticism here was mild but positive: that a person should not buy these fine automobiles until he has at least provided a decent place for the wife and family to live.

Victor places more emphasis on color and expresses great hostility to whites and to "mulatto bastards" who are snobbish about color. Francis shares these feelings somewhat but also expresses his antagonisms in terms of class and religion.

He said that he had never missed a Mass on Sunday in his entire life, and he felt quite contemptuous of those professed Catholics who did not adhere strictly to the religious rituals.

It seems likely that in general the people with a primary loyalty to family may be more sympathetic to agencies like the church, which bolster familism, than to the antifamilistic demands of occupation or racial etiquette, but this does not necessarily imply extensive participation. For many of these people, in fact, familism is a restrictive withdrawal reaction. All but one of them have absolutely no stable social ties beyond job and family, and the prevailing pattern of nuclear family residence effectively reduces their social worlds to the microcosm of a small household. Thus their reactions to color, class, or other important dimensions of the society outside their homes are phrased in terms of denial.

Mary almost got angry when she was invited in so many words to express dislike of whites because of discrimination. She went to great length to state emphatically what boiled down to, "I don't dislike white people," and "I don't feel discriminated against."

That very strong sentiments may be controlled by this process is made clear by Victor, who expressed the strongest hostility toward whites encountered in the study:

He said that he is glad . . . that Negroes do not hate white people any worse than they do, because, he said, if they did they could kill white people wholesale, and (he) mentioned, pointing to his food, that, "after all they do fix food for a large number of them, and just think what they could do if they decided to poison all the food they fix for white people." He went on to point out that white people live in communities all by themselves, and all Negroes would need to do would be to shoot into their houses or to throw dynamite into their houses or burn their houses in order to create a great deal of terror and disturbance. The subject seemed upset even by the thought that Negroes might do this, and expressed more than once that he was glad Negroes did not hate white people as white people hate Negroes.

Victor fantasied on another occasion planting a bomb in the building where he works, since it would blow up mainly white people. As in Mary's transparent denial, it is clear that Victor's color attitudes are strong and disturbing. Francis, too, expressed strong color feelings. On repeated occasions he said that no one could possibly understand the Negro's position in society unless he were Negro. And William makes a graphic charge against Negroes for their lack of solidarity:

(He) feels that the main reason Negroes are discriminated against in this country is because of themselves. He said that Negroes are like crabs. You can put them in a bowl together and no one will ever get out because the others will pull him down.

A striking feature of these attitudes toward the social meaning of race is the juxtaposition of intense feeling with a diffuse patterning. Lacking the middle-class rationalizations (color prejudice is stupidity), the matriarchal opportunism (exploit the exploiters), or the gang's vengeance (fight back: you have nothing to lose), these respectable familistic people appear to share a positively phrased familistic attitude toward race: all men are, or should be, brothers. There are, however, some suggestions of what such familistic attitudes might be like if they were to become widely shared, as in William's remark:

I asked him if he got along well with the white fellows on his (baseball) team (at the Naval Training Station) and he said, "Very well indeed . . . they treated me like a brother."

A somewhat similar detail crops up in Ellen's and Vera's family:

Vera was able to find some pages in the (old family) Bible on which were the names and birthdates as well as dates of marriage and dates of deaths and burial of her father's kin dating back to 1852. . . . The first name entered, in 1852, was that of a white ancestor. . . .

It would be tempting to dismiss all these people except William as isolates, marginal to their society, but for the circumstance that the structure of their lives is demonstrably part of a viable tradition, passed on to them by their parents. The family Bible in the Hill family is a particularly dramatic evidence of this continuity, but it is equally dramatic that five of these six subjects came from homes in which both a father and mother were present up to the time the subjects were adolescent, whereas this is true of only three of the remaining fourteen cases. Both by precept and by example our "family members" were taught by their parents to prize the values of stable family life above other goals, and they in turn are well embarked on transmitting these same values to their children. Four of them have children, and all their children have had the experience of living in a home with a complete set of parents all their lives. None of the seven other subjects who have had children have provided them with this fundamental and formative experience.

We may conclude that while the complex of attitudes and allegiances inherent in nuclear family residence are not determined for the individual by any specified particular of his past, they are nonetheless combined in a segment of the New Orleans Negro community into a separable tradition quite distinct from those we have already discussed, a tradition with its own premises and standards and its own customs and rules.

The members of our nuclear family group share a strong feeling of dependency. In attempting to meet the ego identity crises at adolescence, they adjusted by regressing to earlier childhood patterns of relationship. For all the subjects in this group, marriage has been a solution by default to the problem of ego identity, for marriage and the strong solidarity of family life are ways of gratifying their dependency feelings. Going along with this is their marked social isolation from groups outside the family. All of them have chosen mates who have in common a rather strongly mothering attitude toward them. This is true of both the men and the women. It may be appropriate in this connection to consider first the history of William Leon, the exception to almost all the rules we have been able to formulate for the familistic working class, the only current member of a stable family who did not himself come from one, probably the most deprived child and the most mature adult in this group—in short, the despair of the deterministic scientist.

WILLIAM LEON: BASEBALL DADDY

William Leon is a 34-year-old postman, born and raised in New Orleans. He is married, has seven children, and owns his own home. He is a faithful Baptist and an active Mason.

William was raised in a rather stable and secure lower-class environment in a house owned by his maternal grandfather. His father was a longshoreman who supported his family fairly well, but was hospitalized for a psychosis when William was three, and died only two years later. The family's economic support after this came from William's older sister and his two older brothers, whose income was supplemented by welfare grants. The family never wanted for food, but there was a shortage of clothes, a source of humiliation to William since his classmates ridiculed his poor clothing. One pair of pants had to last him all year.

Practically nothing is known about the personality of William's father. His mother apparently had a good deal of maternal feeling for her children and was solicitous about their welfare. She was crippled with arthritis and diabetic ulcerations all through William's formative years. Two of his aunts were of special importance to him. His mother's oldest sister lived with them and was the primary disciplinarian in the house. Apparently she was punitive at times and would deprive the children of privileges even after they had been beaten or otherwise punished. They were whipped severely and sometimes made to kneel on hot bricks. There was another side to her character, however, for she rewarded their good behavior as well. She gave them ice cream and candy and money for movies, and was the only source of such rewards. She took a special interest in William, since he was the youngest, and often discussed his future with him. She also inculcated certain values, the most important of which was staying out of trouble with the law. William developed a good deal of affection for this aunt despite her punishments. He had another aunt who was completely indulgent. Though she never lived in the same house, he remembers her very fondly. William's mother worked as a seamstress and was thus able to be home with her children but his aunt is a more important figure to him, because of his mother's illness. William very much admired a cousin ten years older than he, who lived next door, and who had a lot of influence on him. This cousin was an expert baseball player. He taught William a love for sports and a desire to maintain certain standards of sexual morality.

Although the family was hard hit by the death of William's father, who was the chief breadwinner, and by the fact that there was no steady employment for any members of the family during the depression, William's family was nevertheless a stable unit, living together in a home they owned and finding security in this unity. In 1938 various members of the family were on WPA off and on. William's older brothers went on to steady employment. One of them became a union steward, earning a good salary. All the children married and have maintained stable marriages.

We know little about William's early development, but more about his school years. He was an excellent student despite a rebellious attitude toward some of the teachers and a tendency to play hookey. In 1938 he was in trouble because he had stayed away from school for a month. Nevertheless he had positive feelings toward many of his teachers and idealized some of them. He went to school until he was fifteen, quitting in his sophomore year of high school when he had only a few weeks to go to complete the year. He left because of economic difficulties and his feeling of need to help his family support itself.

In school he had a great need to conform to gang activities and had belonged to several gangs and clubs, though apparently never as a leader. He frequently expressed violent attitudes in the

1938 interviews, mainly in an attempt to impress the interviewer with what a tough guy he was. He may have had some feelings of inadequacy about his masculinity, for he bragged about his love-making and his toughness. He boasted about drinking hard whiskey and showed the interviewer a knife with a four-inch blade that he carried in his pocket. He said he hoped that the police would not try to hurt him "because I always carry this in my pocket." He belonged to a racially mixed gang called "The Black Legion" and talked about fighting with white boys. "You see, when you fight a white boy you're really fighting more than him; you're fighting the policeman too." He was cynical about religion: "I just go to the Catholic Church to see the girls, anyway," and he expressed an aggressive interest in white women, "Some people say Negroes shouldn't fool with white women, but don't white men fool with colored women? If I get a chance I sure am going to fool with one. . . . I think the Negro men ought to lynch white men for fooling with colored women, just like the whites lynches the colored man for just looking at the white woman hard." He attempted to outrage the interviewer in 1938 by saying that he would like to be a pimp and have the interviewer marry his girl friend and take care of the children that he and his girl friend would have. He figured his girl friend could turn over to him the money the interviewer gave her. It is clear that he was trying to be just as outrageous as possible, although this appears to have been an expression of his gang's stereotyped attitudes rather than his true feelings. The other side of his personality came out when he said, "But seriously, I'd like to be a mail carrier or a mail clerk. I could be a pimp, but I couldn't stand up under it."

Despite all his talk about white women, he indicated his desire to marry a black girl. "I don't think I could get used to a bright woman. I've been going with dark girls all my life. They're sweeter anyway." His desire for conformity is expressed in his ambitions: "I don't want to go to college. High school is enough for me. I want to be like my people. You see, if I finish college, I might be high-hat, and I don't want to be like that. I can live all

right with that money that the government will give me for being
a mail clerk or mail carrier."

After reading through the 1938 data, the psychiatrist who made
the "blind" analysis of these data on William described him as a
rather likable adolescent, somewhat given to bragging, whose life
was regulated almost exclusively by his adolescent peers. He felt
William made a great effort to effect a stable pattern of sexual
behavior, and found no evidence of any marked homosexual preoccupation. Noting that William's hostility was estimated by the
1938 interviewer to be at a very high level, the psychiatrist re-
viewing the material was not impressed that it was a great problem to him, but felt that William was able to maintain important
relationships rather easily and that he channeled his hostile impulses in directions that were quite acceptable in his group. He
noted that William had a great deal of preoccupation with color
gradations within the Negro group and with the relationships between whites and Negroes and that this was obviously of great
importance to him but that he expressed no great bitterness
about it. William was anything but isolated in Negro society, and
was most aware of the limitations and opportunities around him,
but was able to see the progress of Negroes in a limited way. The
psychiatrist expected these attitudes to persist.

He also predicted that William would complete high school,
"or nearly that." He did not believe that he would adopt antisocial
patterns of behavior, and expected that he would be "a fun-lov-
ing, not too ambitious person, interested in family life and capable
of a stable marriage." He predicted that William would stay close
to home throughout his life and continue his real interest in getting along with people. His free expression of affect tended to
make him likable then, and the psychiatrist thought this would
probably apply to both white and colored associates now. Em-
phasizing the degree of contact that William had had with whites,
the psychiatrist felt that the fairly effective general adjustment
that he had made by the age of fifteen had largely been determined by this fact. The other important determinant of his ability

to adjust to a difficult situation seemed to be his relatively secure and stable family life.

Although the depression came along when William was about eight, there were no sudden shifts in the family fortunes. His two older brothers were providing for the family. Despite the fact that he was first in his class, he quit school at fifteen to work in a grocery store for two years between 1937 and 1939 and made extra money shining shoes at night, earning a total of $10 to $15 a week. In 1940 he went into a factory, where his job was to make the bands with which cotton bags are tied. He was paid $20 to $25 a week for 60 to 70 hours' work. In 1942 he went into the Navy and served for three years, seeing considerable action in the Pacific, including the invasion of Okinawa. He went through seven typhoons and had some pretty close calls. He was a gunner's mate first class but was "busted" to second class a few weeks before his discharge, when he broke into the officers' locker where the beer was kept and told one of the officers to go to hell.

He had married when on furlough from the Navy and had gone overseas immediately after his marriage. On his return he did nothing for two or three months until he found some temporary work at the Port of Embarkation and at the dock. Following this he worked steadily in a warehouse for four years. During that time he also went to night school under the GI Bill, where he studied for the civil service examination for railway mail clerk. He failed the examination, but in 1952 he passed the examination for letter carrier and has been working in the post office as a letter carrier since October 1952. Since returning home from the Navy in 1945 he has had seven children and has bought his own home and a car. He is making over $300 a month and is able to save a little bit each year.

William is a friendly and agreeable dark-skinned Negro of medium build who nevertheless gives the impression of solidity. He is generally happy, smiling, affable, and friendly, and almost never grouchy or complaining. He is extremely eager to please his interviewers. He dresses very neatly, and when he is wearing his postal uniform it is generally well pressed and looks as if he had just put it on for the first time. He is generally restrained in his movements, sitting quietly during interviews with very little indication of anxiety. When angry responses would be indicated, William sometimes laughs, even inappropriately. He appears to work at giving the impression that he is hardly ever angry. His content of thought reveals adequate reality testing, although some grandiosity is evident in the goals he sets for himself. This is offset by the fact that his actions are perfectly consistent with reality and that he doesn't altogether believe in his own grandiose schemes. Sometimes the interviewers were surprised at the quality of his thinking. His awareness of political and racial nuances was striking. His intellect is high average (Wechsler-Bellevue IQ 114). William elicited friendly and positive reactions in virtually all who contacted him.

William's job as a letter carrier fulfills the ambition he has had since early adolescence. He usually works on the night shift. After leaving work at midnight he generally spends an hour or two drinking beer with his fellow employees before returning home. He occasionally has upper abdominal pains after drinking but is reluctant to stop because of his need to be "one of the boys." He obviously likes his job very much and enjoys the companionship of his peers. On returning home he generally finds his wife asleep. Because of her fear of pregnancy their sexual activity is at a minimum. William does a great deal around the house, including some of the tasks ordinarily performed by women: cooking, cleaning, dressing the children, and shopping. He prides himself on these activities and particularly on his ability to cook. Nonetheless, he is resentful toward his wife for her "laziness." He seems to be the primary disciplinarian in the house, and it is he who rewards and punishes the children.

His community life is quite varied. He takes a leading part in church activities and sometimes goes to church a number of times on Sunday. He generally attends all the church's social functions. He takes great pride in being a thirty-second degree

Mason, and belongs to a veterans' organization as well. These group and club activities are supplemented by his interest in baseball. Most of this interest is now passive, although once he was an active player. He watches baseball on television and goes to the ball park occasionally. He and his family frequently take rides together or go picknicking, and they have a good deal of unified family life. William takes an active interest in politics. In a recent election he helped instruct prospective Negro voters in the proper method of registration. He also attempted to persuade his fellow employees to vote for a man running against the incumbent senator. He is fairly well informed politically and much of his political activity is based on what he feels will be good for Negroes. He was against the incumbent senator from Louisiana because of his poor record concerning civil liberties and racial matters. Most of his associates are salaried working men of the upper lower class. He is very friendly with his neighbors and frequently drinks beer with them. It is clear that he makes friends easily.

In his home William seems to take a dominant role. He has a protective attitude toward his wife, as well as toward his children, but he is oftentimes authoritarian and orders his wife to do things for him. Sometimes she sulks and refuses to comply, but in general she plays the complementary role of a passive, obedient child. When emotionally upset, she withdraws by sleeping much of the time. One interviewer described her as being one of the children. Still, William has a good deal of pride in his wife and respects her opinion—in financial matters, for example—though he objects when she does not comply with his wishes. William has many responsibilities around the house, which he carries out rather well, including repairs to the house as well as the domestic duties already described. The children are very respectful and obedient, but the indications are that this respect and obedience are not entirely out of love for their father. Psychological tests of the children indicate their inhibitions, shyness, and fear of aggression. Neurotic patterns are already developing in the oldest child.

Much of their obedience, we can then suppose, is based upon guilty fear, the fear of punishment. This indicates that William must be much more authoritarian than he acknowledges himself to be, but there are also many positive features to his paternal role. He does not seem to have any residue of hostility toward his children. We don't know much about his wife's role with the children. She may be a source of fear, inasmuch as their oldest boy's reaction to the maternal figure in tests was a fearful one, and he seemed more trusting of the male figures.

Although William tends to be the dominant figure at home, it seems that outside the house signs of leadership appear only in his church and club and not in his other social activities. It is hard to know how much leadership he really exerts. He certainly tried to give the interviewers the impression that he was an important guy. With his beer-drinking pals he apparently has a strong need to conform, and he conveys the same feeling of passivity toward his two older brothers, particularly the one who is a union organizer. We know very little about his current relationships at work except that he seems to get along very well with everyone and is well liked. This has been his dominant pattern throughout his life. Wherever he has worked, in the Navy or on civilian jobs, he has gotten along well with both his employers and his peers. There have been no indications of any serious trouble.

In his interviews with a Negro psychiatrist, additional information came out that he was having two extramarital love affairs. He seems to be using these women without giving them very much in return, and he seems to have a narcissistic approach to women in general and to be more concerned with what he was getting than with giving.

The general impression one gets of William is that he is happy and contented, yet there are some evidences indicating inner turmoil. He is preoccupied with rather grandiose omnipotent fantasies, such as having a house for each one of his children, or a fourteen-room house for the whole family, or winning large sums of money in contests. Other information from psychological testing indicates that he has rigid defenses and that he is repressing a good deal of rage. Nonetheless, his defenses really do work well, and in most of his life he seems to be fairly happy and able to get along well with people. William's marriage is probably the least comfortable of his relationships. He seems to have a great deal of resentment toward his wife, and his extramarital affairs are probably an indication of dissatisfaction in this area.

His attitude toward color is a healthy one. He does not derogate himself because of his skin color, nor does he ingratiate himself with whites. He seems to be working actively for the advancement of Negroes. He resents failure of Negroes to take advantage of opportunities, and he resents their manners when these are inappropriate. He senses the limits of what can be accomplished in a given period of time but nonetheless wants to do what he can to achieve the possible goals. William still has some of the fantasies of his adolescence of having sexual relations with white women. This seems to be about the only remnant of self-derogation in his make-up, although a more important element in this is his hostility toward whites and a wish to revenge himself upon them for the relative ease with which he feels white men have sex relations with Negro women.

William does not suffer from racially based self-hatred. He is positively identified with Negroes; he is proud of his race. This positive identification presents an interesting problem. Kennedy[1] has asserted that the Negro brought up among whites develops a "counter" white ego ideal and is perpetually frustrated because he cannot change his color, while the Negro raised "in the Negro neighborhood develops the abstract" white ego ideal, which allows for some symbolic substitution or modification, and hence has a better chance of developing a healthier ego ideal. William's case contradicts Kennedy's hypothesis. He was reared in a mixed neighborhood in which white and Negro children played together. Indeed, most of his playmates and closest friends outside

[1] Janet A. Kennedy, "Problems Posed in the Analysis of Negro Patients," *Psychiatry*, 1952, 15:313–327.

school were white; they would visit each other at home regularly. His next door neighbor was a white baseball coach who was a close friend and adviser, and William played with his children almost daily.

Indeed, it is probable that this association and acceptance by white friends had a profound influence in developing William's positive Negro self-image. The geographical "distance" between Negroes and whites is not as significant as the emotional "distance." Our data suggest that it is erroneous to suppose that every Negro develops a "white ego-ideal." As Bernard[2] has suggested, this is also a stereotype, and like all stereotypes, a distortion of reality. William's whole attitude toward color, and perhaps toward life itself, is captured in the statement he made in 1938. "You know, one time I wished I was white, but it didn't seem to help any so I just stopped wishing and decided to be what I am, a Negro."

William was hospitalized in 1951 for a suspected ulcer. There are possible indicators that his dependency needs are stronger than might be suspected from the interviews. He has strong defenses against these needs, as evidenced by the dominant role he plays in the household. His resentment toward his wife is probably related to the fact that she is not the "feeding mother" that he unconsciously hopes for. We have no material on his feeding in childhood, but it may be relevant that his primary method of rewarding his children is alimentary. He certainly is concerned about feeding guests in his home. He usually served lemonade to the interviewers who visited him. Whenever he sends his children for a treat it is for ice cream. This fits in with the idea that his dependency needs are somewhat, though probably only slightly, exaggerated; and in view of his exaggerated show of independence, these needs may be responsible for his gastrointestinal symptoms. This show of independence was one of William's prominent traits in 1938, and the dominant note in all his interviews,

[2] Viola W. Bernard, "Psychoanalysis and Members of Minority Groups," *Journal of the American Psychoanalytic Association,* 1953, 1:2, 56–267.

but it was really pseudo-independence, actually representing conformity to the demands of his peer group.

William's ego processes are working adequately. His reality testing is pretty generally intact except for the grandiosity previously mentioned. His selection and sorting of stimuli seem adequate. There is some overuse of fantasy as a compensatory technique for reality failures, although in view of the realistic deprivation, it is questionable whether this is abnormal. He has above average intelligence, good ability to think logically, and better than average capacity for learning. His ability to plan for the future is normal, and it is noteworthy that he does plan for the future rather than live in a series of present moments, as many lower-class Negroes seem to do. He is concerned with savings, insurance, and real estate investment. William seems to have an adequate mastery of his environment, as well as fairly normal self-discipline, concentration, and endurance. His purposiveness is indicated by his concentration on family goals, to which he returns over and over again in conversation, and which he actually attains. His purchase of a house as soon as he came out of the Navy is typical. He has some difficulty in reconciling his wishes and needs with outer reality, but this is not extreme. In reconciling these wishes and needs with the demands of conscience, as in the problem of his extramarital affairs, he reacts casually and with very little, if any, evidence of guilt. He seems to have a rather effective control in the use of his emotions, although his need to control his angry feelings outside the home probably causes him some discomfort in personal relations. This latter inference is based almost entirely on the projective tests; clinically it is not much in evidence. Indeed, one's strong impression is that he seems comfortable most of the time.

The things that seem to be significant in William's sexual life are an expression of what we might call "middle-class attitudes" toward individual sexual activity. He idealizes his cousin's refusal to have sex relations with his wife until after marriage, yet he himself had premarital intercourse, is frequently promiscuous, and has had at least two extramarital affairs. Certainly there must be a problem in his marriage, since his wife is reluctant to have intercourse because of her fear of pregnancy and has actually voiced her desire to shy away from it. William seems to be exploiting his wife in this regard because he wants to produce at least nine children so that he can have his own baseball team. This rather humorous foible is a very serious matter to him. He really intends to have his children form a baseball team. A number of his children are named after major league baseball players. His second son is Jackie Robinson Leon.

One of William's girl friends is a childhood sweetheart whom he has been seeing since 1951. The other girl is very tall, about six feet two inches in height, and very well built. He developed an interest in her because of their mutual interest in sports. He has taken her to baseball games and finally to dinners, and then they began a sexual relationship that he continues without disrupting his relationships with the other girl friend and with his wife. He doesn't wish to have his wife know about these relationships because he doesn't want her to be hurt. He once called these girls' names in his sleep and his wife accused him of having affairs, but he admitted to nothing.

William's competitiveness appears in his desire to get ahead in various groups such as the church or the Masons, but it is not extreme and is offset by a strong desire to be coöperative. He seems to be able to work very well in joint enterprises. His desire to dominate the group only comes out in his home. He seems to be able to subordinate himself in other enterprises, probably because of his need for conformity and acceptance.

The variety of his activities and interests is striking. His group and community participation is more extensive than that of any of our other subjects. Of the six subjects who make the family their chief focus of interest, he is the only one who is really involved in group activities outside the family. His family is not, as it is with the others, a fortress erected against the dangerous outside world. It is a family that participates, joins, and engages in community affairs. From all the available evidence this is a result of William's personality. His wife passively "goes along" with his extrafamilial interests.

William is something of a happy-go-lucky, immature kid with rather grandiose desires for status, prestige, and material possessions. His lack of these attributes and possessions does not seemingly produce any feeling of depression or frustration, perhaps because he is convinced somewhat unrealistically that he can obtain anything he wishes to. He states this over and over again. To be sure, he has obtained many of these things, such as a home and a car; nonetheless, his conviction in this area is somewhat magical. It is this which probably sustains him, because what he hopes for is always right around the corner. On the basis of this perceptual distortion, he functions well in his job and is stable in his work activities, and reliable and responsible at home and in his group activities. His ego ideal is to be a stable family provider who obtains through the course of his life many of the conspicuous evidences of success. He is interested in bigger and better motor cars, bigger and better houses, and—to a lesser extent, perhaps—better clothes. This may be based on the fact that his father was sent away to a mental hospital when William was only three, and it may be an attempt to do for his children what was not done for him.

William probably has some conflict over dependency and independence. In relation with his wife it is apparent that he unconsciously treats her as a mother-substitute. He does the same things for her that he did as an adolescent for his mother. He was very devoted to his mother and helped her, for example, by doing many of the chores around the house. Nevertheless, he unconsciously expects from his wife the same kind of care that his mother provided for him, and he resents the fact that his wife is primarily interested in sleeping. Just how abnormal William's needs are in this area is hard to tell. The evidence seems to point to the fact that his wife is somewhat less than adequate insofar as she does retreat to bed. Although interviewers who visited the home never found the children poorly clad or neglected in any way, the question remains whether this is William's doing or whether his wife is so competent that she can take care of seven children and still spend a good deal of time in bed. In any case, his wife probably withdraws this way as a kind of passive reaction to her husband's domination and control.

There is probably some conflict, too, in William's unconscious attitudes toward women. His extramarital affairs are probably a hostile derogation of women, and with his ambivalence toward his wife may represent a residue of the buried rage he had against his punitive aunt. The consequences of his aunt's severe, even brutal, punishment are not otherwise apparent. His contempt for his wife is, to be sure, mixed with a good deal of pride and respect, so the case is not clear-cut.

His only other source of neurotic trouble is his need to be at the top, to be a leader. This is in conflict, probably, with his need to conform. At home, apparently, he can exert this leadership without conflict, while in his group activities this tendency is inhibited by his need to be liked by everybody. He has a very strong desire to be thought of as a good guy and to be liked and admired by all people with whom he comes in contact. It is doubtful whether he can be an effective leader because of this conflict.

In general, William is making a very adequate adjustment. He is perhaps the most normal of all the subjects we have interviewed, and one is hard put to it to find evidences of basic conflict or of any kind of severe psychological strain. Apart from his conflict over dependency, some ambivalent feelings toward women, and conflict over his need for leadership versus his need for conformity, there is very little evidence of neurosis in William. He handles even these conflicts very well, and he has no outward signs of anxiety or psychoneurotic symptom formation. In his functioning on the job and his responsible behavior at home, his is a very good working adjustment to his world. This is also true of his attitude toward skin color. William's image of himself is healthy.

The expansiveness and affability of William's family-centered life do not appear to be typical or even frequent among familistic people. For a considerable variation on the family theme, we may leave William, on the front steps, beer in hand, worrying about the World Series, and pick up the deep laughter issuing from a more sequestered third floor apartment in Chicago where Mary Hopkins now lives.

MARY HOPKINS: LAUGHING WIFE

Mary Hopkins was the adolescent "Laughing Girl" of *Children of Bondage*.[3] She was originally selected for special attention because she seemed to be a typical lower-class adolescent girl who was neither mobile nor disturbed but placid, unresentful, and unprotesting. However, with the inestimable advantage of hindsight and the perhaps more incisive and perceptive examination techniques available today, we do not see in Mary exactly the stereotype that Davis and Dollard considered her to be. In fact, we have sometimes thought of her as a "social isolate," an interpretation remote from that of the original study. Many of Davis' and Dollard's predictions for her future life were far off the mark, but one important consistency does remain: Mary is still superficially untroubled and unhampered by neurotic conflict, and hers is not a disintegrating personality. She has found socially tolerable ways of maintaining her personal security at the cost of restricted ego function.

The 1938 interviews were conducted by an intelligent upper-class light-skinned Negro woman, a fact that may have determined Mary's responses significantly. The interviewer questioned Mary aggressively, especially about color and sex. The material thus obtained was used to support the class personality theses of the original researchers and perhaps lent some distortion and overdetermination to them, but it gives us a good picture of Mary's adolescence. Her retorts to the original interviewer's prod-

[3] Allison Davis and John Dollard, *Children of Bondage*, Washington, American Council on Education, 1940, Chapter 3, pp. 44–67.

ding questions concerning aspirations, status, and sex indicated that she had a fairly good appraisal of her opportunities in life and was not shaken in her self-esteem by the interviewer's veiled insinuations that Mary should want to be better than she was. The original researchers interpreted these responses as evidence of Mary's lack of ambition to rise socially. This is broadly true. In Mary's case being Negro is not a motivation for driving ambition, but it does have other meanings. A more detailed look at some of the significant experiences of Mary's developmental years and later life discloses the existence of a connection between her skin color and significant interpersonal relationships, especially with her mother.

"Laughing Girl" was a facile name for Mary, as she was a fairly typical, well-adjusted, upper-lower-class girl. Her family life was stable and all the family seemed to get some fun out of life. When interviewed she was a dark brown 15-year-old in the eighth grade. Her father had been a laborer of various sorts, and her mother was intermittently employed in a pecan factory or as a domestic worker. Mary had two older step-sisters by her father's first marriage, but apparently never met them. She lived with both her parents, as is apparently usual in the upper lower class, and was the oldest of six children. For a time they lived with her maternal grandmother and this grandmother's second husband. Mary's grandmother was indulgent toward her grandchildren and was the dominating person of the household. Mary lived there her first four years of life, and even after her parents moved out she spent a lot of time with her grandmother until she was 13. Then she moved back into her parents' home permanently. Mary says that she loved her mother the best, then her grandmother, father, and grandfather in that order. Her mother was a tremendous woman who weighed 269 pounds. We have no direct report of her mother's character, as she was not interviewed. Both Mary's mother and grandmother worked away from home a good deal of time during her childhood. A paternal aunt substituted from time to time for her mother and grandmother through the early years of Mary's life, but this aunt's death, which occurred during the time of interviewing in 1938, seemed to have little effect on Mary. Mary's father was evidently a moral sort of person who worked fairly steadily even during the depression. He was rather sturdy and reliable, was interested in his children, and took them places with him. In general he conducted himself with a good deal of integrity. Both he and Mary's mother had extramarital sexual unions, though we know little of the particulars. Mary's two next younger siblings both died, one in infancy and one at age six. On the basis of Mary's personality, and because the death of a sibling, especially a younger one, is a portentous event for a child, one may imagine that their deaths influenced Mary's developing ego.

One of these two younger siblings was a girl, but Mary denied the existence of a sister to the psychiatrist, saying, "I'm the only girl." The next four siblings were boys ranging in age from ten to one. Mary expressed a good deal of rivalry and contempt for the older two of them, and a good deal of affection for the next youngest. All the children slept together in the same room. Mary's mother was literate and helped the children with their lessons. Her father was almost totally illiterate (as is her present husband). Their family life was that of a stable upper-lower-class family, adjusting relatively successfully to the pressure of the depression years. Her father, her mother, and her grandmother were all working. Her father actually joined the NAACP and even attended PTA meetings in spite of his illiteracy. He was an amateur preacher of some note in a local way. Mary's mother belonged to some similar groups, and Mary herself attended church. There is no indication that she belonged to any social clubs or other organized groups. After entering high school she worked part-time as a domestic worker; then in 1940 she moved to Chicago, without finishing high school. She worked for a while in domestic service there. In 1942 her youngest brother was born. (He died in a fire when he was about seven years old.) It was also in 1942 that Mary quit working and married. She was already pregnant at the time. She had only one child by her first husband. She married again in 1946 and again in 1951. There have been two children from her last marriage, a boy and a girl, both born in the early 1950's.

The 1938 material makes Mary's family appear to be composed of stereotyped individuals rather than of real people. It is difficult to ascribe to them the significant attitudes and personality traits that are pertinent to Mary's later life. Mary withheld from her aggressive interviewer a great deal of pertinent information that she has later revealed. She did express some interest in moving away from New Orleans and has subsequently done so. She had a wish to become a nurse and actually did undertake some nurse's training later on in life. It was our initial impression that her personality was fairly well integrated and sta-·ble. Her wishes were moderate, reality-bound, and possible of achievement. She had a realistic appraisal of the discriminatory practices of the South, and wanted to get away from them. She laughed easily, and she distinctly had some capacities for enjoying life.

On the basis of Mary's experiences up to adolescence, the psychiatrist predicted, indeed, that she would be a fairly happy person and would make a reasonably good adjustment. He expected her to become a nurse, marry, and have not more than two children, "since her maternal interest, though definite, is limited . . . she herself often likes to act like a baby." He further felt she would be a reliable and disciplined person, adjusting harmoniously to racial situations, and capable of self-assertion even despite her somewhat inhibited reactions to authority. Without being sure why, the psychiatrist thought Mary might from time to time have mild periods of depression, and would use her laughter to hide such feelings.

After entering high school, Mary worked part-time as a domestic worker. In 1940 she moved to Chicago, where she lived with her grandmother's sister and entered the eleventh grade. Shortly thereafter she quit school and did domestic work for about two years. She was married in 1942 and had a son in 1943. Her husband was in the Navy, and they soon separated. In 1946 she married again. Her second husband worked in a laundry. In 1951 she divorced him and married for the third time. This third husband is a driver's helper in the city sanitation department, thirteen years Mary's senior. Their daughter was born in 1952, and a son in 1954. The marriage has been disturbed by Mary's feelings that her husband tricked her, passing himself off as an educated man when he is in fact illiterate, and also by Mary's continued interest in a long-time boy friend from Brazil. Mary had six months' training in practical nursing, and actually worked as a practical nurse in 1951 and 1952. She has not worked since.

During the current study, Mary was interviewed for a total of fourteen sessions, which were conducted once or twice a week. For five of these she sat up; for nine she lay on the couch. The analyst did not continue with them because he did not want to get Mary too involved in a therapeutic procedure that would have to be arbitrarily terminated. He afforded her supportive therapy for problems that she brought out during the course of the interviewing. At the time of the interviewing Mary was living in an all-Negro neighborhood in Chicago where she has an apartment in a government project building. Her style of life is upper lower class. She has impressed everyone who has seen her currently as a laughing, jolly person. Her laughter comes easily and spontaneously, as it did when she was a child.

Mary could be characterized as a smiling depressive. Her defensive smiling and oft-asserted desire to help others and to be a nurse does not entirely cover up her equally conscious need to have a reliable source of succor. When some support is given in the interviews she readily admits her need for help and her wish to have others make decisions for her. She feels, for example, that she should have more children, in spite of gynecological difficulties and child-rearing problems, because otherwise she might lose support from her husband, who is proud to be a father. Yet as early as her third interview she also talked of what she'd do as a grandmother when she'd be free of the "burdens" of child rearing.

Her depression stems from two sources, one historical and one current. Historically, it is probably a defense against her strong hostile feelings toward her younger siblings. Her mother certainly impressed Mary with the idea that she had to be a substitute mother, and that she could not be allowed to indulge her own needs for maternal affection. She still has strong desires both to mother and to be mothered. In particular, the death of her sister probably has a great deal to do with her ambition to do good as a nurse. In spite of her protests about liking to nurse her own babies, she dreamed of a dead infant at the time her own nursing child was starting to cut his teeth. In another dream she expressed considerable ambivalence about breast feeding. Her desire to be a professional nurse carries implications of social prestige and financial independence, but it also expresses a need to help herself through identification with patients. Here, again, she is ambivalent, and prefers to nurse men because women are too demanding.

The current factor in Mary's depression is the loss of self-esteem and lack of sexual gratification involved in her marriage to an older, illiterate man for the sake of economic security. Her outward anger is directed at her husband, although she has almost given up fighting with him about his illiteracy and has decided to accept him as a meal ticket for herself and the children. Mary at first denied that she needed or enjoyed sex, though it was not painful, and she said orgasm didn't matter to her. She blames her first husband for seducing her and getting her pregnant. Later she admitted that with one man, a very light colored "Brazilian" who was her boy-friend, she did have orgasm, and as she talked about this she rolled her thighs in a masturbatory manner.

Mary's attachment to her father was very strong and tinged with considerable masochism. She provoked beatings from him in lieu of sexual contact. Her association between sexual contact and masochistic provocation was again revealed when she described the time she walked out on her second husband and he broke her jaw. As she related the incident she giggled and seemed close to orgasm on the couch. As often happens, her father's strictness encouraged her to "step out." It is not surprising that she had to get pregnant before marriage.

Despite all this turmoil, Mary functions well in many ways. She is more modern in social and child-rearing attitudes than one would expect in view of her trapped dead-end feeling about her husband's waning sexual desires. She has sexual fantasies about other men, and says, "it's hard to be good," but her husband is dependable and supports her efforts to be a good mother.

Mary's Rorschach depicts her as a cheerful, capable person with a realistic appraisal of her own capacities, who has adapted rather well to the life she leads. The test also revealed her ambivalence and need to be cautious, and some phobic ideas and counter-phobic reactions. Her outwardly cheerful mood was extensive enough to suggest reaction formation. The psychologist felt that treatment would be helpful to Mary since she had ego reserves available to her in both her psychological structure and her interest in health, as well as in her capacity for reaching out to others. The psychologist suggested supportive psychotherapy looking toward relief of anxiety from her inner stresses as the logical treatment. No great degree of depression was brought out by the Rorschach. Many responses indicated preoccupation with oral sadistic impulses, corresponding perhaps to the mood of bitterness that prevailed in her psychiatric interviews. Surprisingly, in view of her quite adequate vocabulary, her various test scores on the intelligence tests were grouped around the high nineties. All the TAT stories project an emphatic person, cheerful, appropriately conciliatory. A minor undertone of gloom was present, and also some suspiciousness, but on the whole the record was that of a healthy, normal, and generally adaptive person.

Mary's reaction to her skin color deserves special attention. She is clearly representative of the stable upper-lower-class level of Negro social structure both as a New Orleans schoolgirl in 1938 and as a present-day Chicago housewife. Her color attitudes are expressed in platitudinous terms; her interracial relationships are limited but anxiety-free; and the "self-hate" evidenced by her depression stems from internal stresses not related to skin color in any significant degree.

Mary is dark-skinned, and has "bad" hair and decidedly Negroid features. As an adolescent she expressed her own attitudes, and presumably those of her family, in emphatic terms that were designed to keep her free of any troublesome situations with others, whether white or Negro. She denied being discriminated against in any way and was critical of Negroes who made an issue of the caste system. This attitude was emphatic in her statements to her interviewer in 1938, and again in the questionnaire she filled out at the onset of the current study. She was taught by her mother to be nonaggressive to whites and she accepted this maternal dictum without question. It seems surprising that her father was at one time a member of the NAACP, but we may note that this organization is now much more controversial and vociferous than it was almost twenty years ago. There is no reason to believe that her father had sufficient education or intelligence to be aware of the more far-reaching social problems with which the NAACP now contends.

Mary was uninterested in contrasting Chicago and New Orleans in terms of segregation practices. She was matter-of-fact in stating that there was more segregation in night clubs in New Orleans, but she showed no antagonism or resentment in doing so. It may be remarked that she does not attend night clubs in any case. Throughout the original study of "Laughing Girl" there is a wealth of lower-class New Orleans lore, and, characteristically, Mary and her family are committed to a stereotyped lower-class compliance with caste customs. They denied that caste had any very immediate or personal significance. The information gathered from her in 1954 is strikingly expressive of the same attitudes. Mary was most insistent that she was more discriminated against in Chicago than she was in New Orleans. In probing this point, we found out that Mary was using the term "discrimination" to refer to a restriction of interpersonal relationships be-

tween whites and Negroes. She felt that she had been less restricted in such relationships in New Orleans than she was in
Chicago. She readily admitted that in terms of participation in
the activities of social institutions, such as going to the movies,
Chicago was less restrictive than New Orleans. The picture of
Mary's life suggests that race is not the only outside reality from
which she retreats in familistic isolation. She joins nothing.

There is no trace of shame or disappointment to be found in
Mary's admiration of her children, although they are Negroid in
appearance. The ambivalent feelings toward her children which
did emerge in distorted form during the interviews, especially
in dreams, were determined by her reaction to her long succession
of younger siblings. Mary was required by her mother to be a
substitute mother for these younger children and consequently
was denied adequate gratification of her own needs for maternal
affection. This prototypical maternal attitude was expressed later
in Mary's instruction in caste etiquette, as here, too, strong hostile feelings were allowed no overt expression. Her mother specifically instructed her (and this remained conscious until Mary's
adolescence at least) to avoid temptations to fight white people
in any interracial situation, no matter how strong the provocation might be.

Mary has some specific concern about her "bad" hair and the
fantasy that it would have been all right if only she had not cut it
close when she was young. Part of her memory of this event is of
her mother's punishing her for the act. The prominence of this
seemingly race-determined idea of what she might have been
also suggests a screen memory that stands in front of a repressed
and distorted childhood fantasy to account for loss of or absence
of a penis. Supportive evidence for this hypothesis is found in her
picture of men as brutal, aggressive, or damaging. In addition,
there are some indications from the dreams she reported during
her psychiatric interviews. For example, in one interview she reported a dream with her analyst pictured as a physician in a
mental hospital. In the dream she was waiting to see if he would

give her permission to go home and nurse her baby. She was told that she could call him, and she described the telephone as being "funny, very different." She was unable to work the phone and described it further in her associational material: "It's all mixed up. The telephone—it was a box with a whip on the side and [I] found little holes underneath—there used to be iron things which would hang down and you'd push them to get the number but now they were broken off and there were holes like soft drink machines you had to put your fingers in instead of money in a certain way from underneath, a woman told me, but I couldn't work it—then [my little boy] came in." Earlier in the same dream she pictured a number of women in restraints and described all the attendants as men. A woman gave her a breast binder and instructed her to use it or her breasts would get flat and dry up. It was then that the analyst's name appeared in the dream in connection with his anticipated permissiveness in letting Mary go home to nurse her baby. The suggestion of maternal injunctions for restraint seems fairly clear. The transference implication bears out the picture of her mother as a castrating aggressive woman. The historical data on her mother's physical assaults on her father and her domineering role in the household have appeared throughout the material collected in 1938 and the present.

In any event, Mary has effectively internalized her mother's injunctions, particularly in matters involving hostile and aggressive impulses. The oral quality of these is designated beyond question by repeated references to nursing, breasts, and teething in her dreams. It was no accident that she chose practical nursing as a vocation. It was her mode of ambivalent compliance with her mother's requirements and it also satisfied her need for help of this sort through identification with her patients.

The theoretical implications of Mary's life and personality are particularly interesting in relation to race. Her conscious ego identity as a Negro is almost entirely compatible with her pattern of life. This pattern is somewhat restricted, as would be expected of a person who is chronically depressed. The restrictive pattern of Mary's life, in fact, has actually protected her from direct frustration by caste system practices. When she says that she is not discriminated against, it is apparent that she is telling the truth. Her personality makeup actually protects her from situations in which she might suffer indignities because of her race. Her neurosis does not function to her advantage except in a feeble and unsatisfactory way, but her extreme inhibition of aggression has permitted Mary to avoid some of the discriminatory practices of which many Negroes are more acutely aware.

Mary's discussion of race is made up largely of clichés, which do hide some antagonism to Negroes, but the bulk of Mary's depression does not stem from this. It reflects rather internalized family stresses, oral sadistic impulses, fear of retaliation, and later oedipal guilt.

The very considerable variety of color reactions and the subtlety of the influences that shape them are amply illustrated even among people whose social worlds are similar. Despite their common commitment to family life, William Leon's active participation in racial uplift efforts stands in sharp contrast to Mary Hopkins' withdrawal from and denial of "the problem." Francis Gregory takes yet another tack, and illuminates with particular poignancy some special problems of finding one's self in a social environment confused by race and rumors of race.

Francis Gregory: Creole Mister

Francis Gregory possesses a number of unique characteristics. He is a New Orleans Negro Creole. He presents a personality that is truly neurotic, in contrast with the rather severe character disorders observed, for example, in Chester Olivier[4] or Edward Dodge.[5] Most importantly, he is more nearly in a socially intermediate position between Negroes and whites. This inbetweenness is due partly to his heritage as a Creole, partly to his professional training and ambition, and partly to his self-con-

[4] See Chapter 8.
[5] See Chapter 6.

ceived social position in the community. His primary social identification is clearly with his family and he is rather markedly isolated from other contacts. In a psychodynamic sense he has problems involving his sense of identity, or identity consciousness, which are strongly organized around the fact of his being a Negro with fairly light skin, and he is plagued with conflicts involving his work and sexual functions.

Francis is a pleasant-looking, neatly dressed young man with dark curly hair. He is almost painfully self-conscious when unsure of his acceptance by others, but is quite affable and self-contained when he feels secure. He is of slight build, about five feet six inches tall, with rather large hips and long legs. His features are perhaps more Caucasian than Negroid in quality, but his skin is a light brown or "coppery" color, and is distinctly Negroid. There is a slight scar on his forehead caused by the removal of a cyst in infancy. His voice is high-pitched and soft and tends to have a feminine modulation. An almost unceasing half smile is characteristic of his demeanor. His speech is easy to understand and his grammar and vocabulary are those of an educated person, though he uses colloquial and idiomatic Creole expressions at times. His accent can be described only as distinctive. It is neither southern, nor Negro, nor educated white New Orleanian. Petulant in repose, Francis' facial expression is not unlike that of an excessively indulged child. He walks bent slightly forward.

On his initial contact with the psychiatrist, Francis needed nothing more than the briefest indication of interest to launch him into a rather complete and well organized summary of his life history. He talked about his current problems, especially those pertaining to his marriage, with the purpose and intensity of a person who needs to find relief from a severe anxiety. Although the interviews were originally solicited by the interviewer for the specific purpose of accumulating scientific data, Francis quickly made use of the opportunity for personal psychotherapy. His hopeful and enthusiastic attitude quickly ran its course in some 30 visits over a five-month period and finally ended with a luke-warm acknowledgement of "some help," a feeling of great relief that he was stopping, and a conscious fear that he would get "too dependent" on the analyst if he continued the relationship.

After an interval of a few months we began to hear from him by mail. His letters referred to some money he felt he had been promised by one of the members of the team for participating in the project. He expressed open resentment and anger because of "broken promises." An attempt was made to utilize his complaint to reinitiate interviews with him, but it was only partially successful. He was bitterly angry at the psychiatrist and consented to only two more interviews with him. A Negro psychiatrist later saw him about six times but Francis did little more than review the injuries he felt the white psychiatrist had done to him, and attempt to prove that he was the victim of racial prejudice. Still later he was seen twice by a second white analyst. This final effort to establish a therapeutic relationship failed before it got started, though without the rancor that had resulted from the first termination.

Francis Gregory was born in 1923 in New Orleans, the oldest of six children. His father was a bakery helper and delivery man, his mother an ex-school teacher, then employed as a seamstress. By 1938, his mother held a good secretarial job. His father had a sixth grade education and his mother had graduated from high school. The family was staunchly Catholic and, at least on his mother's side, staunchly Creole. His mother was a member of the Knights of Peter Claver auxiliary, and the older members of her family spoke French. His mother's father, a Creole, had deserted his wife when Francis' mother was about six years of age. He was a Pullman porter at the time. He later "passed," and became a highly successful businessman in another city. He never communicated with the family again.

Neither of Francis' parents had siblings, but the household was a large one nevertheless, and included Francis' maternal grandmother and her second husband. This man was light skinned, as her first husband had been, and according to the memories of people interviewed, "could have passed." Two maternal great-aunts with their husbands also lived with the family at various times, and Francis' maternal great-grandmother lived with the family the first few years of his life. Another great-aunt, who apparently never lived with the family, took care of Francis and his younger siblings off and on from 1930 to 1933, when Francis was seven to ten.

This discontinuity of residence, and of significant adults in Francis' environment, has been a major determinant of his character as an adult. Techniques of adaptation to nonfamily representatives of authority are established in our culture during exactly these years of the early school grades, and Francis' problems with authoritarian figures dominate every aspect of his adult life. His repeated separation from his mother has further contributed to the intensity of his ambivalent attachment to her. At present, his mother states that she spoiled her first child terribly, and Francis is aware of how openly his siblings regard him as his mother's favorite. There were five younger children: a sister, a brother, and then three younger sisters. They were spaced about two years apart except that the youngest is four or five years younger than her next older sister. There was also an orphan boy nine or ten years younger than Francis living with the family. Francis' next younger sister was and still is the object of his intense hostility. In the usual pattern of sibling relationships Francis was congenial with the others, and he idolized his youngest sister.

When Francis was about six or seven years of age his father became ill. He eventually died of a carcinoma of the stomach in 1938, but the illness in 1929 may have been of another sort. At any rate, Mr. Gregory was employed irregularly after 1929, and in 1930 Francis went to live with his great-aunt. He had apparently already started in a public school, and was now transferred to a Catholic school for one year. He was finally transferred back to a public school for reasons that we do not know. He resented these changes bitterly, especially the final one. His adult memories of the bitterness he felt about this indicate his childhood awareness of the significance of this sort of environmental discontinuity.

When he was interviewed in 1938 he was 15 and was in the ninth grade. He was working part-time as a delivery boy for the same bakery that had employed his father. He also had a paper route and was a member of several teen-age clubs. He had been an indifferent student up to this time and was very resentful toward his teachers. His mother and grandmother were support- ing the family, his grandmother as a seamstress at a clothing factory and his mother as a secretary. Francis grew up in a section of New Orleans that was the center of concentration for Negro Creoles and his friends were drawn mainly from the middle-class families in that section. His mother's friends were almost all working women, though none of them was a domestic.

The 1938 interviewing was started at a particularly critical time in Francis' life. His father's death had occurred a few weeks before, ending a siege of illness that had dominated the family atmosphere for ten years. Francis' own interests and direc- tion were then crystallizing in the form that they have since maintained. It is significant that his family had been stable, even though there had been a good deal of discontinuity in the particular circumstances of Francis' life. His parents lived together until his father's death. In 1938 Francis was quite certain that his father didn't have any interest in other women, even when the interviewer suggested this possibility. His large circle of relatives must have lent a great deal of solidity to Francis' feeling about family ties. There were many authorities in his life, and discipline was apparently divided among them. Francis seemed vaguely aware of a lack of useful, orderly influence in his life, which sug- gests that none of them was dependable and consistent in authoritarianism.

After his illness, Mr. Gregory worked less frequently and be- came much more active at home. He cleaned the house industriously, often did the cooking and shopping, dressed the children, and did the many other things that a housewife customarily does, a common Creole pattern for men. The children were afraid of him, Francis remembers. His discipline, which was probably limited to the confines of the house, was enforced without physical punishment. At the same time he was capable of being a warm person, possibly more so than any other of the array of adults in Francis' early life. He played with his children, took them swimming on the lakefront, and bought them as many toys as his income would allow. Francis stated a few weeks after his father's death that he was much more attached to his mother, but this may have been an effort to deny the importance of his father. The remark suggests that he was using the defensive maneuver of identification with the aggressor. Until his father's death Francis felt that he had not been given much by his father. He took it for granted that fathers did all these things for children, and it was only after his father's death that he perceived the magnitude of his loss. Several weeks after his father's death he reported a dream that he said had occurred the night his father died. It consisted simply of his father's being dead. He was awakened from sleep by his mother, who told him that the event had actually happened. The interviewer asked Francis what he thought about it. He replied, "Well, I guess I had this dream to strengthen me so I wouldn't be shocked when they told me he was dead."

Francis' avowed feeling about his mother in 1938 is remarkable. He said he had no wish to get married and felt that his main role and obligation would be to take care of his mother and younger siblings. He told the interviewer then that there had been a shift in his attitude toward his siblings after his father's death. He said that he used to fight with them, but now he would give them what they wanted, and try to assume his father's role in the family. This adolescent renunciation of a life for himself with almost overt incestous feeling for his mother was strongly motivated by the guilt associated with his father's death. The experiences of his disrupted earlier years doubtless contributed to the strength of his complete reversal of the usual adolescent striving for emancipation. Overindulgence by his family, an overprotective mother and an inadequate father, and his discontinuous school experiences all left him deficient in techniques of maintaining self-esteem, with consequent insecurity in the face of the stresses and tasks of adolescent development.

Francis eventually found that he could gain a measure of self-esteem and security by exploitation of his own superior native intelligence through intellectual achievement. He transferred to high school soon after the 1938 study, and from then until his graduation from college he pursued education without interruption except for a break of service in the Navy. He graduated from high school at 18, in the first year of the second World War, and went on to a Negro university for two years. He was drafted and entered the Navy, where he applied for V-12 training, although he was never accepted for it.

During his basic training at one of the large naval training centers, something about his behavior attracted the attention of a psychiatrist. He was put in a psychiatric ward for observation for several days, but was discharged from it as fit for duty. He remembers that the word "tension" was used to describe his condition, and that it was also noticed that he cried easily. Without further difficulty he became a petty officer, second class, and was assigned to a small ship that was one of the few desegregated vessels in the Navy. His war service involved no combat and was otherwise uneventful.

When he got out of the Navy in 1945, he returned to college. This was a highly significant moment for Francis, since it led him to make a major effort to become independent of his mother. He registered in a nonsegregated university in the north for the express purpose of continuing the life away from his mother begun by his naval service. During the single semester he was there he got the very best grades of his college career, but he regards this as a paradox. He returned to college in New Orleans because he was unable to tolerate being away from his mother. The separation entailed by the war had been more tolerable for a variety of reasons, not the least of which was the substantial allotment he sent home monthly. Francis graduated from college in 1948 with a degree in business administration. He worked for a few months in a vocational guidance office. During his last year in college he became acquainted with his future wife, a girl from Texas who was studying nursing. Following her graduation in 1949, she went to Chicago where she lived with relatives. Francis joined her there. They were married, and returned to New Orleans to live. For about three years after his marriage he worked as a social worker. His wife became a "first-of-race" Negro by becoming employed as a registered nurse in one of the hospitals in the area. She had begun Catholic instruction before meeting Francis. The early years of their marriage were stormy because of both marital adjustment problems and the "social problems of Negroes" that Francis encountered in the course of his work. In 1952 he sought personal aid from a social agency and during the three or four months he was seen by the worker there he decided to leave social work. He obtained a job as a temporary postal employee, first as a mail carrier and later as a night clerk. At present he earns approximately $4,000 a year, and his wife earns approximately $4,100. They have one daughter born in 1954.

Francis' siblings have been quite successful in their endeavors. One sister has a Master's degree from a northern university, is married to a professional man, and now lives in a northeastern state. A second sister became a social worker and is employed by a hospital in the west. A third sister attended college, but did not graduate. She is now married and living in the west. A fourth sister is married and living in New Orleans. All his sisters married while in school and have children. His brother, like Francis, is in the postal service.

Francis has remained in the middle class into which he was born, though occupationally he is downwardly mobile. He bitterly attributes his failure to maintain a professional level of employment to racial prejudice. He plays up his associations with "professional people," and is proud of his wife's achievement in her work, but he refuses to admit the obvious fact that Negroes are increasingly able to push through the barriers of racial prejudice to significant positions and achievements. In the interest of the neurotic and infantile rage that he unconsciously directs toward both parents, he is forced to distort his appreciation of this reality.

There can be little doubt that Francis identifies thoroughly with the "happiness and morality" ideals of the middle class. He is upset by deviations from standards of sexual morality, including some that have occurred in his own family. The standard he sets for himself is ambivalent, and his own sexual adjustment in marriage is not satisfactory to him. He envies men who have extramarital adventures and dominate their wives and, viewing even his difficulties with his wife in terms of her occupation, is dissatisfied with his own achievements.

Faced with frustration of his class ambitions, Francis considers color as the cause. He insists that no one knows what it is like to be a Negro unless he is Negro, and feels that progress in race relations in New Orleans is stagnant. He is proud of his wife for being the first Negro in her job, but he does not identify himself with the aspirations and goals of Negroes in general. He has, in fact, much hostility and contempt for lower-class Negroes. At times, he seems to be clearly identified with Negroes and expresses intense and explicit resentment of whites in general, but he also seems to feel that he deserves at least the equal of what the white man gets, while the lower-class Negro deserves the treatment he receives.

The pattern of Creole family life fits Francis very well. He came from a home dominated by the mother, in which the father had relatively low occupational status. His own behavior in marriage is stereotypically Creole: he cooks, stays at home, takes a real interest in home-making, and is subordinate to his wife in occupational prestige. All these things are part of Creole tradition.

As with all our subjects, an analysis was made of Francis' 1938

interviews by one psychiatrist before he had knowledge of
Francis' current life situation. The speculations about Francis'
future were remarkably accurate. Two interviewers saw Francis
in 1938, a woman and a man. Francis was constrained, artificial,
and inhibited with the woman. With the man, however, he was
frank and outspoken, and freely expressed hostile attitudes. This
pattern allows us to see that he is much less afraid of his own
hostility in relationships with men than with women.

The predictions made from the 1938 interviews were that
Francis would go on to college under pressure from his mother
and the ego ideal which he himself had incorporated, and that
he would pick an occupation which offered him status and
prestige and in which he could avoid competitive struggles, such
as under Civil Service or in professional work. The psychiatrist
specifically suggested "teaching or perhaps social work" in view
of his mixed sexual identification. Noting Francis' attachment to
his mother, the psychiatrist found it hard to predict whether he
would marry, but if he did, guessed that he would marry "either
a nurse or a teacher." He felt Francis would be torn between
selecting someone he could lean on and marrying someone he
could protect (in view of his inflated self-picture), and predicted
that his sexual adjustment would be precarious "inasmuch as he
has inadequate masculine strength and his sexual fears are quite
strong." The psychiatrist saw promiscuity as a conceivable prop to
Francis' deficient masculine pride, and expected Francis to continue his identification with whites and his self-hatred for being
Negro, and to reject specific Negro identification and membership in Negro groups.

He predicted some increase in Francis' use of projection
mechanisms, and more frequent exploitation of his dependency
gratifications as props to his faulty ego, and "if life is cruel," he expected an increase in Francis' distortion of reality to the point of
paranoid development. On the basis of a hint that Francis was
unusually concerned with his body ("repeated reference to
how his mother saved his life with an eye operation in infancy")

the psychiatrist even forsaw Francis' "ulcer": "physical symptoms and the use of the physical symptoms in terms of the secondary gain he could achieve through them might be a future adaptation."

It is interesting that Francis initially declined to identify himself as Creole, though he was frank enough about it as the forty interviews progressed. At first he assumed that the interviewer had the typical white New Orleanian attitude toward Creoles: that Creoles were white, that they were of French and Spanish descent, and that for a Negro to call himself Creole was local blasphemy. This was an immediate indication of his confused racial identity. Francis wanted to be both white and Creole, but could afford to be neither in any situation where he was called upon to be something racially definite. He could not afford to offend the white interviewer, since he wanted to exploit the situation for personal therapy by being as ingratiating as possible. After about ten interviews or so, he was able to say, "I am what most people call Creole as you know of Negro Creoles."

As one member of our research team once remarked, Francis is "a real neurotic." He is an intelligent, sensitive person, with highly organized defenses and some very specific and crippling neurotic symptoms that tend to be psychosomatic. His symptoms become severe in times of family crisis, as they did when his wife was pregnant, and they respond to the usual medical measures for treatment of a peptic ulcer. There is something about him that suggests an "ulcer personality." He affects great independence, but it quickly proves to be spurious, a trait also found in his adolescent interviews. He feels forced to deny his dependence with a façade of pseudo-autonomy, and is always acting as though he did not need other people. He has never actually had an ulcer, however, and at times he frankly succumbs to his dependent needs. At other times he has demonstrated a sustained, driving ambition.

Among our subjects, Francis is uniquely ambivalent over his racial identity. This is more striking than it has been even with such subjects as Chester Olivier, who have aggressively attempted to erase caste boundaries (see Chapter 8). Even Chester is definitely Negro when he thinks of himself. Francis thinks of himself mostly as white, and conceives of himself as distinct from Negroes. At first glance Francis would seem to be a personality who follows at least the general outlines of a psychology of self-hatred. On a conscious level he hates Negroes and being Negro. With Francis, however, this is not a settled issue. His personality organization has not solidified around this conflict and there is actually a great deal of flux within him over his self-evaluation. Socially speaking, a Negro as an individual is forced to make up his own mind as to whether he is to be a "race man." It is a matter of explicit decision on conscious issues whether or not one will join the NAACP. Francis has refused to join even the Knights of Peter Claver because, he says, "It's ridiculous for the Church to differentiate between white and Negro in this particular way." He says that there should be just the Knights of Columbus, with no "separate but equal Negro section at all." If Francis expresses self-hatred, it is self-hatred for personal defects that he has rationalized in terms of Negro-white relationships. The self-hatred comes first. The fact of his being Negro is merely a circumstance that has augmented and permitted rationalization of it. To type Francis as a case of self-hatred is merely to assign a more specific designation to the familiar dynamics of neurotic depression. Francis' assertion that "I could have passed but I didn't" may be factually true or it may be only fantasy, but it was based upon the fact that *perhaps* he could have, and it is this social definition that is the important one for it reveals that culturally he is neither Negro nor white.

During the early part of his current interviews, Francis became very much interested in what he was saying. It appeared to the psychiatrist that he was embarked on a therapeutic process that would of necessity carry to some logical end point. He identified various crises in his life, particularly the one that occurred while he was working as a social worker. At this time, he said, he became "so identified" with the troubles and trials of his clients that he would become overcome with emotion. He was apprehensive about his relationship with the interviewer as he began, but once he started to talk he felt he could not stop. He possessed considerable skill at extracting opinions from the interviewer, which he then would incorporate subtly into his thesis that, like all whites, the interviewer could not understand Negroes and must be treating him badly because of the expression of his various opinions. After only half a dozen sessions, he began to dwell exclusively on the tragedy of his having been designated Negro by birth. An interpretative question about the purpose of this resulted in a rather rapid switch to discussion of his job, and later to some contemplation of his feelings about himself as a householder and husband. He saw that he had a tremendous longing to establish a firm male identity and to feel himself the dominant person in his household. He was frightened by the implications that this had for changes in his way of life, and promptly managed to cut down the frequency of visits on the rationalization of increased work in the post office.

In Francis' case an interpretation led to a most dramatic change in the content of the sessions. The first 13 sessions were filled with obsessively determined content about racial discrimination that contained considerable paranoid overtones. The nine sessions following the interpretative remarks were almost completely free of this subject. From preoccupation with racial issues, Francis shifted to preoccupation with his particular important intrapsychic functioning and how it was determined by important relationships in the past, particularly his relationship with his mother.

The dramatic shift in content is clouded by the fact that at this time he was already involved in formulating a thesis about the interviewer of which the latter was completely ignorant. He had found that subjects were occasionally paid for their interview time, and decided that it was his "right" to receive therapy as a paid patient, if he wished. He began to accumulate data through these interviews, which later supported a violently accusatory outburst against the interviewer and against everyone else he knew who was connected with the project. During this period he maintained an attitude of utmost friendliness and coöperativeness toward the interviewer. He continued to speak of his very real need for psychotherapy and characteristically said that he feared becoming so dependent on therapy that it would be worse than if he had not had an opportunity to undertake it.

After 31 visits and the passage of about five months, Francis interrupted the regularly scheduled interviews. They ended on a note of friendliness and he was invited to return if and when he wished. Up to and including this time he spoke with evident sincerity of being "much stronger" and having greater insight into his life. He spoke of his determination to have his wife quit her job and of finally becoming a true householder and the dominant member of his family.

About three months later Francis' mother contacted the interviewer by phone and requested an interview for her son. It was arranged, and at the interview Francis expressed interest in continuing with the sessions as before, but he used his time primarily to complain with extreme bitterness and rage about the bad treatment he had received from other members of the research team. His principal complaint was that a promise of money had been made to him for appearing for his interviews. The alleged promise was dated at about the time he had interrupted the interviews. This session revolved chiefly around his extreme sensitivity to the feeling that he was being misused and exploited by the research team to the point that he had developed gastric symptoms in connection with the experience. At first he included the interviewer in his vituperation only to the extent that he felt that the interviewer had failed him by not recommending a plastic surgeon to his wife for removal of a keloid.

A final interview was held a few days later. This was devoted entirely to his feeling that he was a victim of circumstances. When exception was taken to this, he launched into a tirade about the mistreatment of Negroes in general and of himself in particular. He castigated other members of the research team as he had before. Because of Francis' rage and bitterness, it seemed that it was useless for him to continue with the initial interviewer, and he was informed of this. He seemed rather startled by this attitude and continued to nurse his resentment.

Francis was a valuable contributor to the understanding of interracial relationships in a psychotherapeutic setting. The difficulties and failures encountered with him dramatically pointed up the pitfalls of trying to bridge the color gap with a severely neurotic person. His paranoid-like defense of feeling misused, of being taken advantage of, disliked, and persecuted was ready-made, and was promptly brought into play whenever Francis began to perceive the approach of anxiety. His basic neurotic problem was a severe one involving his relationship with his mother. The highly charged atmosphere of anxiety and rage about this mother-child relationship quickly invests any other in which there is even the most distant kind of parent-child parallel.

Early in the course of work with Francis complete psychological examinations were done. The tests brought out his tenseness and lack of self-confidence. His test intelligence, though in the bright normal range, was lower than the clinical estimate. His Wechsler-Bellevue IQ is 115. There was a wide scatter of the scoring on the various subtests, which perhaps accounts for this. His Rorschach brought out well-defined neurotic patterns, and a great deal of tension, which the test indicated would be expressed primarily in psychosomatic ways. There were strong suggestions that he was not secure enough to permit himself free expression of his own ideas. Absence of human figures indicated poor relationships with other people and lack of acceptance of himself. The record was that of a constricted person who has a great need to control all aspects of his behavior. His neurotic defenses served to inhibit both his responses to his impulses and his expression of his stronger feelings. The neurotic adjustment he achieved, as indicated by this record, is far from a satisfactory one. There seemed little hope for modification in it.

Some aspects of the case tend strongly to indicate that Francis suffered from a paranoid state, as differentiated from merely having a paranoid "racial" slant on life. Perhaps the most significant evidence of this was his retroactive distortion and misinterpretation of his experiences with the first interviewer. All his accusations of mistreatment were carefully organized around bits of data gathered from here and there, which permitted him to feel that his experiences with the interviewer had led to a "great failure." He spoke frequently of "broken promises." What is lacking that might really clinch a diagnosis of a paranoid state is the element of grandiosity. It is neither overt nor implicit. Nor does he imply a clear-cut conspiracy against him. Francis does not have, either, the relative freedom from anxiety that a truly paranoid personality can enjoy as long as his delusional system is maintained. His tendency to get involved in long, drawn-out quarrels and bitter disputes with people, particularly white "salesmen or merchants," indicates a definite litigious bent. This is also of interest since his mother was recently engaged in a lawsuit over an inheritance. The clinical study and the psychological tests do not support a paranoid state diagnosis. They do reveal an extremely low opinion of self but that is, after all, only the first step toward a paranoid organization of personality.

Francis' marriage is of particular importance in his adaptation. He married with a definite need to be the powerful protector, but he is frightened when he himself is not protected. If he marries a wife who is strong enough to protect him (as indeed he did), this only exacerbates his need to deny his weakness by protecting, or better, dominating her. No satisfactory adjustment in marriage could obtain from this impossible situation. Francis explicitly avowed that he wished to marry "not a wife but a mother." He has managed to maneuver his wife into a situation where sexual contacts are few and far between. She works days and he, nights.

The result is a great deal of complaining and bickering. The complaining tends to center around such housewifely activities as his wife might carry out: cooking, housekeeping, or caring for the baby. Francis acts like a spoiled, indulged child. He complains that his wife won't let him drive the car, yet he manages to do so often. He asks her to take care of all the accounts and check-writing in the family, and then carefully goes over her totals to see if he can find errors. Often he can. He complains that she tries to manipulate him by withholding sex, but then gets himself a job that leaves no room for sex. This same type of complicated self-deception appeared in his relationship to the psychiatrist. In his account of his mistreatment in the interview situation he seized upon the interviewer's remark that his wife must be proud of her "first-of-race" status in her occupation, and distorted it into an indication that the interviewer was prejudiced against Negroes.

Francis constantly depreciates himself whenever attention is drawn to his achievements. He belittles his first jobs, even though they got him considerable prestige and recognition and were in fact in fields where intelligent, educated Negroes were extremely valuable. Francis distrusts other people, "particularly Negroes," because "they [*sic!*] borrow and don't repay you," and he frequently talks about liking his white co-workers better than the Negroes. He lives in a kind of chronic identity crisis typical of late adolescence. He feels inferior to women, "even to my daughter," and deceives himself that he is subordinate to his wife and mother in all ways, then bickers with them, checks up on them, and finds them in as many errors as possible. This satisfies in a neurotic way his need to feel superior. In 1938 he announced to his interviewer: "I'll make the best husband in the world if I ever marry," an opinion that hints at his sense of inferiority to women. Trained in business administration, employed as a social worker and later as postal employee, he is unable to identify himself occupationally. At the post office he has maintained a temporary employee status, thus depriving himself of the benefits enjoyed by regular permanent civil service employees. He has aspirations to become a schoolteacher, and to go into business, but he has been unable to realize them.

Francis identifies himself as a Creole cautiously, but he feels the identification very strongly. He is highly narcissistic, particularly about his physical appearance, and wants his child to have his own looks but his wife's intelligence. It is significant that his wife is much darker than he. His continuing failure to establish any secure sense of identify for himself is obvious. Although he wishes that he could leave the New Orleans community he feels genuine fear of leaving his mother, and is sure he could not survive away from her. He has the experience of going north to school to substantiate this feeling, and it is painful to his self-esteem to contemplate that failure. As his mother or wife is a restraining influence to him unconsciously, he has to erect defenses to prevent his rage toward either from exploding. Even as a 15-year-old he was outspoken in his devaluation of himself when he said, "I'm not a leader." He has recognized at times, both in adolescence and adulthood, that his mother force-feeds him. He felt that his father was only an agent of his mother, and believed that his mother actively encouraged him to let his father carry the blame for any failures in their life. His father certainly was directed by his mother in matters of discipline.

The pattern of the family's life prior to 1938 was similar to Francis' own since he has been an adult. He has lived most of his life in a kind of discontinuous atmosphere. This accounts for his failure to have any security in his relationships with people. His pattern is to isolate himself behind a façade of bitter hostility. It is probable that this stems mostly from his discontinuous juvenile experience, especially between about five and ten. He is possibly perpetuating this pattern of discontinuity in his own daughter by sending her to nursery schools.

Family-centered people such as William, Mary, and Francis share certain socialization characteristics with our other groups. Like members of the middle class, they have had a stable family life. Like the matriarch or the gang buddy, they have strong dependency feelings. In the middle-class pattern, a base of pre-adolescent security permits adolescent rebellion and subsequent autonomy, and the lack of strong ties of dependency facilitates just this outcome. In the matriarchy and the gang the dependency drives are overwhelming and more or less determining, though the ultimate identification is different for men and women. The psychosexual unbalance of matriarchal family organization and the inadequacy of the gang as a stop-gap substitute family leave the dependency bonds established in early life unchallenged and uncontrolled, and hence they become the primary forces in adjustment. People who center their lives on the nuclear (and more or less egalitarian) family, as do William and Mary and Francis, have both the strong dependency and the experience of stable family life, and their resolution of the riddle of identity seems to be frequently determined by the restrictive character of family life—the reluctance of each generation to let the next one go its way. All our familistic subjects lived significantly longer with their parents than did those of the middle class.[6] William's life reminds us that this pattern need not preclude all flexibility and maturity, but it is also true that William's experience is distinctive in several respects.

As a culture or way of life, then, a social world confined to a nuclear family is isolated and withdrawn, apathetic toward wider social issues, and intensely ingrown emotionally. Yet it is a viable structure, difficult but tenable psychologically, and demonstrably enduring from one generation to the next. It may also be very widespread. (Despite the equivocal nature of our "sample," it is worth remarking that fully 30 per cent of our cases are familistic.)

The importance of patterns, models, and persisting structures of this type in the configurations of identification and identity that center on the family, the gang, the middle class, or the matriarchy is dramatized when we consider people whose lives have no such focus. Varied as the influences are that play on the individuals we have examined, they are at least patterned and orderly in some respects: restricted as it is, the world of the family is yet more extensive than complete isolation. It remains for us to explore the concomitants of marginality.

[6] See Figure 6, p. 85.

Marginality

A true marginality coupled with alienation from the life around them is the characteristic pattern of primary role identifications of four of our subjects. Two of them seem to share a self-conception that may be fairly described as "bohemian," and both of them have gone a long way toward building a consistent social world based on bohemian premises. They are handicapped by the lack of a bohemian tradition in New Orleans Negro society, but they have succeeded not only in defining and defending for themselves a bohemian way of life but also to a degree in finding their friends among people of similar outlook. This success remains partial, and both Alma and Chester express inconsistencies of attitude that reflect clearly their marginality to several of the social worlds we have discussed. Their struggle to create a consistent world is all the more interesting. Alma states the classic bohemian premise very well:

She said that one of the things that makes her most unhappy is the fact that people tend to accept rules and regulations of a particular group or a total society almost without question.

And Chester, who lost his job at a Southern college for Negroes after (among other things) giving his students a rousing pep talk on homosexuality, obviously feels deeply the same need for revolt:

I asked Chester why, if he liked teaching so much, he behaved as he did at State, when he knew that what he was saying and doing would prevent his getting a job there. Chester went into a very excited defense of his position: "What you are asking me to do is to give up my principles, and that is all that I live by. . . . You're asking me to sell out."

Alma and Chester, though they do not use the term, loathe philistines. They do a good deal of talking about "conventional morality," all of it strenuously negative.

But for all her brassy self-assurance Alma often reveals the pull of matriarchy, and when she brought her college career down about her ears, it was to her mother that she fled. After months of excuses for not being formally interviewed, she offered this interesting distortion:

[She] began to insist that if [the psychiatrist] really wanted to see her, it seems to her that he should have come to her home, or come to see her at school, rather than to call her and ask her to come to his office. "Because," she said, "after all, there are ways to seek women. . . ."

Chester's involvement in gang life exerts a similar pull. He is a gambler of professional ability as well as the holder of a Master's degree from an Eastern university, and he can forget neither the one nor the other:

. . . he seems to excuse himself for not succeeding because, he says, he has always known and liked the common man. The truth is, he said, even now he walks down Rampart Street and people on "The Ramp" refer to him in this way: "You know, here is a boy that college didn't spoil."

It seems likely that if a strong bohemian tradition existed among the Negroes of New Orleans, Alma and Chester might have been strongly enough attracted to it to break off these other ties, but New Orleans' Negro Bohemia is still too fragile an adaptation to absorb and support them. When Alma gets into real trouble, it is still Mamma she goes back to, and Chester is so wrapped up in his attempts to form a professional identity, to maintain the gang friendships he prizes, to validate his manhood through extra-marital conquests, and to rebel against his mother and the class values that already enveloped him in 1938, that no one of these conceptions of himself allows him a durable sense of personal security.

It is interesting that the general confusion of their lives is reflected in Chester's and Alma's views of race. Alma, who has passed for white on repeated occasions, ignores or denies the social implications of race:

She said that she had another experience in passing for white by working one summer as a laboratory assistant in a hospital . . . where they did not hire Negroes in such capacities. . . . She worked there for three or four months, and each evening after work she would go home with a friend of hers who was obviously colored. . . . She said this in order to indicate to me that she did not have the least bit of frustration over passing for white.

Chester's position is similar:

We are perfectly willing to accept the "desired and forthcoming integration" as Negroes. Our fight is rather for the "integration of opportunity" and not the complete loss of identity and absorption of a race that we happen to be proud of, despite the inconveniences.

Neither Alma nor Chester, however, has elaborated a thoroughly satisfactory intellectualization of this attitude, and their reactions to racial symbols are neither as casual nor as clearly positive as these statements would indicate.

The distinctively marginal position of Alma and Chester is clearest in relation to the question of the genesis of their attitudes and patterns of role identification. The social institutions that might facilitate the creation of a bohemian world and the transmission of its traditions simply do not exist in their lives. They have become bohemian intellectuals by default through rejection of the multiple alternatives with which their experience presented them, and their tenuous establishment of a social niche for themselves has taken place on the fringes of the least objectionable social groups in their experience—the circles of university life and the recreation and entertainment fields. Even these choices have not detached them from previous ethnic, family, class, and peer group loyalties. Alma is still significantly a Creole and a matriarch; Chester is still a "self-made man" and a gang buddy. There are limits to the degree to which an individual can found his own society.

Our bohemians emerged from the identity crisis with contradictory partial ego identities. What in their background led to this kind of situation? Both of them continue to act out repressed rage they felt toward their mothers. Their mothers had in common a marked status awareness. They were anxious for their children to get ahead, and pushed them to the impossible. They did not permit Alma or Chester any kind of realistic goal-setting, nor did they provide them with any moratorium during the identity crisis to integrate their achievement with past experiences. Hence for these subjects, greater and better achievement became a goal in itself, and they charged off in all directions, achieving here and achieving there, with a net result of partial, fragmented identities. Going along with these partial ego identities is a corresponding sexual confusion. They are college graduates with rather superior intellectual endowment. Yet they were not able successfully to resolve their earlier psychosocial crises and when they reached the one at adolescence there was no solution for it. Hence their lack of ego identification. Alma's and Chester's attempts to build an ego identity have also been blocked by the habitual ways they have used to defend and enhance themselves. These ego defenses had been established at least by adolescence and were still actively and stably operating in adulthood.

George Morgan is superficially somewhat similar to Chester and Alma. Being a professional man, he has a clearer social position than they, but he uses it as a front for a way of life just as alien to "conventional middle-class morality" as any bohemian might wish. In a sense, however, his doing so is more gratuitous, and he himself attempts no intellectual rationalization comparable to the shrill rejection of Babbitry voiced by Alma and Chester. George's classic marginality is partly suggested by his equivocal

family position[1] but its full measure can only be savored in detail.
He came from a stable family and has established one. His
mother instilled strong social ambitions in him and he is a class
"success"—by marriage, by status, and by income. Despite the opposition of both his parents he was emphatically exposed to gang
life, and his adult playboy activities are compounded of typical
gangland promiscuity and hostility toward women. Although his
father was around until George was adolescent, no one who has
met his mother could imagine any family she lived in as being
other than matriarchal, and George is still living with her despite
the psychological strain on both his wife and himself in such an
arrangement. One almost gets the feeling that George's life is
made up of a random sample of the patterns and mechanisms observed in the lives we have already examined. And in some respects this is precisely the case, since George has indeed been exposed to a wide swath of New Orleans Negro society, and no one
way of life has had sufficient impact or appeal to influence him
for very long.

For many men in George's profession, the profession itself
would constitute a primary role identification. Indeed, there is
every reason why this should be so, for the special and prolonged
education necessary to qualify for a professional career is frequently both a traumatic and a formative experience, and a man
may well come to build his social conception of himself around
the code of ethics, distinctive traditions, and general social evaluation of his profession and the role models he follows in it. Not
George. He has too many other roles to play. In a strict sense his
position is analogous to that of the marginal man caught between
the European peasant culture of his immigrant parents and the
Anglo-Protestant culture of the United States, but in George's case
the alternatives are more numerous and more vaguely defined.
Further, the lack of focus to George's social participation is
matched by the diffuseness of his ego identity. He is not rejected
by the professional class to which he is educated, nor does he have

[1] See Figure 6, p. 85.

to reject his family or the other social institutions in which he has participated. But the very variety of his social experiences and some specific rather crippling patterns of his emotional adjustment combine to leave George an actor without a character to play, and without even a favorite mask in his collection of false faces.

Unlike Alma, Chester, and George, who manage to present a superficially plausible impression of real participation in the society around them, Ruth is a completely marginal member of society. Abandoned by her parents before she can remember, and cared for, but unloved, by an aunt and uncle, Ruth grew up without real emotional attachment to anyone. Although she did fairly well in school, she disliked her teachers and had no close friends. As a teenager she did housework for a series of employers, but liked none of them. Eventually she became a hospital maid, a job that isolates her almost completely except for her contacts with one much disliked supervisor. For a while she belonged to a casual social club, but it withered away. She is a faithful Catholic but hears mass alone and has no friends at her parish church. The only social relationship in which Ruth really participates is an organization for Catholic Negro women, and she has no intimates there either. Several of Ruth's relatives live in her neighborhood, and some of them helped her build her home, but she paid them for the work. She often asks for overtime duty at the hospital to escape the emptiness of her life, and she works compulsively at home on a variety of projects (gardening and the like), but she rejects the idea of being a homemaker, and denies with heat that she can cook. Intensely fearful of men, she has nothing to do with them. She spends Thanksgiving and Christmas in bed.

It will be apparent that when we interpret Ruth as socially marginal we imply a very restricted participation in the life around her. This is not the same thing as total isolation, however, and even our brief review of her life in the preceding paragraph points to some genuine social involvement. Considered in detail, however, Ruth's social world reveals no organizing principles of role identification that come to dominate her life: all her roles are secondary roles, and her participation in them is temporary and provisional. If there is a conflict between her view of herself as a woman and her job or her religion, it remains unrecognized and unresolved, and she seems to be able, like a species of social chameleon, to take on whatever attitudinal coloration is demanded by her role of the moment, and to offer therefore little or no resistance to the world around her. If someone structures the situation for her in terms of color, she reacts in terms of color; if class is under discussion, she reveals convenient class attitudes.

Only in her religion does Ruth appear to find some sense of affiliation, placement, and identity. She disapproves of people who do not keep the Sabbath, never misses a meeting of her church society, and is significantly influenced in her attitudes toward color by the publications and activities of this society and of the archdiocese of New Orleans. Ruth places a high value on education, but she specifically puts "morals" above education in her scheme of values:

I asked Ruth if she thought she would have been better off if she had continued in college. . . . She said, "Perhaps so, but it all depends on what you do with your college education. Some students that I was in high school with did something with their education when they went to college, and some didn't. I'm better off than some of them, and I guess some of them are better off than me."

Later Ruth makes it clear that the class implications of this remark are to her a matter of moral classes:

I asked Ruth about social class and social status. She seemed to be very interested and anxious to talk about it, and this is what she said: "I feel that a person's social class should depend on how they act. Some people are more moral than others. There is a woman around the corner who is unable to read and write, but I think she is one of the best women I have ever known. I think a person like that belongs to the upper class."

There is little indication that Ruth's concepts of morality are specifically Catholic; rather she tends to talk in terms of "good" and "bad" people as though these were objectively defined status categories:

Ruth does not think that all white people are bad or that all white people must be distrusted. She said on almost every occasion when I interviewed her that there are some good white people, and she expressed the very definite belief in today's interview that these good white people might be able to do much more for Negroes than Negroes can do for themselves.

There is here the germ of a social identification, but Ruth has been unable to develop it into a set of categories from her real experience. She temporizes, exposes one set of color attitudes to a Negro and an opposite set to a white interviewer. She reacts with anger when her religion is attacked, but is not dogmatically or denominationally intolerant. There is no group of her associates whom she considers generally "good" and no definite group of "bad" people. Because she has been weakly exposed to matriarchy (living with her aunt during most of her adult life), to class aspirations (a good high school education and practical nursing training), and to stable family life (part of her childhood was spent with her grandparents), she remains aware of at least some aspects of many alternative ways of life going on around her. She is unable to make any of them her own.

Through casual participation in her society, then, Ruth maintains an unintense and shifting set of loyalties. She never allows herself to become involved or committed. It is striking that in this respect she is unique in our sample. Possibly only the disruptive features prominent in Ruth's life—her orphaned childhood, her thorough fear of sex, her progressive isolation from intimate human contacts—could create a person who could be as persistently detached and as completely restricted to shallow and superficial identification with her fellow man.

RUTH LOWELL: SOLITARY MAID

A social isolate, leading a barren, empty life, who nevertheless has fantasies of being accepted into the elite of New Orleans Negro society; a hospital maid who served champagne to one of the interviewers who visited her home—this is Ruth Lowell.

Ruth is one of those people who run from competition because of a poor self-esteem, only partially warranted by real inadequacies. The competitive failures that result only serve to increase Ruth's low opinion of herself and create a vicious circle of increasing failure and self-derogation. To see this in sharper focus, compare Ruth's adaptive techniques with those of Emma,[2] a successful competitor. Unlike Ruth, Emma is not afraid to compete. Despite being faced with overwhelming trauma in her early twenties, she was able to change the whole course of her life and lift herself to higher levels of accomplishment and ego integration. In contrast, Ruth did not take advantage of her opportunities and retreated whenever slight obstacles came along. Her poor self-esteem is directly related to her reactions to the poor social status of her tenant farming father and grandfather, and of her aunt, a domestic worker, for these are the important people affecting her processes of identification.

Ruth is 40 years old, single, and Catholic. She lives with her aunt in her own five-room house, and works as a hospital maid. She is a medium-sized woman, on the obese side, with a round, rather homely face and a pleasant smile. Her skin color is intermediate, perhaps more dark than light, and she is definitely Negroid in her general appearance. Her hair is kinky; her skin is splotchy. She wears plain spectacles. Often she had difficulty in looking straight at the interviewer, and her inability to do so indicated some embarrassment in the relationship. Her speech is slurred and often indistinct; at times it becomes unintelligible. Sometimes she appears to be under some pressure and will speak at length, but most of the time she is not very spontaneous. She has difficulty in abstracting and talks constantly about concrete situations, as if the interviewer already knew all about them, and she takes no pains to make these situations understandable from

[2] See Chapter 4.

his point of view. She sometimes has difficulty in associating, or in doing even simple arithmetic.

The dominant theme of Ruth's reactions in all interview situations is her desire to please the interviewer. She refuses to express an opinion of her own and avoids saying anything that could be considered argumentative or even controversial. On one occasion she said to the interviewer, "I am not going to vote. I never have. I once went and was confused. You have to reason things out for yourself. They didn't tell you nothing." Another time she said, "I cannot argue with anybody. I can't stand it." Speaking about the Supreme Court decision on desegregation, she told the white psychiatrist, "It's like not being welcome at someone's house," a tacit expression of her fear that she might say something that would disagree with the interviewer's viewpoint. The interview in which she denied her feelings regarding the Supreme Court decision was followed by an attack of diarrhea that night and two nightmares that week, and even then she could not acknowledge that she had any angry feelings at the time of the original discussion.

Ruth was always polite, and always on time for her interviews. Any hostility she expressed was indirect and subtle. Most of the time she is not even aware of having any angry feelings. Her hostility is revealed, for the most part, through her dreams, in which the dominant theme is violence. The first dream she reported was one in which a chimney was being knocked down and a white person severely injured. Many of her dreams concern accidents in which people were taken to the hospital.

The attitude she unconsciously expressed toward the psychiatrist was, "If I am a good girl I will be taken care of." This, indeed, is her attitude toward any authority, white or Negro. She still retains her childlike faith in obtaining love through obedience. Her tremendous need for approval caused her to buy a new wardrobe before the interviews with the psychiatrist began, and to return home from her job at the hospital (an hour's bus ride, each way) in order to take a bath and change her clothes for her appointment, although the hospital where she works is next door to the building in which the interview sessions took place.

Ruth's life revolves about her job and her church. She works as a hospital maid on the night shift, from 11:30 at night until 7:30 the following morning. She is home by 8:30 and generally spends an hour and a half or two hours tidying up around the house. Then she goes to sleep for three hours, awakens at 2:00 P.M., and does some more work around the house, or occasionally goes shopping. She has a light snack and then returns to bed and sleeps until about 9:30. She gets up, has supper, and dresses to go to work. Despite the fact that she is home from 8:30 in the morning until about 10:30 at night, she rarely has friends at her house, and even more rarely visits anyone else. Her life is drab and empty; her personal relationships are sparse and superficial; her friends are few, and never intimate. She is mainly occupied with routine tasks: her work as a maid, and making sure that her house is clean, neat, and pleasant.

The only other important area of activity for Ruth is her religious life. She is a devout Catholic, and never misses Sunday Mass, even if she is ill. She will get up at four o'clock on Sunday morning in order to get to Mass on time. A staunch Catholic since adolescence, Ruth frequently attends church during the week. She has been a sergeant-at-arms and a member of the funeral committee of a chapter of the Knights of Peter Claver auxiliary. In sharp contrast to her reticence on almost all subjects, she has strong and confident opinions on matters touching on religion and will defend them even to whites when she hears them attacked. Curiously enough, none of her relatives or forebears appears to have been Catholic. Her aunt is a Baptist.

Ruth is also a member of a sewing club, and most of her friends are members of this organization. There had been a dozen members originally; there were four during the period of interviewing, but only three when the interviewing was ended. During most of this period the other members of the club included two domestic maids (for well-to-do white families), a cook, and a life insurance "writer." By the end of the interviewing, the club was on the verge of dissolution, and Ruth seemed scarcely sorry to see it go. None of these friends appeared to be really close anyway, and there apparently was no visiting among the members apart from the monthly meetings.

Ruth has a rather large number of known relatives, but almost none of these has any real meaning for her. Her younger brother is married and has two daughters; and although it appears that Ruth sees them with some frequency, she hardly ever discusses them and seems to have no emotional involvement with them. She has a number of cousins, including one young woman who frequently comes for extended and unwelcome visits. One of her uncles and one cousin live in her neighborhood and work as carpenters. They helped her build her home, but it is indicative of her lack of closeness to them that she paid them for their work. Other of her cousins live in the North or in other parts of Louisiana. Ruth's mother had five sisters, but Ruth sees them only rarely, has never liked them, and has even expressed a limited amount of resentment that they didn't help take care of her when she needed them.

She works compulsively, both at the hospital and at home. She seldom takes time off for Christmas or Mardi Gras. During the time that she was interviewed she either worked on holidays or spent them in bed. She had accumulated so much vacation time at one point that she had to work only two days a week for several months in order to "work off" her accumulated vacation time.

Her lack of recreational activity is striking. Though she likes opera very much, she goes to the opera only once a year. Perhaps once a year she goes to a football game. Although she complained bitterly to the Negro psychiatrist who interviewed her about the lack of recreational opportunities in New Orleans, her isolation is so extreme that we may doubt that she would notably increase her recreational pursuits even if more opportunities were available to her.

Even at church there are only a few people whom she knows and who know her. She mentioned one woman friend with whom she goes out, but they are not close, and she has never visited this woman in her home.

Ruth has a constant concern with the society world—the elite of the Negro community. She talks endlessly about people she has known slightly or whom she has heard about who are getting married or making a financial success, but she talks about these people as if they lived on another planet—as if her social world and theirs could never merge or have even peripheral points of contact.

In short, Ruth is a person who is emotionally isolated. Although she has a number of contacts at church, at her job, and in her sewing circle, they are all superficial. She is not emotionally involved with anyone else, even with her aunt who lives with her. Though she is in daily contact with her aunt there is no real intimacy between them, and they never do anything outside the home together.

Nowhere is Ruth's social isolation more marked than in her complete lack of any interpersonal sexual life. When asked about an interest in men, she talked about a rather superficial relationship with a boy she knew while she was a high school student twenty years ago. At that time she apparently had some hopes of marrying him, but when she discovered that he was interested in having fun and not in marrying, she dropped him. Still virginal, her only sexual expression is in self-stimulation, which she has carried on since puberty. She hasn't had a date in twenty years.

Ruth Lowell was born in 1915 in a small town on the Mississippi River about forty miles above New Orleans. When Ruth was only four years old her mother died during the influenza pandemic. Her father died of tuberculosis when she was seven. Ruth had never lived with her parents anyway. She had been placed with her father's parents when she was an infant and was reared by them. They died when she was about ten. She describes herself as a sickly child, nervous and frightened, with unspecific "spells" up to the age of eight. Since then her health has been consistently good. Her only hospitalization occurred at 17, for a tonsillectomy. She has few memories of her father, mostly concerned with his death and funeral, and even fewer of her mother; but she remembers her grandparents very well and has happy memories of their farm in Mississippi, their kindnesses, and the good food. Her grandmother died in 1926 at the age of 90, and her grandfather a year later at the age of 89. Her mother's father lived until 1950 and died at the age of 89, but she had practically no contact with him. Ruth remembers nothing about her maternal grandmother, even though she had been named after her. She has one sibling, a brother one year younger than she, but they actually lived together only briefly.

Ruth has always described her early experiences as extremely happy, since her grandparents, and particularly her grandfather, apparently showered a good deal of love upon her. She felt that she was actually preferred to her brother when she was a child. She remembers trying to make this up to him by saying, "Never mind, I'll buy you a Cadillac when I grow up." However, since she overidealizes her grandfather in this particular period and has also described herself as being sickly, nervous, and frightened, there is some question about just how happy this period really was for her. Certainly her own parents, particularly her mother, must have seriously rejected her. If this period had really been as happy as she states, one would not expect to see the serious psychopathology which she reveals in her adult life.

Ruth's grandfather owned a four-room house and five to eight acres of ground on which he grew corn, cotton, sugar cane, and vegetables. Apparently Ruth's father was downwardly mobile, as he was only a tenant farmer and owned no property. He was employed at odd jobs on a sugar plantation.

The rapid succession of deaths in Ruth's family must have been severely traumatic to her. By the time she was 11 her mother and father, three uncles, and her beloved grandparents had all died. This accidental situation had a determining influence on her social and emotional isolation. Her refusal to commit herself to any one person for fear of being abandoned became a crippling inhibition in her relationships.

Until she was ten, Ruth attended a one-room schoolhouse in Mississippi in which the teaching was very poor. This was a severe handicap when she shifted to the New Orleans school system. She never got over her feelings of inadequacy in school, even after graduating from one of the best high schools in the city.

This wasn't the only adjustment Ruth had to face in moving to New Orleans. She came to live with her father's sister, a very stern, strict woman with a severe, obsessive character who insisted on obedience, cleanliness, and neatness. Her aunt was very suspicious about Ruth's sexual life, and indicated that she thought Ruth had been fooling around with boys when she had her menarche at about the age of twelve. She was constantly accusing Ruth of going out with boys and of being pregnant, and even into adult life, if her period was late, her aunt immediately accused her of being pregnant. Ruth thus came to see sex as something dirty, to be avoided at all costs. Her aunt kept very close check on all her activities and refused to let her go out to parties and dances or to have any kind of companionship with boys. Ruth says now, "My aunt bossed me. She wouldn't let me go out. She wouldn't let me visit the houses of my friends if they had brothers." From her aunt's fear that she would be sexually attacked, Ruth learned to perceive sex in terms of violence. As a consequence she has had no sex life in which there is any shared experience. In one of the sessions she told the psychiatrist that she takes a purgative called "Black Draught." "My aunt says that I'll lose my nature. I replied to her: 'What's the difference? I don't use it anyway.'" At one point she expressed to her aunt a desire to adopt two teen-age girls, but her aunt objected, saying that they would do nothing but run around with boys, so she dropped the idea. It is clear that she never was too serious about this and only brought it up when she was certain that her aunt would object. She now states that it would be too much trouble to rear teen-age girls.

Ruth's fears of sex were augmented and confirmed by the character of her uncle. He was a mean, vindictive, and sadistic person who was constantly chasing Ruth out of the house, sometimes with a knife in his hand. She was so afraid of him that she would go to her aunt's place of employment after school in order not to have to walk into the house by herself. Her uncle was altogether a colorful and irresponsible character, who told the 1938 interviewer: "Life don't owe me nothing. For 14 years I haven't worked a single day. I got good clothes, plenty to eat, tobacco to smoke, and anything I want. I hear men worrying about the rain. I tell them it don't bother me, it don't rain in the house where I am. I have nothing to do but rest, eat the best, and live better than anybody else." He said this laughingly. He also related his sexual adventures with white women in France and Belgium in World War I and told how he stabbed a "nigger" with an ice pick and pretended his shirt had been torn in the fight so that the police would charge him only with disturbing the peace. His attitude toward society was clearly expressed in these words, "I always get the crooked bunch in any club—that handles the money, and I pull with them. I get the president and the secretary off together, and between them we'll spend up some money." This uncle was filled with stories about voodoo, which he told to scare Ruth. He told the interviewer in 1938 that he was going to a voodoo woman who was trying to separate him from his wife. Ruth's uncle died in 1938, but it is quite clear that the 13 years that she had lived in the same house with him must have had a decisive influence in shaping Ruth's conscious and unconscious ideas about men and what behavior she might expect from them.

In 1938 Ruth was a senior at the best high school for Negroes in New Orleans. She told the interviewer then that she was 19, although she was really 22. She was ashamed of being so much older than her classmates and of having done so poorly in school. Apparently she did have a great deal of difficulty, and just managed to graduate that same year. Over and over again in the 1938 interviews she expressed resentment of the preferential treatment she felt the teachers gave to the children of wealthier business and professional families. She could not assign their academic success to anything but this preferential treatment, for to do so she would have had to acknowledge her own intellectual defects. She was keenly sensitive about the disparity between her social status and that of the wealthier children at school. This projection of blame on the principal and teachers was so necessary to her that she bitterly expressed these feelings to the interviewer, despite her usually extreme caution about committing herself to a definite point of view. Though the projection permitted her to deny her intellectual deficiencies and her class inferiorities, it never bolstered her self-esteem to the point where she could feel accepted by the more favored children. She was hypersensitive to rejection and manipulated situations so that she would never have to be faced with the possibility of it. She refused to participate in any extracurricular activities because of this fear. Already in her young-adult life she was an extreme social isolate.

In 1938 the interviewer was particularly interested in her attitudes toward race and color. Although at one point she said, "I hate white people and they hate me," it was quite clear that she reserved her greatest resentment for the "uppity" Negroes by whom she felt snubbed, and the lower-class Negroes of whom she was contemptuous. Her discussion of passing clearly indicated a desire to have a higher class position and the perquisites of being white, but had little to do with color as such. In general, her attitude toward the caste system was extremely passive. She would just as soon sit in the segregated balcony of a white movie house and had no ill feeling about it. Her other major focus of resentment, besides the rich children and teachers who snubbed her, was the immorality and violence of lower-class Negroes. This class-oriented attitude is still prominent today. She spends a great deal of time talking about these feelings, particularly with reference to the Negro patients in the waiting room and emergency clinic at the hospital. She still resents "uppity" Negroes, such as her classmates or teachers who pass her by without recognizing her. Her anger toward whites always has a class slant.

Ruth learned many of these attitudes from her aunt, who worked as a domestic in the home of a wealthy white woman in the Garden District for several decades. When this woman died she left Ruth's aunt a good deal of antique furniture, china, glassware, and pictures, all of which are prominently displayed in Ruth's home today. Her aunt also took over many of the values of this white family, and taught them directly to Ruth. It is as if she and her aunt have been trying to live in two social worlds at the same time: upper-middle-class white and lower-class Negro. This cultural conflict accounts for much of Ruth's social isolation. Since she cannot attain the one world and rejects the other, the only course open to her is isolation.

As an adolescent Ruth was interested in church and in school, though she placed less emphasis on religion then than she does now. She was attending church regularly and had already adopted the tenets of the church in a fundamentalistic fashion. Her interest in school was in the social implications of graduation, and her ambition was to be a nurse and marry a doctor. Unfortunately she was not much of a student. Recent psychological tests indicate that she has average intelligence, but emotional difficulties interfere with her maximum use of her endowment.

The only indication Ruth gave of an emotional involvement with anyone came in a discussion of her relationship with her aunt. Her brother is mentioned only in terms of his giving her some of his CCC salary to help her finish school, but there is no warmth or closeness indicated in her remarks about him. On the other hand, she was somewhat defensive about her aunt and was inclined to blame the circumstances of their household on the other members of their family. This positive attitude was probably derived from the fact that Ruth and her aunt shared the same social ambitions. Her aunt taught her to do light housekeeping but deliberately avoided teaching her to do heavy work—

washing and ironing—because she didn't want her to become a domestic servant. Devoted to the values of the white family for whom she worked, Ruth's aunt expressed pride in her niece's chastity, and was very protective of it. She described one incident in which she had called up a neighbor who had made advances to Ruth and told him to stay away.

The psychiatrist who was not seeing Ruth currently, and who knew nothing about her current adjustment or her life experiences since 1938, reviewed the 1938 data and made this forecast: "I think one can predict mainly a life which would be scanty in its scope and satisfaction and generally carried out in a rather restricted way in all areas. I think that she would be expected to be an intensely hostile person but with very strict, rigid control over this, with a good bit of emphasis on being morally indignant about distant situations perhaps, but not able to express very much about things too close to her. I suspect that she would be the kind of person who would be able to show her hostility only by just disappearing from a job. If she married, I think it would be only on the basis of some kind of social convenience. There is certainly very little in this old record to indicate that she has the personality that is capable of any warm, meaningful relationship with a man. Occupationally, I suspect housework, since that is the only thing that she was doing then, and one could expect that she would be likely to continue in that to some degree. College is only remotely possible, and then would prove a failure if it were tried. I would predict that there would be no antisocial behavior in this girl's life."

These predictions are almost 100 percent perfect. The only minor discrepancy is that Ruth has been a very stable worker and generally loyal to her supervisors and to her position. It is true that on one occasion, when she was intensely angry with her supervisor at the hospital, she quit without saying anything about it, but she returned after a week at the supervisor's urging. The interpretation of Ruth's adolescent interviews indicates that her social isolation could be seen very clearly at that time in her life, 18 years ago.

Ruth told the interviewer in 1938 that she had spent two years at a public school between the ages of 10 and 12, then had gone to a parochial school between 12 and 16, and finally to a Catholic high school until she was 19. She had had to repeat the tenth grade. She finally finished high school at 22.

Following her graduation, Ruth spent two years working at an old folks' home, took a six-months' course in practical nursing, and then did practical nursing for two years. Despite the ambition she expressed when she was a senior in high school, she gave up nursing to work as a hospital maid for seven years between 1943 and 1950. She was laid off in 1950 because she was not a veteran, and then worked for six months in a fashionable restaurant until that was closed in January, 1951, because of the Kefauver Subcommittee investigation into crime. After this she worked for some time doing housework in a private home. Later she worked as a maid in another hospital in New Orleans, then again as a maid in a private home, and finally started to work at her present job in 1952.

The interesting thing about her occupational history is that she actually followed up her ambition to become a nurse by taking a course in practical nursing. She could have gone on with that career as a practical nurse; she could have taken a regular nursing course and become an R.N., but she returned to her work as a maid. There are two primary reasons for this. One has to do with the conflict over her social status, and the other with her defenses against anxiety. Ruth was afraid to strive for increased social status because of a fear of failing. This was too much of a threat to her self-esteem. Continuing with practical nursing, on the other hand, was offensive to her. Nursing seemed to her "untidy" and "unclean," and sick people "disgusting." She would rather be a maid than take care of the sick and face the unpleasantness that she associates with bodily functions, operative procedures, blood, and excretions. Here we see her obsessive-compulsive character structure in operation. On the one hand her occupation as a maid permits her to stress cleanliness and neatness, just as she stresses these things in her own home: the disciplinary emphasis of childhood is still the emphasis of her adult life. On the other hand, the same factors produce overreactive feelings of disgust with aspects of bodily functioning. This is a clear-cut case of fixation at the anal level of psychosexual development. The "battle of the chamber pot" is still the most important battle of her grown-up life.

In addition to her preoccupation with cleanliness and order, a prominent characteristic of Ruth's obsessive-compulsive personality is her denial of hostility. Her angry feelings are below the surface; often she does not even feel them. A typical example of the way she handles anger is her frank expression of such feelings about her white supervisor to a Negro interviewer and categorical denial of them to a white interviewer, to whom she stressed only the supervisor's good points. She refused to acknowledge discrimination against Negroes to the white psychiatrist until pressure was applied. Her obsequiousness and tremendous need to conform are aspects of the same personality structure. She would do anything rather than argue or fight. Sometimes she substitutes physical symptoms for anger, and frequently develops a band-like headache or diarrhea in place of angry feelings.

As a consequence of the inhibition of her anger, Ruth's affectionate feelings are also inhibited. She seems to have little capacity for love. Her interest in her religion, particularly as it involves ritualistic types of experience, is part and parcel of this character structure. If frightened at night (and Ruth is frequently afraid of ghosts), she repeats the rosary or says the Lord's Prayer.

Ruth has handled her competitive failure and her isolation by denial. Over and over she stressed to the interviewers how content she feels and how pleasant and satisfactory life is to her. Once in a while this Pollyanna attitude breaks down and she has crying spells. This is rare, and generally occurs when she feels that people are taking advantage of her, as when her cousin spent the summer with her, but declined to help her with the household chores, and finally departed leaving her a few dollars. One of the reasons for her resistance to psychiatric interviewing was her fear that this defense of denial would break down under pressure from the interviewer. She was very much frightened lest she have to face the real barrenness of her life.

Her other prominent defense is projection. Projection of blame appears in her referential ideas that other people may talk about her and accuse her unjustly. Ruth wishes to keep all her thoughts and actions private. These ideas certainly are consistent with paranoid tendencies. She was afraid to tell any of her co-workers that she had got a raise, lest some of them object and complain to the management. She constantly expressed the fear that her aunt was prying into her affairs. She feels that a teacher for whom she worked many years ago flunked her on purpose because she quit her job, and she details long, incomprehensible stories about colleagues at work who impose on her. Over and over again she asserts that her teachers discriminated against her because she wasn't as rich as the others. She is still afraid of retaliation from the principal of a school she attended 18 years ago, and asked the psychiatrist not to say anything to the principal about whom she was talking. Although some of these ideas have elements of validity, they are mainly distortions of reality. The whole impression is that she feels unjustly accused, picked on, and discriminated against. These feelings of persecution are not allowed to interfere with her feeling that all is well with the world, for her use of denial is even more prominent than her paranoid ideas. Any time that she expresses the feeling that her lot is unhappy or that people are unkind to her, she immediately follows this by denying it and saying that the world is a good place to be in, and that most people are kind and considerate. In this balance of forces we see that the mechanism of denial is a safety factor and one that is essential for maintaining her adjustment at the present level. If the denial mechanism was seriously interfered with she would become much sicker.

Psychological testing confirms Ruth's compulsive and paranoid tendencies. Her Rorschach pictures an individual who utilized compulsive defenses in an effort to maintain control over her anxiety. Her concern was reflected by her frequent turning of the cards and her need to qualify everything she said. She ignored the main issue of the card and constantly changed details to avoid having to set forth a final, clearly defined concept.

Paranoid trends were also present in her Rorschach material. Her adjustment to her environment is precarious. Poor ego strength was reflected in the inadequateness of many of her responses: 42 percent of her F responses were F minus. The absence of human movement responses indicates that Ruth cannot use fantasy as a means of overcoming some of her anxiety. Her entire record reflected the personality structure of an exceedingly inhibited individual, and since she never really came to grips with the things she saw, she gave the impression of wanting to withdraw from situations.

Ruth's sexual confusion and distortions were detailed in the Rorschach record and there were definite indications of her inability to express aggression openly. A most important test finding was that Ruth shows no real capacity to relate to others, although there is a superficial responsiveness that serves to make her appear friendly. All the tests used with Ruth set forth compulsive patterns. They also repeatedly illustrate her inadequate relationships with other individuals. Isolated factors in the Rorschach and the Machover point up suspicious or paranoid trends. She maintains tenuous compulsive defenses but is basically an anxious person with a poorly integrated personality structure.

Ruth is isolated not only from others but also from her own inner life. She is "anti-intraceptive," and mistrusts the "dominance of feelings, fantasies, speculations, aspirations, and imaginative subjective human outlook."[3] Ruth is much more concerned with concrete, objective facts. She is afraid of her own thoughts and feelings, afraid of looking closely at herself or having her inner life exposed to others. This accounts for her indignation against prying, or what she perceives as prying, and against unnecessary talk. She wants to keep busy, to devote herself to practical pursuits; instead of examining her inner conflicts she turns her thoughts to something cheerful. This is a mark of a weak ego, since the anti-intraceptive individual is afraid of thinking about human phenomena because he might think the wrong things. He is afraid of genuine feeling because his emotions might get out of control. This is an accurate description of the way Ruth deals with her own inner life.

In summary, one can see that Ruth's social and emotional isolation has come about because of an interaction between accidental situations and certain cultural influences. The accidental situations were the repeated deaths in her family, the influence of her aunt upon her values and standards, and living with her mean, sadistic, and shiftless uncle for 13 years. The pronounced fear of sex that was produced by the amalgam of these forces further promoted her isolation. On the other hand, cultural factors were exceedingly important. Ruth rejected her own social origins and took as her standard the white middle-class morality and behavior her aunt taught her. This created extreme conflict in her identification, which, coupled with all the accidental factors, produced such low self-esteem and fear of competitive failure that she actually chose a lower-class occupation. At the same time she tries to emulate middle-class standards in serving champagne, in her pride in material possessions, and most of all in her fantasies of belonging to Society.

In this situation it was inevitable that she would develop pat-

[3] Henry A. Murray *et al.*, *Explorations in Personality*, New York, Oxford University Press, 1938, cited by T. W. Adorno, Else Frankel-Brunswick, Daniel J. Levinson, and R. Nevitt Sanford, *The Authoritarian Personality*, New York, Harper, 1950, p. 235.

terns of isolation and of paranoid thinking. Had she had more con-
fidence in her own abilities and less fear of failure, she might have
struggled to attain a higher status, as Emma did, but the crippling
effect of her early experiences, particularly during adolescence,
robbed her of the inner strength to carry on this struggle. Her denial of reality and her fantasy life are absolutely essential for her
security. Any marked interference with them might easily provoke a true paranoid episode and a definite break with reality.
If Ruth is fortunate, her defenses will continue to operate successfully into her old age.

Ruth Lowell's solitude illustrates a marginality of complete
withdrawal. Such a complete separation from society could only
be the result of rather special circumstances, and it is apparent
that Ruth's life pattern was shaped by an unusual concatenation
of damaging events. At the opposite pole of social participation,
as well as of social class, George Morgan is hyperactive, the life
of every party at his own insistence, versatile, successful, even
gifted, but no less marginal, and no less lost.

George Morgan: the Great Man

George Morgan is a professional man, one of only a very few
Negro members of his profession in New Orleans. In many respects he is a true representative of the Negro middle class, even
the upper middle class. His life is a long succession of triumphs.
At the beginning of his fourth decade of life he seems already a
success, and his future is bright. He is married and has children
and a good measure of professional achievement.

George is free to move in the best Negro social circles, but he
is also free to move in the other social direction as well, and does
so even to the dubious edge of propriety. Without exception, his
interviewers were initially impressed with his attitude of interested coöperation, his intelligence, diligence, and stability; and
without exception each interviewer was startled to find later that
all these qualities except his intelligence were a spurious front.
One psychiatrist, for example, felt George was "disappointing"

and "pretty sick." George's sense of identity remains insecure and diffuse, with behavior patterns that are clearly regressive, and in some respects openly infantile. The term "psychopathic" occurred frequently in discussions of his behavior, but the term needs considerable qualification, as will be seen later.

For reasons that will become apparent, our necessary vagueness about George's occupation is less distorting than it might seem. His professional status is only important to him as a general mark of success, rather than being the center of his life or a major determinant of his conception of himself. He is, in fact, remarkably detached about his profession, and while his exercise of it is competent, the mainsprings of his life lie elsewhere. The reader may think of him as a doctor, lawyer, or college professor and not be far off the mark.

George's mother is a remarkable public figure and a leader in Negro civic affairs. George lives under the same roof with her, and always has, except for the time he spent in the army and in school. His mother is a formidable influence. In her public life, she has been showered with accolades. She has served on various municipal committees and is active in numerous civic or religious organizations. Once, she was given an award as an outstanding mother. She is also a university graduate, a remarkable achievement in itself for a Negro woman of her generation.

Our first-hand glimpses of Mrs. Morgan, Sr., at home reveal a personality that is cold, paradoxically disorganized, and often remarkably hostile. She has always been rather indifferent to the details of operating her household, and though she managed to keep her husband in debt most of his life, the family home is in a rather poor district, old-fashioned, crowded, and run down.

Mrs. Morgan has always placed marked emphasis on scholastic achievement and social status. She is decidedly unaware of or indifferent to the severe psychopathology of one of her daughters, though this daughter, George's youngest sister, has overt psychotic symptoms that are obvious to the most casual and untrained observer. Mrs. Morgan is inclined to dwell on the scholastic achievements of this daughter, as well as those of her other children. She speaks of her children in a self-flattering way as if she were talking of herself and her own achievements.

In 1938 Mrs. Morgan naïvely described her pride in having spied out and detected the failure of mothers of delinquent boys, while she was working as a volunteer in connection with Juvenile Court. Her interest in the parents of delinquent children revealed a need to reassure herself of her own maternal adequacies by drawing attention to patently bad mothers, and also showed a good deal of thinly disguised hostile aggressive feeling about motherhood. The attitude she displays toward George, her oldest child, is one of possessive pride coupled with a dedication to the theory that his every whim should be gratified immediately. She describes the achievements of her sons, and especially George, as she does her own civic success: with glee and self-admiration.

George's manifest relationship with his mother is one of bland acceptance of her admiration. Perhaps he is not more rejecting and antagonistic because of his marked dependence on the attitude she expresses. At one point he said laughingly that she was out most of the time and didn't bother him much. In social gatherings he acts like a pampered talented youngster showing off at his mother's request. He enjoys his mother's attention enormously and has no apparent recognition of the fact that observers might secretly laugh at his performance. Among the several women in the household, George's mother is certainly the number one personage. His wife is abject and subdued in her servitude to her mother-in-law and defers even to her psychotic sister-in-law.

George's father is a somewhat obscure figure. He was a steady wage earner, employed by the Post Office Department as a mail carrier. Family unity was maintained well. He owned his own home and they had a car, even in the depression years. Mr. Morgan was less overprotective and solicitous than his wife, and probably a much less potent factor in the family. One gains the impression that he simply furnished the money for his wife to use as she wished. Many statements of his attitudes are quoted in the record but they are aphoristic, stereotyped, and weak. He expressed disapproval of some traits in George's character to the interviewer in 1938, and complained of "this late sleeping habit of George's" but did not enforce any change in it. George in turn gave lip service to obeying his father. He says he joined the army at his father's wish. His father told him he should not marry a woman he could not handle (or at least Mr. Morgan told the interviewer that this was his feeling about the matter), and George seems to have utilized this suggestion in his choice of a wife. There was some parental disagreement in regard to religious matters. George's mother is Catholic. His father went to the Baptist church, though he had originally been a Catholic. He gave it up when George was 11, following the death of George's younger brother in early infancy. We get the impression from this and other hints that he made some sort of feeble protest at the power his wife exerted in the family. Though Mr. Morgan was nominally the disciplinarian, he was actually assigned this function by his wife when she thought punishment appropriate. As an adult, George commented about this: ". . . my Dad was a strict disciplinarian. . . . I always lived under his thumb." George's distortion expresses his wish that his father had been a stronger person, capable of dealing with his ambitious mother. George also recalls how much emphasis his father put on the value of "personal dignity." He did not want George to do rude, "undignified" things like being a cheerleader in college.

The picture we are given of George's early home environment is one of remarkable stability and normalcy. It is remarkable because of the high degree of present malfunctioning of the family as a whole and of the various individuals in it. The solution of this obvious paradox is suggested by some of George's mother's remarks, which indicate the early psychopathological influences she had on her offspring. On one occasion she was excessively critical of George for putting some stolen green peaches in his mouth because they might have made him sick, but she implicitly condoned his stealing by simply not mentioning the theft as a crime. She consistently disparaged the success of her children's contemporaries in school, and she openly called a teacher incompetent who had given George low marks. On another occasion she spoke of the inadvisability of exciting her children when they do something wonderful lest it discourage them from trying it again. In 1938 she made the interviewer her reluctant ally in setting strict patterns of behavior for George.

At the time of the earlier interviewing George was 13. He was preadolescent both socially and physiologically. He was rather small physically, and closely attached to a group of male friends about his own age. His interests included baseball, books, stamp collecting, and boxing, all thoroughly normal and healthily diversified hobbies. George expressed highly stereotyped attitudes to his interviewer that reflected both the rigidity of his own thinking and the strictly imposed attitudes of his mother. He tells us now that he was pulling the interviewer's leg in regard to the questions he was asked about sexual matters. He was decidedly malevolent to his next younger sister, two years younger than he. His second younger sister and his younger brother attracted little attention from him, hostile or otherwise, as far as we know.

In some formally prepared statements obtained from George in 1938, he indicated that his feeling for his mother was predominantly hateful, and that he regarded her as punitive and restrictive, though these attitudes were somewhat obscured by his stereotyped statements about what a good mother she was and how much she did for him. In regard to his father he reveals something rather different. His father showed him how to shoot marbles, for example, and in a discussion of his parents' divergent views on fighting he said, "My father is actually right, and my mother is only partially right." He dreamed prolifically throughout the period of interviewing in 1938. Many of the dreams involved some current interest in money and material possessions. Others were anxiety dreams concerning falling, being chased, or being threatened with physical injury. The theme of castration anxiety was central. He was excessively interested in competitive activities.

For example, he freely spoke of his intellectual superiority to most of his contemporaries, but he also showed himself to be a good judge of reality in these competitive situations in school. His intensive competitive drive was related in part to his developmental state at the time, as competition with contemporaries is a major preoccupation for juveniles and preadolescents, but George seems to have had more competitive spirit than the usual preadolescent. One of George's sisters died as a two-months-old infant during the time of the interviewing. His reaction to this seems to have been spontaneously one of sadness and disappointment. He described her as, "The sister I liked best—she was so cute." This could scarcely have had a realistic determination, so probably his grief was unconsciously meant as a jibe against the other siblings. It is possible, too, that the seemingly inappropriate affect stemmed from reactivated oedipal conflicts.

His feeling about whites was clearly hostile but expressed in common stereotypes. He said of white people, "Get all you can from them." He pictured himself as superior, and rationalized segregation practices as best he could. He said of segregated seating in church, "It is the same sermon no matter where you sit." He felt the same way about the seating arrangement in street cars. He said Negroes were their own worst enemies and spoke of whites as superior to them because "they are able to stick together." He was aggressive in his feelings toward white people, but feared retaliation for expressing these feelings openly.

George was more or less continuously aware of the fact that his mother required him to make a good appearance, both literally and in school activities. He had already decided on a profession. The prestige and income of professional people seem to have been the prominent factors in determining his decision.

In attempting to predict the course of George's life on the basis of its tenor in adolescence, the psychiatrist noted that he had chosen his profession, and that three members of his gang had the same ambition. He expected George to become "a substantial citizen with an interest in Negro activities and civic affairs . . .

anxious to improve the general welfare of his own group." He noted underlying feelings of inferiority and questioned whether George's defenses were adequate to cope with them, particularly noting the possibility of some difficulty in his relationship with whites and guessing that he might become sullen or overtly hostile. He predicted that George would marry and have children but expected him to have some distrust and suspicion of his wife. Noting that George's hostility toward his mother was "pretty well repressed," he wondered whether this, too, might come out in a pattern of defiance and hostility toward his wife. On the whole, these hints and guesses come closer than the outright predictions.

When George graduated from high school, his reputation as a scholar was already firmly established. He went to a Negro college for the next two years, where he was rather active in extracurricular activities, though he did not participate in any organized sports. He was also a cheerleader during this time, and boxed some for his own amusement. He enlisted in the Army Reserve and was called to active duty in 1943. Although he had scored well on the classifying test and probably could have gone directly into the Army Specialized Training Program, he preferred to keep his test score to himself because he was "tired of school." He took his basic training, and then requested a transfer to the A.S.T.P. when it was rumored that his unit might be called overseas. The request was granted, and he was sent to an unsegregated university to finish his undergraduate work. He enjoyed this period a great deal. It was the first time he had ever had an opportunity to live in a part of the country that was not legally segregated, although he had once visited in Chicago. He finished college six or seven months later, and a few months after that began his advanced training at a Negro college in the South. He got his professional degree in 1946. He had married in the meantime, and he and his wife moved to New York City for a year and their first baby was born there.

George wanted to settle in the West where he had gone to school, but returned to New Orleans to be with his family. After his second period of service in the Army, he again wanted to return to the West, but he says he was unable to do so because his father had died in the interim, and his mother and unmarried sister could not tolerate his moving away.

In discussing his experiences in the Army, George expresses some opinions, but little discernable feeling concerning racial practices. In basic training, during his first period of service, he was in an all-Negro unit. Later he was in an integrated unit as an officer and thoroughly enjoyed his prestige and status. On one occasion he told Negro friends with some glee that many of the white men must have thought he was "an uppity little nigger" because he liked to pull rank and assert his power.

Our most valid information about George's color attitudes comes from reports of social gatherings in which he entertained his guests with accounts of his war service. He is an amateur photographer and had collected a number of very well executed color slides of various battle positions and landscape scenes overseas. He gave accounts of his friendship with Southern white officers, and even reported that he and a white officer from South Carolina found themselves allied in defending social practices of the South. In the same vein, he claims that segregation and racial discrimination in New Orleans are "not so bad" and that he could excuse any that he was subjected to, because it was his home.

Following his return to New Orleans from New York and before he was well settled, George was recalled into the Army. He served approximately two more years, mainly in Korea and Japan. His rank during most of this time was First Lieutenant, though he was discharged as a Captain. He served for the most part with combat units, and had considerable front line experience. He had a number of sexual relationships with both Japanese and Korean women. He was pleased by their subservient attitudes toward the male in sexual matters, and still enjoys telling his male companions about this. Following his return from Korea, George got a job suitable to his training, and rapidly found himself involved in numerous professional activities. He found all of this time-con-

suming but he seems to have no lack of opportunity to indulge
his liking for nocturnal excursions with his male cronies.

The present status of George's marriage is of considerable interest and is remarkably informative as to his character. The marriage is not happy; there is chronic crisis and strife. George's wife
is in constant conflict with his mother and his psychotic sister.
His wife is a light brown-skinned girl, small, and rather quiet in
manner. She affects complete dependence upon George, while he
openly and guilelessly expresses contempt of her competence in
almost any area of feminine behavior that happens to occur to
him. She subordinates herself both to her husband and to her
mother-in-law without signs of open objection. Indeed, she seems
quite defeated.

In talking of his marriage, George gives the impression of ap-
preciating the flaws, disruption and discontent in the situation. He
regards this as mostly the result of his psychotic sister's behavior.
However, it finally dawns on the listener that he does not necessarily have any real feeling of interest in his wife's welfare. He regards her rather evident misery as an irritant to his comfortable
existence. Although he speaks of the possibility that she might
benefit from psychotherapy, he is really concerned only with how
her treatment would benefit himself. Curiously enough, young
Mrs. Morgan confidentially gave the information to one interviewer that she regards her husband as utterly dependent upon
her. He needs to have her attend to his clothes and his meals, and
even his bath. She speaks of him as simply "another child in the
house," and she makes this statement not with bitterness, but with
resignation. She also mentions that George prevents her from
satisfying her ambition to go back to college where she had finished only one year. At this time she had three children and was
pregnant again.

George's description of his courtship is instructive. He says that
he first noticed his wife as a "dejected" girl at a party that he attended in company with her older sister. He wonders if this kind
of depression, which was his first conscious memory of his wife,

might have to do with her mother's "peculiarities," though he does not elaborate on this. Even though he discusses his wife's depressive symptomatology at great length, he minimizes it and certainly is not impressed with its seriousness. He regards her bitterness about repeated pregnancies as the sort of complaining that one can generally expect from women. Within the first year of their marriage she suffered from an attack of hysterical blindness. George and his wife had known each other since she was 11 years old. They seriously dated while he was in graduate school after the war, as a result of the "dejection" incident noted above. He described a series of ultimatums that she issued to him about his behavior with other girls, the final one of which was that they get married before he got his degree. They did.

The striking feature of George's sexual behavior is his need to have immediate sexual gratification on his own terms. The only time he expressed genuine anger at his wife was when she attempted to force him to stay home more of the time by refusing him her sexual favors. This occurred shortly before his reëntry into the Army. Unlike the ultimatums of their courtships days, this one failed. Its direct result was that George arranged for a "secretary," whose work consisted almost entirely in being handy for his sexual use. Eloquent evidence of his attitude and basic orientation toward women, and perhaps toward all other people, is his praise for his wife's ability to please him sexually more than his secretary does. Similarly he admires oriental women immensely because "they really know how to please men." The conscious, enduring, consistent pattern of his relationship to women is on this basis. He has a consummate need to be admired, a need so great that he carefully selects associates and activities to allow him to feel a more or less continuous inflow of admiration. He is unaware of the criticisms, amusement, and disapproval that his antics provoke in many of his acquaintances, because he holds himself quite free of any intimate association with them—evidence enough of the anxiety he experiences when his conception of himself is threatened.

In George's character structure phallic traits are predominant. He is resolute, superficially self-assured, intensely vain, and probably very sensitive. He will not leave his mother, and he avoids situations that might damage his narcissistic evaluation of himself. His basic oral dependency is revealed in reaction formation: his self-deception that he is complete unto himself. He boastfully asserts that he can cook or sew as well as any woman. This sort of pronouncement brings direct praise from his mother. Obviously, too, his strong undercurrent of feminine identification comes into the open in this sort of statement. George's behavior is overtly aggressive and inconsiderate. He consistently lets people wait on him, literally and figuratively: professional associates, interviewers, friends, and women. He is casually, even rather defiantly unconcerned about it, too. He walked jauntily into his house after an unexplained absence of two days and asked his mother and wife what all the commotion was about. On another similar occasion he said, "Why all this fuss? I'm here, aren't I?" This and similar incidents dramatize his symbolic use of his penis. That is, "loving" his secretary or his wife and the other women of his life serves his revenge and his need for sadistic domination. Such behavior also enables him to deny his castration anxiety, which is extremely intense. The primary target of these feelings is his mother.

George is fond of amusing himself by deceiving others. This is evident in his retrospective comments about his 1938 interviews, in which he thoroughly enjoyed pretending complete ignorance of sex and playing the role of the nice boy. Today he shows remarkable skill in playing the role of the altruistic busy professional man. Although he seems to be unaware of it, this is a role that is especially useful in his intimate relationships and as a technique for his high-handed renunciation of his duties as a father and husband.

In the community at large, his prestige and professional role serve as a convenient blind for gulling husbands of women who interest him, and leave him free to exploit women in a highly vengeful way. His cleverness or perhaps his own self-deception in these matters fools many people. Certainly most of the current interviewers did not suspect the degree of his pathology and the extent of his personality disorder during their initial contacts with him. George rather naïvely regarded the Negro psychiatrist who interviewed him as a man of similar interests, and consequently much more revealing information emerged rather quickly.

He has a passive satisfaction with his life, and evinces little interest in changing it, except to eliminate such irritants as he finds in his day-to-day existence: the behavior of his psychotic sister or his wife's depression. He gives lip service to interest in such matters as segregation, but it is minimal. Perhaps what seems to be passivity in his makeup is more his refusal to countenance the realities of his life that do not fit his narcissistic needs.

In George's professional orientation there is much that is psychologically akin to that of a religious charlatan, particularly one who has no very clear awareness of his duplicity. There is no evidence whatsoever that he neglects his professional work, or that he engages in any sort of illegality. His professional activity is simply devoid of work requiring a high degree of skill or responsibility.

George has a very effective skill in ingratiating and flattering people so long as his contact with them is of short duration. He was initially interested in the activities of his various interviewers, both in regard to the study and in other ways, but he lost interest quickly as the contact developed. He was never able to "find the time" for psychological testing. His narcissism is evidenced by any number of things. He loves military pomp, uniforms, and the authority of officers. He is amused and pleased by his ability to deceive others. All of this stems from his mother's training: her emphasis on appearances, the trappings of success, and the importance of manners.

George has developed a remarkably efficient technique of self-deception in order to maintain his narcissism. His great need for power, or at least for a feeling of superiority, he gratifies by selecting his activities and friends so that he can always be the most intelligent person in the group, or the one with the most money and prestige. He likes big cars and fast driving. On one occasion he spontaneously announced to the interviewing analyst, "I suppose I'm the most individualistic person in town." His dependence upon this sort of thing contributes to his desire to stay in New Orleans. He loves this city, he says, and is unable to leave. He shows a remarkable ability to ignore or deny the importance of any problems arising from segregation. He gives lip service to the problems of the isolation of Negro professionals from general professional life, but he is obviously quite unconcerned about it. His feeling and attitude toward women in general and toward his wife, mother, and mistress in particular are probably the most revealing of all. In each of these relationships he is in a strongly oral dependent position. The one method his wife mentions of exerting some control over him is refusing him sexual intercourse.

The family emphasis on prestige and intellectual or educational achievement fortunately found George and his siblings quite intelligent. Even his father carried a certain amount of prestige as a mail carrier during a period when this occupation ranked fairly high in the Negro society in this community. That the father should be a mail carrier and the son a professional man is not at all surprising.

George speaks in an easy way of his skin color and its significance to himself, in both interviewing and social situations. There is a noticeable similarity of his attitude in 1938 and in 1955. In 1938 he spoke of the "good racial situation in New Orleans." He finds the position of the Negro in New Orleans at the present time "not so bad." At the same time he is aware that able men in his profession tend to leave the South. George's attitude seems stereotyped and devoid of deep personal involvement. In 1938 he told his interviewer that if Negroes had their own street car company, the whites would bomb it. In 1955, he said he thought "passing" was a poor idea because of the risk involved, and the serious consequences to be suffered if one were caught. In both cases, he was expressing his deep concern with retaliation for aggression.

Though George's mother has been active in race relations work since his childhood, we have surprisingly little comment on the specific character of the training she gave George regarding race. He himself has revealed only a few memories about it. One of these was an injunction from his mother not to play with white boys, though George was raised in a mixed neighborhood and did play with them. Some sex play with a white girl when he was eight years old especially aroused his father when it was discovered, and strong measures were taken to prevent a recurrence.

The Negro psychiatrist who interviewed George warned us not to consider him as "typical" of Negro professional men. In this he is certainly right. George does not have the need for acceptance and recognition common to many, perhaps most professional people. There is a regressive quality to this lack. George has little regard for keeping appointments on time, a trait that bespeaks the arrogance of a spoiled child. He is distrustful of close emotional relationships with women except as he can dominate them sexually, or ruthlessly command their attention and care—much as an infant might dominate its mother.

An interesting aspect of the personalities of many of our subjects has been a paranoid slant on life. George is an exception. He does not invoke the "second-class citizen" reason for being a failure, as Francis Gregory does. He has no need to, simply because he does not feel that he is. Like Mary Hopkins, George reveals an ego deficit, a pathographic defect. He restricts his living pattern so as to deny the limitations imposed on him by his skin color. His only objection to New Orleans is that he does not like the climate! George has no paranoid tendencies because he just denies or ignores feelings of inferiority, and is therefore free of having to project or rationalize them. He arranges his life so that he almost never has to face anyone as an inferior. If he does, as he may in social gatherings, he just shows off his "parlor talents," by playing the piano or showing his war pictures. When he was arrested for a traffic violation he had a temper tantrum, a highly dubious and dangerous foible, even for an educated Negro in a Southern city as relatively easygoing in racial matters as New Orleans. These antics, together with the obvious limitation of his defensive patterns, suggest the degree of psychopathology in his makeup.

George has given us no evidence of racially based self-hate. Although our interviews would certainly have allowed him to "identify with whites," none of his interviewers elicited any observable transference. He found the psychiatrists useful only as a possible means for removing his troublesome psychotic sister from his immediate presence.

George's social activities are worthy of special comment. He carries on extramarital sexual affairs and consorts with a group of male cronies who frequent various bars and gambling places in the city. He is not a good father; like his mother he has always been an absentee parent. In many respects he appears to be downwardly mobile and treats his position in the Negro community in a way that is bound to depreciate his status. Up to a point, George's activities are typical gang activities but the other dimensions of his life preclude any purely gang-centered identification.

There is practically no evidence that George feels anxiety or discomfort. In his interview with a Negro psychiatrist he exhibited a good deal of axillary sweating, but even then he seemed to have his usual aplomb and self-confidence. There is a kind of psychopathic or sociopathic quality to George's make-up and life pattern, but the total organization of his personality is not sociopathic. He maintains his family relationships in a consistent manner, and even satisfies some of the responsibilities that might be expected of a householder. His family life and background are both unified and stable. The term "character disorder" is applicable to the psychopathological or clinical syndrome that he presents.

George's current social activities have the strong flavor of rebellious adolescence. He flouts the sentiments of society in general and of his female family in particular, albeit in a nocturnally limited way. One is reminded of a bright high school or college student who gets the admiration of his contemporaries for being both a "brain" and an accomplished rounder. The fact of being Negro has furnished George's mother an organizing or focusing point for her pursuits, but George is rebellious here too: he is only remotely concerned with race, and even finds his place outside the truly active life of his profession by using color as an excuse to escape tiresome responsibility to his associates or to his professional integrity.

George's mother is clearly the important, relevant and significant person in the determination of his personality, as is true also of the mothers of Francis Gregory and Chester Olivier. Each of these subjects is differently hampered and inhibited as an adult because each had a different relationship with his mother and a different pattern of techniques for dealing with her, but the three mothers had one thing in common: a driving, determined, unceasing need to use their sons as a means of personal gratification without much respect for the sons as individuals in their own right. The rebelliousness generated by this treatment is strongly inhibited in Francis because of his strong dependency, and is therefore turned inward in a painful and crippling way. In George, too, the process is largely unconscious, and emerges mainly in symbolic irrelevancies that are also disruptive and maladaptive. In Chester, the rebellion has become overt, and he has done his level best not only to rebel noisily but also to make converts and transmute his adaptation into a social movement: a bohemian way of life. Chester has even had some limited success in this endeavor, and has managed to find some other people willing to join him in his idol-smashing assault on authority.

CHESTER OLIVIER: SELF-MADE ICONOCLAST

In the person of Chester Olivier we are presented with a complex of factors that bear directly on a critical problem in the understanding of the contemporary well-educated urban Negro. In 1938 Chester was on the threshold of success or failure. He could either achieve his ambitions for advanced education and a famous career or fail in the face of the overwhelming odds against him, with possible personality disorganization under the stress of such a failure. Since then he has reached two main goals of his adolescent life: marriage into a level of society higher than his own, and achievement of an advanced college degree, but his marriage rather quickly went on the rocks and he has been unable to utilize his education for constructive, meaningful living. He is unhappy and patently disorganized in his efforts to find occupational identity. A long trail of failures of ambitious schemes for acquiring money or fame began with completion of his college education.

Why should an intelligent, well-educated young man be employed as a part-time waiter or shoe salesman? We might say, "because he is Negro," but Chester does not admit of such a simple explanation.

Chester is a small, medium brown-skinned man, trim and athletic, but weighing only about 140 pounds. His face is scarred, but not really disfigured to any significant degree. His manner to a new acquaintance, at least if status is involved, tends to be effusively ingratiating. His mode of dress falls just short of being dapper. He walks with a light, springy gait and an exaggerated arm swing. At times he affects a flowing pocket handkerchief and large quantities of cologne. His voice is remarkably expressive. It is deep and decidedly resonant, and he makes the most of it. He enunciates his words carefully, but gives one the impression that he meticulously avoids any possibility that Negroid articulation might creep into his speech. His accent is "Eastern" rather than Southern and tends to have a theatrical note.

In 1938, Chester Olivier was 16. He had achieved a remarkable degree of success in school, work, athletics, and social relationships. Davis and Dollard and their co-workers were justifiably impressed by his achievements, speaking of him as a "Self-Made Man"[4] who "has made the American dream a reality—,"[5] and defining him, perhaps significantly, as a warrior engaged in battle

---

[4] Allison Davis and John Dollard, *Children of Bondage*, Washington, American Council on Education, 1940, Chapter 5, pp. 99–126.
[5] *Ibid.*, p. 99.

with an oppressive society. Although the authors of *Children of Bondage* gave a glowing picture of Chester's winning ways, they were not entirely fooled since they noted many disturbing inconsistencies in the way he presented himself. Most of the questions they raised were derived from their subjective impressions of Chester's personality, since it was difficult then to assail his itemized achievements. In considerable degree, it still is. Davis and Dollard question at one point, "Does he protest [his success] too much? What kind of person makes such a statement ['Don't get the idea that I am inferior'] when he has not been challenged?"[6] Most significantly, Davis and Dollard suggested that Chester might not be able to endure frustration without personality disorganization. It should be emphasized that these ominous questions have been culled from a mass of material that was predominantly outspoken in its admiration of Chester's "success" as a 16-year-old.

The psychiatrist who attempted to forecast Chester's adjustment from the data on his life up to 1938 expected conflict over his choice of occupation, since Chester's ideas about it were vague and conflicting. He also expected disturbance in Chester's marriage: "he might be tempted, for example, to marry a girl of higher social status and then find her sexually uninteresting." He expected Chester to have difficulty with authority figures, and thought his feelings of inferiority might lead him to identify with whites, or "again, if this failed he might be forced into self-defeating mechanisms such as are motivated by coercive rage." If Chester were thwarted by realistic discrimination or unforeseen occurrences, the psychiatrist expected him to take a subordinate role in his work, family, or other relationships and then blame the world for his difficulties, denying his own feelings of inferiority and inadequacy in a somewhat paranoid way, while at the same time suffering feelings of depression and self-contempt. These predictions are remarkably confirmed by Chester's later life.

At the time he was first interviewed, Chester was a junior in

[6] *Ibid.*, p. 100.

high school. His father had left the family some years before. Mrs. Olivier came from a rural district where her family had descended from slaves. She had some education and probably carried some "bright blood," since she was described as light brown in color. She was very heavy and rather strong. She was described as a most determined and ambitious woman with high ideals and considerable stability. Mrs. Olivier ruled her family with a heavy hand and employed a wide variety of techniques to insure her domination. Her attitude toward her children seems to have been that they would succeed and rise in spite of anything, and assuredly at the cost of any discomfort to themselves. She imposed rigid restrictions on all their play activities, a difficult task in a lower-class neighborhood such as theirs.

Chester was the oldest child, and received a much more effective dose of heavy-handed guidance from his mother than did his three younger siblings. Chester had to make considerable use of his mother's aggressiveness, since he was widely known as a sissy as a young child. Mrs. Olivier shielded him as completely as possible from the influences of his playmates, wedging him "between fear of his mother and fear of his gang."[7] There is evidence of a type of maternal indulgence, probably excessive, which has etiological significance in the later development of character disorders, including psychopathic behavior and homosexual preoccupation, both of which Chester manifests.[8] Chester's mother taught him to work and to save, but she managed all his money. Her driving force and domination in the family appear in almost every aspect of the past as we know it from Chester now and from the 1938 interviews. Again and again such words as "bossy," "demanding," "dominating," "powerful," "driving," and "ambitious" are used by her family and associates to describe Mrs. Olivier. This applied to her religious attitudes as well. She was a

[7] *Ibid.*, p. 103.
[8] Helene Deutsch, "The Imposter," *Psychoanalytic Quarterly*, 1955, 4: 483–505; Lawrence C. Kolb and Adelaide M. Johnson, "Etiology and Therapy of Overt Homosexuality," *Psychoanalytic Quarterly*, 1955, 4:506–515.

spiritualist and enforced her children's attendance at church for almost the entirety of every weekend.

In the early years of their marriage, Chester's parents had a fairly stable relationship with each other. They lived and behaved according to the precepts and standards of the lower middle-class New Orleans Negro community of the thirties. Chester's father had a good job and managed to save money as well as to acquire some property, but he had left the home by the time that Chester was eight. This was no peaceful separation, but a somewhat violent break. He returned to the family for a brief period several years later. During the interim he was often in the neighborhood, was known to his children, and was an occasional contributor to their financial support. The bitter recriminations that Mrs. Olivier later heaped on her husband belie the rosy picture that she painted of their early years of marriage. Mr. Olivier is of Creole descent. He came from a small French community near New Orleans and was bilingual. His son remembers him as being "about as dark as I am." Chester describes his paternal grandfather as being Indian and French with no trace of Negro. This man married a Negro woman who was a "tremendous mixture of races," according to Chester. The children of the union, including Chester's father, considered themselves Negro. As an adult, Chester emphasizes the importance of the paternal line of his family. He speaks of his father as "highly intelligent," but "terribly frustrated in his ambition," and he wants to present him as a strong individual. Only after a period of months did he reveal his appraisal of his father as an ineffectual man. Chester has a need to find and attach himself to a strong masculine figure, and he wishes that his father could have been this to him. He was severely disappointed over his father's inability to cope with his mother, and the disappointment led directly to rage.

The Oliviers' feeling for each other was hostile. We know little but the bare facts of their early lives, and nothing of the circumstances surrounding their initial involvement with each other. Mr. Olivier was a man with some years of education, and was a tile setter, a trade Chester still regards with admiration. Chester states his father always made an excellent income even through the depression years. After their final separation, Mrs. Olivier was openly at war with him. She described him to her children and others as an impractical and improvident man who chased prostitutes, a poor specimen of a father. Mr. Olivier is not consumed with hatred for his wife. He left the family for a number of reasons, but mainly because he refused to tolerate his wife's insistence on being the central figure of the household.

Mrs. Olivier's attitude toward Chester and her ambitions for him were so identified with her own driving ambition that there was little distinction. Her plans for her son emphasize her narcissism. She must have had an exceedingly frustrating effect upon her husband. Mr. Olivier described his wife as bossy, jealous, and openly aggressive. He could not stand to watch her beat the children, which she did effectively and frequently, especially when they were small. He knew that she had turned the children against him, and was too ineffectual to do anything about it except explode with rage, drink, or leave. Mrs. Olivier openly encouraged Chester to defy his father in small matters, such as the management of the money he earned in his various little jobs as a youngster. And she deliberately intimidated and sissified him, to her husband's outspoken disgust. Thus behind a façade of great motherliness Mrs. Olivier was a hostile and possessive woman whose interest in the welfare of her children reflected primarily retaliatory aggression toward men or enhancement of her self-esteem. Mr. Olivier took the only open route to safety and deserted. He returned to the fold briefly some seven years later. He did not stay long, and left to live with a common law wife. After many years of complete separation he filed suit for divorce, claiming half of the property that Mrs. Olivier had accumulated in the interim. Because of her reluctance to take her husband to court, she capitulated to this demand, just as she avoided suing him for nonsupport when he first deserted. She did not want the unpleasant publicity of a public fight. In sum, Mrs. Olivier's hostility for her husband is hidden, subtle, and coercive whereas his re-action to her is outspokenly contemptuous.

Chester's infancy was dominated by an atmosphere of rigid restriction and control. This is highlighted by the character of his toilet training, which was begun when he was three months old. His mother claims not to have washed another diaper for him after that. She kept him on her lap over a little pot, used an enema syringe to start the action, and petted him so that he would not cry. By early childhood he had an established reputation in the family for "selfishness." Mrs. Olivier's characterization of her son refers to his "acquisitiveness" and describes him as "hard." Ac-quisitiveness is a normal trait of a talking preschool child. Chester slept with his mother until he was two years old. After his brother was born he slept with his grandfather. His mother concentrated most of her attention on Chester because she "did not have time" for the others. She consciously wished him to be perfect. She spanked and beat him for such things as a tendency to masturbate. She saw Chester as anything but an infant or little boy with re-quirements of love and affection.

Mr. Olivier's occupation as a skilled artisan kept him away from home much of the time, even when Chester was young. Chester did manage to work for his father on some of his construction jobs as a water boy, but openly defied him (at his mother's suggestion) by collecting his wages for himself. Chester's mother's sabotage of his father's status in this bit of history is striking. Pain, punishment, and fright filled this little boy's early life, and he was unable to expect good will or respect as an individual from either parent. The natural result of such an early life would be a disturbed adult personality.

As an adult, Chester has a greater need to revenge himself than to further his own best interests. The reconstructed picture of his early years plainly indicates his relationship with his mother as the source of a tremendous store of rage. His rage determines Chester's outspoken contempt for the externals of success in the Negro community, since these are exactly the things his mother admired. This reaction throws some light on why he makes a farce of his own advanced education, since this is what his mother sees as the pinnacle of achievement. Thus he can ridicule her at the cost of his own self-respect. His need to distinguish himself from his mother reflects the basic problem of his own personality: confusion about his identity. He has also elaborated a technique of preserving some degree of self-esteem by attributing his failures to anti-Negro prejudice and caste practices. His exploitation of this social circumstance in the service of his suppressed hate for his mother and individuals to whom he assigns a maternal role becomes more and more apparent as his life progresses, at the cost of mobility and freedom of adjustment. The very real tragedy of this sort of neurotic behavior pattern is doubly emphasized by Chester's obvious native talent and intelligence.

Chester's educational history furnishes a central unifying theme in his development as a social person. He has been highly successful in all his endeavors. He attended grade school until he was 14, and in spite of his early timidity and fearfulness, rapidly established himself as an outstanding student. He was the champion orator of his school, editor of the paper, a prominent athlete and captain of several teams, class president, and a member of the student council. We have scant information about how others regarded him at that time. Chester himself probably behaved, then as now, as though his contemporaries were competitors or enemies, reluctant sources of gratification of his own narcissistic needs. Though he gathered many of the laurels of popularity, he literally forced these from his contemporaries and superiors, leaving behind him a trail of resentful, vanquished "friends." Chester's mother managed a matriculation for him at the leading Negro high school in Louisiana, and there the success story continued. Chester was faced with much more competition, especially for social acceptance in groups impressed by family background or wealth, but his record of achievement in high school is in some respects astounding. Currently he is apt to dwell on his high school athletic prowess, especially his achievements as a swimmer and football player. He claims that he was an all-state quarterback on his high school team, and by the aggressive, insistent quality of his claim manages to arouse the suspicion that he was not. Chester also claims to have won the city diving and swimming championships for "one or two years." In discussing his college career he emphasized the athletic aspect of it more than any other.

If Chester expresses a retrospective exaggeration of his athletic ability, this is understandable. Football was the lever he used to separate himself from his mother and her church activities. Before he entered high school, Chester had to attend church with his mother all day each Saturday and Sunday at a Spiritualist Church in an undistinguished neighborhood, rather a long distance from where the Oliviers lived. Chester's father was at least a nominal Catholic, but this appears to have been a notably uninfluential fact. When he went out for high school football, Chester was at least good enough for his coach to make some effort to keep him on the team, and he made good use of this fact to pry himself loose from mother and church. Mrs. Olivier objected violently, even enlisting the aid of other members of the church to keep Chester from giving up his Friday and Saturday afternoons for football. He put his foot down, however, and his mother was forced to capitulate. This is one of the few occasions on which Chester was able to rebel against his mother without concomitant self-sabotage, doubtless because the support of the community, and the prestige athletics brought from his own contemporaries, enabled him to assert constructively his objection to his mother's personality. In addition to athletics, Chester participated vigorously in dramatic activities, debating, and school politics in high school. He did well scholastically, but was not as outstanding as he was in his other activities.

Chester felt that he was denied opportunities in school because of his dark skin color, specifically assigning blame for this color discrimination to a woman who was one of his most important teachers. We hear little of Mr. Olivier through these years, though he told Chester he was saving money for him to attend college. When Chester graduated without a scholarship he approached his father for the money, but his father laughed and told him that he had just spent it all. This is only one of many stories that Chester tells to prove his father's lack of real interest in the family.

Both as an adolescent and as an adult, Chester is disparaging and contemptuous of the social status of others whenever he perceives it as greater than his own. He refers to acquaintances from his high school days as snobs, and pictures his life in high school as almost a conspiracy, in which everyone was attempting to keep him down. He even claims that Dollard made unfulfilled promises of reward for participation in the earlier study. Somehow or another he managed to believe he was promised a scholarship in high school which the school authorities denied him because of his inferior social status and his dark color. Chester had been doing some newspaper reporting, and was responsible for a newspaper account of a party where several Negroes, including a teacher at his school, were arrested for homosexuality. Chester is convinced that this was used against him and insinuates that he was denied a college scholarship he coveted because of it. This is the first of many references to homosexuality, a theme that recurs specifically in important situations of competitive impact. The prototype of these existed in Chester's high school relationships. It is interesting that he described himself as "incorrigible" the first time he was interviewed by the psychiatrist, and that he discussed homosexuality explicitly and at length in this first interview. Subsequently, he has implicated someone else's aggressive homosexual wishes as part of almost all his failures to achieve success.

Chester had two years of college before going into the Army, although he was unable to secure a scholarship to any of the southern Negro colleges he admired. The several accounts of his matriculation in a small out-of-state Negro college vary considerably, but probably it was on the basis of his athletic ability. He weighed about 130 pounds at the time, but claims to have made the first string as a freshman quarterback. He says that he played frequently and that it was necessary for him as well as the other athletes to succeed in the sport or they would be summarily dismissed from the school. Chester has several scars on his face and without specifically saying so, he implies that these are the results of football injuries. He claims astounding success as a quarterback. There may be some measure of truth to this, but one is left with the impression that Chester is both willing and able to embellish the bare facts to suit his own purpose. In college he continued to acquire honors where he might. He was president, he says, of a prominent Negro fraternity. Following his Army service during the war, he graduated from another college, having been refused readmission to the first. Chester accounts for this rejection by attributing it to the "smug morality" of the college authorities, and their specific selection of him as a scapegoat for the misdemeanors of "most of the students." He continued a strong interest in drama while in college, but he actually majored in fine arts and English because there was no formally organized drama department at either college. He acted in many plays, which he claims he directed. With a hint of grandiosity, he states that he was actually doing the work of an instructor even before he got his bachelor's degree.

Chester was married for the first time just before he was drafted. He had known his wife in high school. She was the daughter of a prominent Negro professional man in New Orleans, who had been ostentatious in his display of power and wealth, but who had been dead about a year when Chester married his daughter. They had one son, born only a few months before their divorce, which took place just after Chester was discharged from the Army, in 1945. Chester does not dwell on his sexual prowess, marital or otherwise, but he does emphasize his other physical powers, and he alludes frequently to the danger and prevalence of homosexuality.

When he went into the Army, Chester was assigned to a special service unit, where he thought the duty was very easy. After two years at this station, he was recommended for officer's candidate school because of his preservice educational record. He attended the school for 16 weeks during 1944. Toward the end of his course of instruction he was washed out. The story he tells of this is a graphic and dramatic illustration of his technique of self-sabotage. Apparently he did well in his training but repeatedly flouted authority by throwing questions back into the instructors' faces when racial attitudes were brought up. He also used his cleverness to tempt the fates by faking reports of field exercises. Curiously enough, he was offered another chance at a commission, but instead of availing himself of this opportunity, he made use of the occasion to tell the colonel involved that he had absolutely no intention of taking any more stuff from any of them. Chester rationalized his behavior very carefully. In addition to innumerable references to racial prejudice throughout his discussion of the OCS experience, he repeatedly derogated the personal qualities of the training officers. One of the chief reasons for his provocative flouting of the stiff requirements at OCS was a very real fear of getting into a particular Negro division slated for overseas duty. He claims this division was badly officered and was subsequently shoved into awkward and precarious combat positions. His account of the whole affair at OCS is a highly paranoid one in which he projects the responsibility for his own failure in all directions. The Negro-white conflict is more at the center of this paranoid construction than the homosexual one. He heaped abuse and contempt upon the Negroes who were instructors or had other positions of responsibility at the camp, just as he castigates and reviles any purely Negro effort to better the race situation. The feeling is reminiscent of the criticism he aimed at the ambitious program of his high school.

When he was returned to regular duty, Chester managed to regain his original special service job. Here, as well as at his later stations, he claims to have been a success as a semiprofessional gambler. He gave all his winnings to his wife to bank and manage, a pattern directly referable to his mother's training. He would then ask her for sums as he needed them for stakes. She accepted the money freely, but protested violently against his gambling. Following his discharge from the Army and shortly after he graduated from college and returned to New Orleans, he and his wife were divorced. He described the circumstances of the divorce briefly, saying only that his wife became extremely jealous and that she interfered at all possible places with his ambitions and career. It was over a dispute about his decision to return to school to study drama that they finally parted. Chester's wife has permitted him little contact with his son, although he has made little effort on his own to maintain a paternal relationship to the boy.

Within a short time after his divorce Chester entered graduate school at a Northern university. His career there was rather successful, as his purely academic efforts have always been. He was the only Negro in the drama department at the time he began, though there were several others before he had finished. He got his Master's degree in three years, not an unusual length of time for students at that particular university. During the course of his studies he met and married his second wife. She had been married previously and had one child by her first marriage. After graduation, Chester attempted to get into several Broadway theatrical productions but was unsuccessful. He places the blame for this entirely on the fact that every time he applied for a job, the director of the company would make sly insinuations that he could have it if he would submit to homosexual relations. Chester discussed the problem with his wife, and she agreed with him that he should attempt no such relationship, even though it meant foregoing a theatrical career.

The next step was to investigate opportunities for teaching in various Negro colleges. About the first place he visited was a small border state school where he appeared on the scene just as a vacancy occurred in the drama department. He was offered a job as an instructor and stayed there for the remainder of the summer semester and into the fall. He immediately became involved in petty campus quarrels and rapidly antagonized everyone he could. An enthusiastic defense of the practice of homosexuality by the ancient Greeks, which he made to a large class of drama students, was especially effective in mobilizing the hostility of the college authorities. As usual, he was playing the role of champion of a revolt against "smug morality." At the end of the fall semester, Chester was fired.

He returned to New Orleans to become a radio announcer for a few months, claiming highly altruistic motives in taking this job. He admires (and sneers at) all the popular Negro disc jockeys who speak in a Negro dialect, and who appeal to the lower-class Negroes in New Orleans. His notion was to raise the standards of Negro radio presentations single-handedly. This plan was thwarted at every turn, he feels, by the white owners and managers of the station. When he was fired, there were again vague references to homosexuals. Since then he has been engaged in a wide variety of activities, few of them commensurate with his education and intelligence. Among other things he has been a manager of a night club, a night club M.C., a shoe salesman, part-time waiter, and an occasional speaker for various Negro clubs and schools. He has also written short articles for a "quickie" Negro magazine, but he is contemptuous of most of them. For a time he regarded his chief occupation as the writing of a book which is to be a history and defense of a prominent lower-class Negro club.

Chester is a writer, but even more, he is an actor. He is sharply critical of Negro performers in general, especially the pretentiously artistic ones, and credits artistic integrity to such persons as Louise Beavers or Hattie McDaniel (both "Mammy" types), defending this type of character against the usual Negro outcry against them. Whenever a Negro has an opportunity to do something well, as these actresses have, Chester says, the official bodies, such as the NAACP, brand them unfairly as "Uncle Toms" or stereotyped Negro buffoons.

When they returned to New Orleans, the Oliviers lived with Chester's mother for a time, but his wife and his mother were totally incompatible, and they moved after only a few weeks.

Chester speaks of his wife in glowing terms that reflect his fantasy of a good mother. He calls her the real backbone in the family, the one who holds him to his altruistic interest of making a career in the South. But the ambivalence and hostility is there, as always. He says, "I'd probably be in the East some place making a lot of money if it were not for her determination."

Chester has little to say about his heterosexual activities and interests. The emphasis he places on the ever-present danger of homosexuality is meant to unify his own masculinity, but does not appear to succeed in this aim. At every opportunity Chester puts on a display of virility and power. Toward the end of the psychiatric interviews he became a part-time life guard at a swimming pool, and was observed literally flexing his muscles and strutting in a more or less continuous display for a presumably admiring crowd.

Chester's wife was working as a secretary in a local textile plant at the beginning of the current study and was obviously contributing the major part of the money that the family needed. Chester effectively minimizes this by referring to it in a patronizing way, giving the impression that he feels that this is only as it should be. There is a remarkable similarity in the way that he speaks of his wife and of his mother. He often describes his mother as an ideal sort of person, but always manages to be superior by looking down on her as amusingly backward and inferior.

A description of the mobile dynamic aspects of Chester's personality must rest firmly on an appreciation of his assets and the amazing degree to which he perverts them. He consistently works to his own disadvantage. This occurred in his dealings with various members of the research staff, and with the other associates of his life, both past and present. Chester can perceive no need to reorient himself in his relationships with others and has never sought psychotherapeutic help in any form. He is capable of hiding his motivations from others very effectively, and it is a remarkable fact that with a mass of material from interviews, tests, candid observations, and beautifully detailed data from his adolescence, we probably know very little of the actual content of Chester's thought or feelings. If something genuinely revealing does come up, it is slipped into his production as if it were inconsequential.

Chester continues to have a keen sense of rivalry and competition. This occurs almost exclusively in his activities with other men and speaks for his profound doubt of his masculine adequacy. Consequently, he seizes every opportunity for destructive, angry criticism of "inferior men" to maintain a sense of self-esteem. This technique of disparagement must certainly have its origin in a maternal attitude, perhaps in his mother's attitude toward his father.

One of the predominantly significant aspects of Chester's adult personality is his profound mistrust of others. The origin of this in his early life experience is clear. Chester's mother was rejecting because she used her son for her own ends in a vicious and devastating way, even though superficially she seemed a large-breasted, benevolent, maternal person who would do anything for her children. She thoroughly devalued her husband during the ten years that the family remained intact. Chester's adult references to his mother reflect the subtle ambiguity of the relationship. He often describes her as a highly overidealized mother figure: "Mother is wonderful." However, a subtle derogation of her methods appears even in such references. While her boys were in the armed service, Chester says she was afraid that they would be hurt and wanted to protect them. She would get "sick" periodically, and then call the Red Cross to arrange for her boys to come home on sick leave. Chester's comment on this gambit: "Well, that's the way a mother who really loves her sons would be expected to behave."

Chester directly equates his mother with the schoolteacher with whom he had great difficulty as a high school student. He described this teacher as a dictator and tyrant, and he constantly defied and insulted her, but he was shocked and hurt when she refused to recommend him for a scholarship. Chester thought this teacher had an extremely low opinion of him. Later he said something similar concerning his mother: "Mother always thinks I did it when she reads in the papers of a person being robbed."

Another very revealing comment on Mrs. Olivier's techniques of controlling others is Chester's comment that "My mother's tears are the hardest thing to handle." Mrs. Olivier frustrated her oldest son by making him a means for achieving gratification for herself. Chester has reacted to this with impotent and suppressed rage that has determined his behavior as an adult. However, he puts his assets and talents to the purpose of frustrating her in a consistent, protean pattern of retaliation that invades all the important areas of his life.

Chester is ambitious and intelligent. He has a variety of interests, most of which are grouped around drama or other occupations involving the construction of a clear public identity. He tends to be both boastful and obsequious in describing these interests. The most striking thing about his activities is their high degree of disorganization—his inability to use his considerable capacity. The lack of ability to integrate his life is reflected in his conduct in an individual interview. He conveys a sense of great purpose and drive at the beginning of the session, but loses the initial thread of thought in an intricate ramification of ideas. He is capable of returning to the original theme toward the end of the session, however. Much of his wandering seems designed to hide significant data. He brings up no dreams, and he obscures any failures in his life with elaborate rationalizations. The deception is essentially self-deception, for he succeeds in hiding his traits from others for only brief periods of time. There is no evidence that Chester now engages in antisocial or psychopathic activity. Perhaps even in his past, excursions into gambling and high living were not as romantically complete as he would have us believe.

Chester's disrupting psychopathological need is to fight with authority, and the strength of this need makes it irrelevant to maintain useful and constructive relationships. He once wrote an article criticizing a professor, sent him a copy, and then applied to the same man for a job. He was genuinely astonished that he did not get it. Chester assumes the "smug Christian morality" of his mother and other authorities only to project it. He wants to shock people "out of their complacency," and is truly at one with himself only when doing so. It was extremely satisfying to Chester to wait on tables, and then claim lack of opportunity to use his Master's degree. The value of the degree here is dramatic, as if he had gone to the trouble of getting it only for this purpose. This may be an attempt to identify with his father, whom he has described as a clever man frustrated by circumstances beyond his control.

Chester's theatrical interests indicate some need to seek a durable sense of personal identity. He defines the theater as a place for actors to work, and acting as an occupation like any other, but Chester's need to play roles certainly reaches far beyond this sort of utilitarian occupational necessity. There is a distinct element of grandiosity in his evaluation of himself. On one occasion when he was speaking of receiving no answer to an application he had made for a job, he said it was because "my progressive ideas . . . frightened that man to death." He added later that he knew the man was "jealous and afraid of me." Again he spoke of not mentioning his degree from college because "people in New Orleans are afraid of a college man."

During the course of the current study it became apparent that Chester was unperturbed by the emotional connotation of his interviews except on occasions when attention was drawn to the disorganization of his life. He would ascribe any such comment to the "smug moral" attitude of the observer to regain his complacency. On one occasion he was troubled and ruffled when one interviewer told him that he could get a job teaching if he wished, and did not have to be a waiter. Chester again defended his position by attacking the "morality" of the interviewer.

The excessive concern that Chester shows with the subject of "homosexuality" is a fairly constant phenomenon with individuals who resort to a paranoid adjustment. It is tempting to say that

Chester has this particular kind of conflict about homosexual feelings because of his intense hatred for his mother. Certainly Mrs. Olivier was extremely thwarting in a subtle way that was difficult for him to combat. However, it seems fairly certain that Chester has had no overt homosexual attachments in his life. There may have been transient overt homosexual experiences, since he hints at this possibility in one or two instances, both at high school and in his first two years in college. By the time he was 16, he was already remarkably preoccupied with the idea that homosexuality existed all around him. He said on one occasion, "Homosexuals have always flocked around me like flies." He made the remark as an adult, but it was in reference to his experiences in high school and college. As an adolescent he spoke of heterosexual experiences in terms of genuine danger to his body: "It's like being drained," or "like losing ten years of your life." This suggests the adolescent failure of heterosexual adjustment that is a feature of the development of a paranoid personality, but there is no evidence that we are dealing with a schizophrenic process in Chester. It seems more likely that he began to feel the necessity to prove his masculinity, or at least his lack of homosexuality, at the same time that he was feeling thoroughly disliked by women, including such mother figures as the troublesome high school teacher. He felt seriously handicapped with the girls that he knew in school because of his dark skin and class background.

During the period of his psychological testing Chester was politely hostile. He was consistently thirty or forty minutes late to appointments, and then had to leave early. His full-score intelligence quotient on the Wechsler-Bellevue was 132. On the verbal scale his score was 134; both scores, of course, are in the superior range of ability. His poorest performance was with the arithmetic questions. He did an exceptionally good job with the comprehension questions, although he did exhibit a need to resist convention. When he was asked why people stay away from bad company he replied with some feeling: "Well, it's a question of contamination, if there is such a thing." On the performance material he earned an intelligence quotient of 122. The psychologist felt that he had done a self portrait when he was requested to draw a man. His portrayal of the dress, general outline, and hair of the figure were strongly feminine in character. On the Rorschach test, Chester's responses indicated a clear picture of an individual with good intellectual potential, whose actual accomplishments are clearly hampered by emotional difficulties. There was evidence of marked volatility, and his controls impressed the psychologist as decidedly precarious. The test depicted a dependent person, capable of erratic behavior under stress. It is interesting that there were no overt indications of anxiety. He was preoccupied with sexual things and evidently confused in this area. Anxiety was predominantly dealt with by intellectual defenses. The psychologist felt that Chester had only fair ego strength, and would be unable to maintain adequate integration if he were to be subjected to prolonged periods of stress. Chester's TAT stories indicated that women were not to be trusted because their emotions were not genuine, and because they wished to control other people, especially men. The psychologist's overall impression indicated that he was a disturbed person, unable to utilize his intelligence to its fullest degree, and required to use a great deal of energy in maintaining some semblance of emotional control.

Ambiguity and ambivalence characterize Chester's life since his high school days. In sociological terms this can be traced to a class dichotomy, since he is in transition from the lower to the middle class. It is difficult, however, to enclose all the extraneous elements of his personality or his behavior in these terms. Socially Chester is an iconoclast, and it is easy to document his warfare on any and all expressions of moral injunction or guides to human behavior. When he is maneuvered into responding to a view he once supported, he will freely take the opposite side, particularly in relation to questions about race or skin color. He defends the stereotyped performances of Louise Beavers or Hattie McDaniel as artistic and a credit to the Negro race, but on other occasions he attacks exactly the same qualities in the performances of dialect-using disc jockeys, and says that their stereotyped performances are an insult and discredit to the Negro. He gives a nice statement of his confusion about such matters on an attitude questionnaire. In answer to the question, "In what ways could Negroes coöperate with each other?" Chester says: "Only if we could develop a race consciousness and pride without oversensitiveness. This could be done only with amalgamation of our position and a complete change of thought. I don't think it will be done to any effective extent. Our only hope is to be absorbed. (Silly question.)" This ambiguous expression of Chester's racial feelings indicates that color is important to Chester, but of secondary order. He puts racial discrimination to a personal neurotic use.

There is a continuing juxtaposition of lower- and middle-class status in Chester's history. On the one hand, his is the status world of a tile setter, a domestic worker, a messenger, a gambler, a disc jockey, a waiter, or a shoe clerk; on the other hand his world is that of the physician, stenographer, college teacher, writer, or producer. The ambiguity of status adds up to an ambiguity of class. He is in the difficult position of a man with a Master's degree who waits on tables. Any unitary assignment of class position to Chester would be impossible. His ambivalence affects all the statuses he occupies. His attempt to convert his job as disc jockey into one of "dramatic producer" is typical of his performance. Chester is a lower-class boy with considerable exposure to middle- and even upper-class values that he has been unable to assimilate completely, at least in any durably useful way. As the ambivalence and ambiguity of Chester's social identification are clear on all sides, the ambivalence of his social values seems a natural concomitant. He prides himself that he is one college boy who never got stuck up. He affects driving ambition to be a success but is unable to control his hostility, a failure that restricts his effectiveness. Chester's highly inconclusive class identification reflects a deep personal sense of identity diffusion, for the chaotic social background of his life, which he has partly created, has its concomitants in his motivations and their history. Chester's world is not really a class-bound world. The institutional context of most of his adult experience is the university or the stage. Both are significantly outside the class system: education because it is a path to mobility, and entertainment because of its bohemian *apartheid*. Thus to the already complex ambivalence of status, of class, and of values, Chester adds a collegiate sophistication and a "jivey" worldliness that complicate the understanding of his social destiny. Under the circumstances it does not seem surprising that he appears a little lost.

Chester's remarkable skills in sabotaging himself confirm that the most serious failure in his personality development is identity diffusion. As Erikson remarks, "The loss of a sense of identity often is expressed in a scornful and snobbish hostility toward the roles offered as proper and desirable in one's family or immediate community."[9] Chester particularly selects the goals his mother sponsored for "scornful and snobbish" derision. He is driven to do so by the excessive ideals her morbid ambition demanded of him. It is probable that his choice of acting as a profession is again dictated by his literal need to find a role to play in which he can feel secure. On the stage, at least, he can be somebody. As Erikson points out, the mothers of individuals of this sort have in common a social ambition and a penetrating omnipresence. Such mothers as this are themselves so hungry for approval and recognition that they burden their children with justifying their own existence. It becomes important to them to be intensely jealous of any sign that the child might identify with his father. The father in such a family situation can do nothing that will not intensify the mother's bitterness and vengefulness. Mr. Olivier left; Chester couldn't, and he is still getting even by tilting at windmills, and pulling down idols—on himself.

[9] E. H. Erickson, "The Problem of Ego Identity," *Journal of the American Psychoanalytic Association,* 1956, 4:85.

C H A P T E R 9

Conclusions: Twenty Years Later

It was in 1938 that Davis and Dollard initiated their interviews of the teen-age eighth generation of New Orleans Negroes. These interviews were completed in 1939. Our current interviews began in 1953 and ended in 1957. The complexity and subtlety of the life lines of 20 of these teen-agers over this period of nearly 20 years have been traced in the preceding chapters, nine of them in some detail. Indeed, we have found it necessary to introduce a special emphasis upon complexity in describing and interpreting them. We have had to analyze not one Negro culture, but several; not one Negro personality type, but many; not one Negro family, but a number of different ones. It remains for us to summarize and sharpen some of our findings which we feel contribute to an understanding of the adjustment of human beings to this complexity.

In brief review, we have traced the life lines of Emma, the rebellious little hoyden who became a teacher after surgery had made motherhood impossible for her; Florence, a fearful passive little girl who has become a reliable matriarchal mother—alone, still fearful, but convinced she is not the easy mark others may believe her to be; Edward, the desperate and embattled petty thief without a father who has graduated from the boys' home to the penitentiary; William, the boy who wanted to be a postman and made the grade, and who may yet raise his own family baseball team; Mary, the little girl of the lower class who wanted to be a nurse and marry a man with a job and some education and who settled for the man, illiterate but employed, and motherhood; Francis, the Creole boy whose ambitions and ambivalences carried him to an education and a good marriage and right on into the ulcer bracket; Ruth, an orphaned, overage junior high student who became a fearful, isolated old maid; George, the overprotected bright little boy whose mother pushed him through professional training, and who is now getting even; and Chester, the ambitious and successful student whose will to failure just matches his ability to succeed.

We should be doing less than justice to our predecessors and to the interested reader of *Children of Bondage*[1] if we failed to mention our follow-up of the other teen-agers whose lives are extensively described in that book. Julia Wilson, a "raddie" little Amazon of the lower class, has somewhat surprisingly achieved an enduring marriage to a sailor, who is apparently a good provider even though he is away a great deal. She has also managed to become a nurse, despite the distractions and interruptions occasioned by the births of six children. Julia has not lived in New Orleans for many years and now owns a home on the west coast. All this seems a surprising end to such a violent and unstable beginning.

Jeanne Manuel, the Creole girl who could have "passed," didn't. She married a Creole boy she had known since she was a third grader. Jeanne herself finished two years of college plus some business training. They are now comfortably settled in the West. Jeanne has two children, and hopes eventually to have a "lovely" home, finish her B.A. degree, and become more active in civic organizations: altogether a middle-class ending to a "middle-middle class" story.

[1] Allison Davis and John Dollard, *Children of Bondage*, Washington, American Council on Education, 1940, *q.v.*

Ellen Hill was an ambitious little girl. She is still ambitious. She is the mother of six children and wife of a policeman in a northern city. Despite holding down a job herself and caring for the children, she is still working part-time at finishing college and intends to become a teacher. Her strong class feelings appear to have mellowed somewhat, and though she still manifests strong determination, her life is centered almost exclusively on her family. In view of her continued efforts, Ellen may yet become the winner.

Martin Neal's family bitterly resented his being described as a "black sheep," as well as other aspects of the published report on Martin. They were almost the only people who reacted this way to *Children of Bondage* and even they had not actually read it but only heard about what it said. The prediction that Martin would go "north" is accurate in its essence. He actually went west. He has never married, and is employed as a fireman in a western city where this department has only recently been desegregated. Martin is not insensitive to the ambitions his family had for him and wishes now he might have become a big-time "first-of-race" college football coach. He is still working part-time at finishing college, but it remains to be seen how far he will push this. He seems reasonably content where he is.

Judy Tolliver's uncontrollable aggression and his complete commitment to a lower-lower-class way of life may adequately explain the fact that he has spent the last 12 years in prison in the North. His father now comments, "I was the first one to have a nervous breakdown and I guess the others just sort of follered me." Only two of Mr. Tolliver's ten children ever married, and at least one is now in a mental institution. We were unable to establish why Judy is in prison, but the length of the term he has already served is suggestive. He has apparently been in continuous trouble all his life.

In interpreting the significance of this all too human jumble of life patterns, we regard our findings as primarily a contribution to what has become known as an "ego psychology," for they

focus on the interplay between the individual and his psychologically real social world, and concern how he evolves his habitual
ways of relating to that world.

It is now axiomatic in the behavioral sciences that social worlds
may be described in a variety of ways. In the folk sociology of
even the modern South, for example, "race" and a vaguely pre-
Darwinian biological conception are still importantly involved.
For some modern investigators caste, or class, defined by interaction patterns or objective indexes—income, education, or home
ownership—is the focus of definition. Others tend to lay heavy
emphasis on the patterns associated with ethnic cultures. Our
approach has been to discover how each individual orders the
social roles he plays along a value dimension.

We do not feel called upon to deny the alternative approaches,
nor, indeed, to prejudge them at all. Ethnic affiliation, class, caste,
even "race" may, in determinate circumstances, define social roles,
and may therefore take their places in the matrix of influences
that play on individual adjustment. We have elected to examine
the differential relevance of these and other social roles to each
individual, and we have found such examination highly rewarding. Often our subjects told us explicitly that one role was more
important to them than another: "I couldn't finish school because
I had to help my family." Even more frequently such choices
had to be inferred from repeated selection of one role over
another: leaving the family for professional advancement, for
example.

Selection of one particular role as the central part of one's social
identification invariably seems to bring into play the cultural
phenomenon of ethnocentrism, structuring it around the symbols
of the primary role. Ethnocentrism is thus an important manifestation of the essentially cultural process that this role selection
represents. Yet in another sense we could with justice call it
"egocentric" for ethnocentrism functions to reaffirm for a group of
people with similar social commitments their common identifica-

tion and their common fears and suspicions of any threat to this self-conception.

We found that we could isolate a primary role identification for most individuals, and that such an identification was intimately related to the quality of integration of the individual's psychic functioning. Further, these commitments are not unique or idiosyncratic but are characteristic of groups of individuals. For one group the primary role identification was with the middle class, and was suffused with the values associated with that class. For another it was the maternal role in the matriarchal family, and in this group sex becomes a more basic fact—even socially—than class. For a third group the primary identification was with older boys and men in more or less age-graded peer groups—gangs; while for a fourth being a family member was the most important of all roles and the family became not only a focus but almost the total sphere of social life.

As would be expected, not all individuals are able to evolve unequivocal identifications of this type; some have only vague or conflicting role identifications. There is a corresponding diffusion or lack of mature integration in the psychic functioning of such individuals.

It seems doubtful that the patterns of identification we have isolated exhaust the field, but we are inclined to think that they are among the most frequent resultants in the community we have studied. We may even guess that the gang, the matriarchy, and the isolated family, specifically, are the dominant social forms in the lives of a substantial majority of New Orleans Negroes, and we would expect the patterns of role identification associated with them to be correspondingly prominent in any large sample of this population.

Our data reaffirm, often dramatically, the great importance of significant adults to the shaping of the individual's personality. The presence or absence of such figures and the nature of the model they present are intimately linked to the individual's development of ego ideals: vague or vivid images of what he would like to become. The development of such ideals takes time, and is subject to varied influences and constant change. It may be compared to the method of successive approximations for obtaining the best-fitting function to describe a given array of observations. The clarity of establishment of ego ideals is an important determinant in the formation of a primary role identification, and this in turn greatly contributes to the individual's particular configuration of psychodynamic organization. For example, Marjorie, whose ego ideal derived in considerable measure from her father, became a successful middle-class business operator, with all the authoritative assertiveness that such a role implies. Her greatest psychic conflicts lie in her roles as a mother and as a wife. Edward, on the other hand, was deprived from earliest infancy of opportunities for shaping a male ego ideal. He developed a largely negative social identity, and at age 30 exhibits an almost schizophrenic organization of personality.

The patterns of identification we have traced clearly center primarily, though not exclusively, on family life, and it must be regarded as no accident that our classification of primary role identifications is also a classification of the institutional agencies of socialization. There is, of course, no necessity that "significant adults" be found within the family, but the cards are clearly stacked to favor that possibility. It seems doubtful, on the other hand, that the middle-class way of life could survive without the extrafamilial institutions that facilitate mobility—perhaps most notably the schools. Even a very strong rebellion against one's family would be doomed in a society where the family was the only organized institution. Similarly, the gang identification is more than merely a reflection of the problems of matriarchal upbringing for a boy. It also supplies positive role models and values of its own. Even in a society as complex and diffusely organized as the one we are here examining, the education of the young for the problems they will face as adults is not left to chance. Adult role models are not random. They are patterned in institutions: the family, the school, the gang. Such institutions tend toward order, and they provide a context of learning in which individuals may come to shape their social relationships and psychic identity in similar ways.

The interrelationships between primary role identification, ego identity, and the techniques used for maintaining ego integrity are not a matter of simple cause and effect nor of independent and dependent variables. Each of them influences and is influenced by the others. The individual does not select ego defenses only to fit his social role; he does not choose his job merely to act out his psychic needs or conflicts; he does not shape his attitudes toward race only in response to "more fundamental" social or psychological commitments. He attempts rather to order these various influences on his life, for they are all operative simultaneously, and he must find a socially and psychologically viable adaptation for every moment that will deal fully with the whole range of pressures upon him.

From moment to moment and from year to year these adaptive efforts of the individual are in a measure both continuous and consistent. Our data indicate that the individual's intrapsychic techniques for maintaining ego integrity are firmly established by adolescence, and that they are stable enough to make possible some measure of accurate prediction even over a period of nearly 20 years. The nature and problems of such prediction are described in the preceding chapters. We may add here a brief summary of the evidence for stability and instability of our other subjects.

The psychiatrist who examined Ferdinand's adolescence expected him to be forced to marry some girl he had made pregnant, and predicted also that he would desert her. He expected a latent homosexuality to continue, and thought Ferdinand's best adjustment would be in a group situation where he could be comfortably conformist. He noted a paranoid tendency, and expected Ferdinand to be sullen, placating, and subtly hostile toward whites. In all these expectations he was quite correct. The "paranoid tendency" has become pronounced, and the prediction some-what underemphasizes Ferdinand's later homosexual involvement. Erroneously but plausibly the psychiatrist expected Ferdinand not to finish college and therefore to have marked job instability and sensitivity to his low status. He actually finished college, and has been stably employed in an administrative job. For similar reasons the expectation that Ferdinand would use racial discrimination as a rationalization for his professional failure has proved wrong. Ferdinand does react somewhat differently to whites and Negroes, but his main treatment of racial problems now is withdrawal and denial.

Nancy was expected to be unhappy and disliked, to make a late, narcissistic marriage, and to finish college unless some other outlet for her competitive feelings were available. Nancy's two marriages were thoroughly narcissistic, though her first marriage was not particularly "late." In other respects the predictions are borne out by events. Nancy was also expected to go into nursing or teaching, or at least into some job where she would not have to be subservient to whites. This is also substantially correct. Nancy finished two years of college, and was studying to be a nurse when she washed out rather dramatically after attempting suicide. It is not clear that the competitive satisfactions of her subsequent jobs (she is now a switchboard operator in an all-Negro agency) fit the prediction, but she has avoided whites. She was the only subject we contacted who explicitly refused to be interviewed by a white man. Nancy was also expected to have a notable fear of childbirth, but although she had a baby shortly before she was interviewed, we are unable to confirm or deny this prediction.

The psychiatrist expected Roland to make an infantile adjustment and to express his problems in somatic complaints. He thought Roland would avoid strenuous or aggressive jobs, marry a domineering wife, and be obsequious toward whites except when he was in safe Negro company. None of Roland's current interviewers gratuitously described him as "infantile," but the description is reasonably apt. His only apparent somatic complaint is a constantly reiterated sensitivity to cold. He is thoroughly contented with a purely passive messenger job, and is far too "infantile" to marry. Roland is not purely obsequious to whites; he is obsequious to everybody.

David was expected to have an unstable work record and problems in dealing with authority. He was expected to marry a wife who would satisfy his strong dependency needs, and to be relatively comfortable with whites. The psychiatrist leaned over backward in these predictions, since he already knew that David had built a successful career in the entertainment field. The other expectations were, however, "blind," and correct in detail.

Gilbert's abiding attitudes were variously described by the psychiatrist as "frightened submission" and "hostile passivity." He was definitely preadolescent when first interviewed, and the psychiatrist mildly questioned his capacity for subsequent psychosexual maturation, and noted that he had little capacity for human relationships. More detailed predictions were not made because the psychiatrist felt the data in Gilbert's interviews were too shallow and too shaky to support them. As far as they go, these predictions seem warranted. Gilbert's relation to his current interviewers is punctuated with broken appointments and other evidences of "hostile passivity." His job record is spotty and his performance as a husband and father irresponsible. His present relations to other people convey also a sense of shallowness and lack of emotional response, though his wife is a partial exception to this.

The primary features noted in Vera's adolescent personality were her rage against authority, her overprotesting reiteration of not wanting to be "bright" or Creole or white, her strong feelings about cleanliness, which she saw in class terms, and "an incipient paranoid development." This predicts reasonably well Vera's current adjustment: she is defiant about color but proud of living in a mixed neighborhood and having rather casual white "friends." She is an obsessive-compulsive housekeeper, bookkeeper, and arranger of details in her life, with a pronounced hypochondriasis that was not specifically predicted. She had just been released from treatment for a schizophrenic break when she was reinterviewed. The current psychiatric diagnosis is "schizophrenic organization along paranoid lines."

Alma was expected to have several unsuccessful marriages, and to use sex in a narcissistic and exploitative way. She was not expected to have any sense of maternal responsibility and her "mild to moderate sociopathy" was expected to continue. Alma has not actually married, and has had no children, but there can be little question about her use of sex as a weapon of exploitation and as a prime prop to self-esteem. Psychiatrically, however, Alma's adolescence does not entirely prepare us for the adult phenomenon. The psychiatrist who reinterviewed her reviewed Alma's hysterical, pychopathic, and paranoid tendencies and concluded that she is headed for a full-blown paranoid schizophrenic break.

The psychiatrist's interpretation of Ellen's adolescence was not entirely "blind," since a number of facts about her current life were unavoidably known to him.[2] Discounting this, he predicted that her overambition would continue and would continue to be frustrated. True enough. The storm and stress of Ellen's adolescence led to the further expectation of derogation of others as a reaction to this frustration, with continued extractive tendencies and demands for indulgence, violent color attitudes, and unsuccessful marriage. These latter predictions fail: Ellen's adult adjustment is much more controlled, restrained, even inhibited, than might have been expected, and while her rage is there, it is rigidly suppressed. Her marriage has proved stable, and while she has not achieved her dreams of being a doctor or a lawyer, she may yet win through to a college degree against considerable odds.

In the normal course of affairs the adolescent is offered a variety of paths for potential future development in his choice of

---

[2] Formal predictions were not made in the cases of Marjorie, Helen, and Victor because of loss of experimental naïveté in this way.

occupation, marriage, recreation, and similar social roles. Such adult experiences as heading a family or performing a job, however, always have elements common to the individual's earlier experiences. They involve relations with authority figures, they have anxiety-provoking characteristics requiring self-defense, or they present thwarting situations arousing hostility. It is the continuity of these elements that permits us to make accurate predictions about the future adult adjustment of an adolescent. In a modern social setting, where the adolescent must make significant and sometimes binding choices, the problem of organizing and systematizing these elements of earlier experience focuses much of the adjustment process on the formation of an ego identity. Such an evolution is strongly dependent on the quality of the experiences of the individual during the previous crises of his life and is further contingent upon the aid or handicaps provided by the web of role relationships in which he passes from childhood into some measure of maturity. As we have seen, a strong sense of self is only one possible outcome. At the other extreme lies a diffuse identity and a more or less severe personal disorganization.

The establishment of a primary role identification is one important aspect of this maturational and organizational effort. It implies the ordering in terms of their relative importance for each individual of an interrelated set of values that have psychic significance for him. This subjective assessment of significance shapes the selection of values, while the values selected serve as anchoring points for the individual's orientation to his psychologically real social world. We have found four different patterns of social identification in our subjects, corresponding to four differing value systems—four different worlds. These divergent premises then determine for the individual the events and experiences he accepts, seeks out, avoids, and rejects.

One set of experiences of particular interest in our subjects is that having to do with being Negro. The variety of patterns of identification we have found correspond to a diversity of "racial" experiences, a great divergence in their evaluation, and a consequent lack of any universal attitudes toward this common yet complex experience. The meaning of being Negro for each subject is strongly conditioned by the values associated with his particular role identification, and these in turn determine, at least in part, what his racial attitudes will do to the quality and nature of his psychodynamic functioning. Being Negro therefore not only has a variety of meanings, it also has a variety of psychodynamic consequences. Some individuals may identify with the white aggressor, with a corresponding loss to self-esteem and an unconscious burden of self-hatred.[3] Emma Fisk illustrates this process, and the somewhat special circumstances that may bring it about. Others may identify with Negroes, as William Leon does, without any apparent feeling of self-depreciation. Yet others may "use" a racial identification as they might use small size or a minor illness to excuse inadequacy feelings that have their roots in other experiences. Francis Gregory dramatically illustrates this technique. The problems posed by being Negro, like the problems posed by being male or being female, are met in different ways and with differing degrees of adequacy by different individuals, depending on the broader framework of the individual's personality organization and its attendant values.

The eighth generation has witnessed change on an unprecedented scale in the world, the nation, the region, and the city. The last two decades have produced important changes as well in the outlook of the sciences concerned with man. Regularity and stability in human affairs can be sought in the face of this new tempo of events only through dynamic concepts in which the changes that occur with the passage of time are theoretically "built in." We have emphasized for this reason the dynamic processes of identification and identity, in the hope that they may make our data relevant and our findings intelligible to our successors who may undertake the study of the ninth generation 20 years hence.

[3] Abram Kardiner and Lionel Ovesey, *The Mark of Oppression*, New York, Norton, 1951.

The Sample and the Universe

In a study that has been concerned with as many different research operations and interests as ours, the biases that may creep into the collection of data are numerous and subtle. Since, moreover, we did not begin with a random sample, and since, besides, we have pursued some particular interests and hunches, it is worth some pains to determine whether the biases we have introduced are those that we intended.

A content analysis of our complete file of case records has provided us with precise information for examining the representativeness of our corpus of data, considered as a sample. The assumption is that we have attempted to sample from the social universe of Negro New Orleans with special reference to a particular age range without unduly disturbing the representativeness of our data in relation to other attributes. Our information makes possible a direct comparison of our materials with three types of statistical information about the composition of the Negro population as revealed by the census: age, sex, and occupation.

It would be possible, of course, to compare the attributes of our subjects themselves with census information in these areas, but the small number of subjects involved makes this a relatively unrewarding possibility. Furthermore, our data have been compiled to be a record of more than this limited number of subjects, and we may reasonably hope that the varied experiences of even a limited number of subjects might yet faithfully reflect a broad sampling of the social context from which they are drawn. We have therefore elected to analyze the content of the cases in terms of an arbitrary universe of "role pages." A "role page" is a description of one social role on one page of typescript data. More than one role may, of course, be described on a given page so that the number of "role pages" of data may be considerably larger than the number of roles or the number of pages. We are concerned here, however, with proportional emphasis on various social roles, compared to the proportion given by the census.

The intent of our study has been in considerable part to examine the importance of early experiences in the social and psychological integration of individuals. We may regard with equanimity, therefore, the emphatic bias of our data toward childhood and adolescence.

We have been at some pains to try to balance our information on the two sexes. It is satisfying to find that we have closely approximated the existing sex ratio.

In comparing the occupational structure of our data with that of the universe it represents, there appear to be three interesting sources of distortion. First, the professionalism of our own interviewing procedures is faithfully reflected in our subjects' reactions to "the psychiatrist," "the college professor," and the like, thus eliciting far more information about professional occupations than would be desirable—assuming we had any way of controlling this. Second, we have more information about middle-class occupations and less about lower-class occupations than the census tells us we "should." Third, the subjects themselves distort the picture of their society as they present it to us by continuing to give the Armed Forces something of their wartime importance, and by continuing to talk about and react to the now defunct WPA: in other words our data are historically more conservative than is the census. We may suspect the possibility of a fourth distortion in the heavy weighting of service occupations, which could be due to the inherent interest of some of these occupations (e.g., sports or entertainment) to the subjects or to us or both.

The occupational class bias in our data is our most serious departure from representativeness. It is not unlikely that some part of this bias is due to the subjects themselves, for both obvious and subtle reasons. We have noted, but cannot always control, the status claims and mobility aspirations that lend an "upward bias" to most interview materials. We have noted, too, but even more helplessly, the difficulty of drawing lower-class people into the net of middle-class participation that our interviews necessarily involved. We may even suppose that an *anti*-middle-class bias of procedure could have given us a sampling that would be more "representative" by the formal criteria we are considering! While, therefore, we may regret the unrepresentative occupational distribution of our materials, we are satisfied that we do have a broad sample recognizably related to the universe it represents. A broad sample with a known bias may with cautious handling be a thoroughly defensible source of many kinds of information.

The comparison of our sample and the census for age, sex, and occupation is given in Table 1. The similar information available to us on the role content of our data in the kinship, religious, and political spheres cannot unfortunately be compared with available census categories.

As a further orientation to the universe from which our subjects are drawn, Table 2 has been designed to illuminate the changes in the makeup of the New Orleans Negro population from 1940 to 1950. In order to sharpen the comparison and facilitate the emergence of the gross trends, all figures are given as a percentage of the total population.

General conclusions about overall changes in the composition of the Negro population may be summarized as follows: the

TABLE 1. New Orleans Negro: Age, Sex, and Occupation
in the Census and in Our Records

	1950 Census (Percent)	Our Data (Percent)
Age (N = 628 role pages)		
0–9	21.8	73.1
10–19	14.8	16.4
20–49	46.0	08.6
50 plus	17.4	01.9
Sex (N = 194 role pages)		
Male	46.8	48.5
Female	53.2	51.5
Occupation (N = 835 role pages)[1]		
Professional	01.3	12.6
Managerial	01.0	01.5
Clerical and Sales	01.7	01.9
Craftsmen and Foremen	02.5	02.1
Operatives	06.9	02.6
Domestic	05.8	02.0
Service	07.3	04.7
Laborer	07.8	04.3
Armed Forces	00.2	01.8
WPA	—	00.5
Other	00.3	00.8

[1] The occupational percentages are converted to a base of 34.8 percent, the proportion of the total population that is employed.

population is growing at about 02.2 percent per annum. The age structure has undergone marked change in this ten-year period: there is a relative increase in children under 10 and older people over 50 and a corresponding relative decline in the intermediate age group (10 to 50). There is a slight increase in the proportion of males in the population. There is a significant increase in the proportion of children 5 to 24 who are in school, and a general rise in the education level, reflected in a proportional decrease of those with a grammar school education or less and an increase of those with seven or more years of schooling. There is a marked decline in the proportion of unrelated persons living in households, and a similar decline in the proportion of single persons. Otherwise the structure of the family, as reflected in these figures at least, remains about the same.

TABLE 2. Changes in the Percentage Composition of the
New Orleans Negro Population, 1940–1950[1]

	1940	1950
Total Population	149, 034	181, 775
Age		
0–9	16.3	21.8
10–19	18.5	14.8
20–29	17.6	16.6
30–39	19.1	15.3
40–49	14.1	14.1
50–59	08.0	08.9
60–69	04.4	05.7
70 plus	02.0	02.8
Sex		
Male	46.1	46.8
Female	53.9	53.2
Education		
Children 5–24	34.7	32.4
In school 5–24[2]	19.8	20.8
Adults over 25	57.3	53.3
0 years	04.7	03.2
1–6 years	32.9	26.2
7–8 years	12.6	13.0
9–11 years	03.8	05.9
12 years	01.9	03.0
13–15 years	00.7	01.1
16 years plus	00.7	00.9
Kinship		
Over 15	74.7	72.0
Householder	27.8	27.2
Spouse	15.5	15.5
Married w/o home	02.8	02.7
Children under 15	25.3	28.0
Other relatives[3]	18.7	18.9
Unrelated	08.6	05.3
Nonhousehold	01.3	02.4
Married (incl. sep.)	44.6	45.3
Separated	10.8	11.6
Single	20.4	15.6
Widowed, divorced	09.7	10.1
Occupation		
Adults over 14	76.0	72.0

[1] Data are from U.S. Bureau of the Census, *Sixteenth Census of the United States: 1940. Population: New Orleans, Louisiana*. Washington, Government Printing Office, 1942; and *Seventeenth Census of the United States: 1950. Population: Louisiana*. Washington, Government Printing Office, 1952, except as noted.

[2] Data from Stuart O. Landry, *Louisiana Almanac and Fact Book: 1951–1952*, New Orleans, Pelican Publishing Co., 1951. The "1950" figure is for 1951.

[3] Includes single children over 14 and other relatives who are single, widowed, divorced, or separated.

TABLE 2. Changes in the Percentage Composition of the New Orleans Negro Population, 1940–1950 (*Continued*)

	1940	1950
Occupation (*continued*)		
Not in labor force	30.0	33.9
Labor force	46.0	38.1
Unemployed	07.0	03.3
(Underemployed)	03.5	—
Employed	39.0	34.8
Employed females	14.8	13.1
WPA	05.2	—
Armed Forces	—	00.2
Unpaid family	00.1	00.1
Self-employed	02.4	01.8
Wage or salary	31.3	32.7
Professional	00.9	01.3
Managerial	00.5	01.0
Clerical and sales	01.2	01.7
Craftsmen-Foremen	02.2	02.5
Operatives	06.3	06.9
Domestic	10.5	05.8
Service	05.6	07.3
Laborer	06.8	07.7
Other and unknown	—	00.3
Services	13.8	09.5
Trade	05.3	06.6
Transportation	04.5	05.2
Manufacturing	03.3	04.3
Construction	02.5	03.2
Professional	01.7	02.9
Government	00.3	01.0
Finance	00.8	00.8
Recreation	00.5	00.5
Agriculture	00.4	00.2
Other and unknown	00.6	00.3
Politics		
Adults over 21	63.4	58.5
Registered voters[4]	00.2	13.4
Religion[5]		
Baptists		75.0
Catholics		10.0
Methodists		06.0
Other		01.0
Unaffiliated		08.0

[4] These figures are estimates. See V. O. Key, *Southern Politics*, New York, Knopf, 1950, p. 519, for 1940 state figures; see Leonard Reissman, Kalman H. Silvert, and Cliff W. Wing, "The New Orleans Voter," *Tulane Studies in Political Science*, 1955, 2:17, for 1954 city figures.

[5] These figures are estimates. See Stuart O. Landry, *Louisiana Almanac and Fact Book: 1953–1954*, New Orleans, Pelican Publishing Company, 1953.

There is a dramatic shift in the occupational structure occasioned by the ending of the depression and the increased prosperity of the war years, as well as by the rising level of stable employment at almost all levels. Unemployment and underemployment have been drastically reduced. WPA workers have been absorbed into the general economy. There has been a proportional decline in the size of the labor force because of the changing age structure and the removal of some women from the labor force, yet there is an increase in the proportion of wage or salary employees. The upgrading of Negro labor is evident in the proportional increases of managerial, professional, clerical, and sales and service employment, even though there are more modest increases in all other categories of employment down through laborers. There is a dramatic decline in domestic labor. Considered by industry, the proportion of employees in every industry is increasing with the exception of service industries and agriculture.

The changing political position of the Negro is dramatically indicated by the revolutionary reappearance of a Negro electorate for the first time in this century.

No figures are available for examining changes in religious membership.

New Orleans
Negro "Folklore"

In order to explore the variability and heterogeneity that exist within Negro society in New Orleans, we settled early on the plan of analyzing representative specimens of the folklore and literature of the group. A number of major genres had to be considered, the most available being the somewhat fugitive literature of the Negro Creoles of the early nineteenth century, a scattered body of materials on Negro Creole folk songs, mainly from the later nineteenth century, the somewhat unwieldy mass of authentic New Orleans jazz songs, a rather scattered and heterogeneous formal literature of recent date, mainly emanating from the Negro colleges, the contents of the Negro newspapers, and the famous Negro spirituals and modern gospel songs. Of these various possibilities, the Negro press, jazz songs, and Creole folk songs seemed the most promising because of their accessibility, their clear association to local circumstances, and especially because they represented local traditions that we had reason to believe were both important and distinct. We selected, therefore, a random sample of the editorials from one year's run of the *Louisiana Weekly* (1954), the lyrics of a random selection of authentically New Orleanian jazz songs, and all the Creole folk songs we could find.

The analysis of these materials was done in terms of psychological variables culled from a wide sampling of the contemporary literature on culture and personality, since we wished to canvass the problem as broadly as possible in relation to this literature. The variables were discussed and defined with some care, and a few subtracted or added for special reasons. Then a subsample of our data was scored independently by two judges and the two scorings were tested for independence, using a Chi-square calculation. Two of the variables, *identification* and *extraversion*, were eliminated as unreliably scored; the remainder were correlated ($p < .01$) and were kept. These variables and their brief definitions follow:

achievement: successful goal striving despite obstacles.

aggression: acts attacking individuals obstructing goals, including polemic and vitriolic language and violent figures of speech.

anxiety: indications of insecurity, including pathological disturbances in individuals or groups arising from distortions in social structure.

competition: antagonistic striving for the same (scarce) goal by two or more individuals or groups.

coöperation: joint activity for a common goal.

dominance: influencing the action of others, especially by coercion rather than exhortation or coaxing.

hostility: feelings of antagonism, or violent language expressive of such feelings.

introversion: concern with inner psychological states, especially one's own or those of in-groups.

rejection: denial of affection or expected gratifications.

submission: acceptance of a situation or activity created or initiated by others, especially one that is undesired or unpleasant.

In addition to these motivational categories, the folklore sample was analyzed for the general use of imagery. This was described by the terms anal, auditory, genital, kinesthetic, oral, tactile, and visual. No formal definitions were attached to these categories, but they were also scored for reliability and proved satisfactory ($p < .01$). Additional scoring categories added later were positive and negative feeling tone, and presence or absence of a racial reference.

The literature selected was broken into scoring units of "lines," more or less corresponding to sentences. The units were made as small as they could be without definitely distorting or destroying the intended meaning. This gave us a total sample of 691 editorial "lines," 334 Creole song "lines," and 440 jazz "lines." The percentage incidence of the various content variables as a pro-

TABLE 3. Percentage Incidence of Various Themes in Three Samples of New Orleans Negro "Folklore" (by "Lines")

	Creole	Jazz	Editorials	Chi-Square Significance
Number of lines:	334	440	691	
Achievement	13.9	07.8	30.2	$p < .01$
Aggression	07.3	08.4	06.4	$.30 < p < .50$
Anxiety	12.4	13.2	06.5	$p < .01$
Competition	08.5	05.3	04.5	$.02 < p < .05$
Coöperation	04.5	03.5	13.7	$p < .01$
Dominance	28.4	22.3	29.9	$p < .01$
Hostility	14.5	12.4	14.3	$.30 < p < .50$
Introversion	19.6	21.6	24.4	$.10 < p < .20$
Rejection	17.8	26.4	28.6	$p < .01$
Submission	15.4	12.1	15.1	$.20 < p < .30$
Anal	02.1	03.7	00.3	$p < .01$
Auditory	14.8	10.2	03.0	$p < .01$
Genital	07.8	15.3	00.0	$p < .01$
Kinesthetic	49.0	48.8	42.9	$.05 < p < .10$
Oral	26.6	11.6	08.0	$p < .01$
Tactile	26.0	12.4	05.5	$p < .01$
Visual	55.4	41.8	21.1	$p < .01$
+Feeling tone	19.3	31.2	52.5	$p < .01$
−Feeling tone	36.2	47.1	29.3	$p < .01$
Race reference	09.4	07.9	59.9	$p < .01$

portion of the total number of lines in each genre is given in Table 3. A Chi-square calculation revealed the significant independence of the groups on 13 of the 19 variables ($p < .01$). There were no significant differences in aggression, competition, hostility, introversion, submission, or kinesthetic imagery.

The Creole songs proved to have the highest proportion of auditory, oral, tactile, and visual imagery, and the lowest proportion of rejection and of positive feeling tone. On all other significant measures they were intermediate: achievement, anxiety, coöperation, dominance, anal and genital imagery, negative feeling tone, and reference to race.

The jazz songs had the highest proportion of anxiety, anal and genital imagery, and negative feeling tone; and the lowest proportion of achievement, coöperation, dominance, and reference to race. On other measures they were intermediate: positive feeling tone, auditory, oral, tactile, and visual imagery and rejection.

The editorials had the highest proportion of achievement, coöperation, dominance, rejection, positive feeling tone, and reference to race. They had the lowest proportion of anxiety, all types of imagery, and negative feeling tone, and were intermediate in nothing.

These findings are presented in graphic form in the text (Chapter 2). It seems thoroughly easy to believe that they are representative of the Creole, lower-class, and middle-class traditions that we selected them to represent, and that these traditions are distinct from one another in many of the ways that ethnic cultures have been found to differ by a variety of techniques more or less analogous to the present analysis, both in the motivational themes they express and in the imagery by which they express them. In detail, the themes we are examining here reappear recognizably and consistently as patterned elements in the New Orleans Negro cultures isolated and described in the body of the present work.

Some Attitudes Toward Socialization Practices Held in the New Orleans Negro Community

As mentioned in the text of this volume, we were unable to substantiate with data on some of our intensively studied subjects the "self-hate" hypothesis proposed by Kardiner and Ovesey.[1] In greatly oversimplified form, their hypothesis is to the effect that the Negroes' basic identification is with the white oppressor and reality factors prevent achievement of this identification; the resulting frustration causes self-hate that, in turn, feeds back to cause them to strive harder to achieve the goal of "being white," and the cycle is repeated. Because our intensively studied subjects did not have the characteristic of randomness with respect to the total Negro population, the possibility arose that we had a most unusual collection of subjects, such that they did not reflect the modal psychodynamic pattern of the New Orleans Negro population.

Accordingly, we decided to draw a random sample of Negro

[1] Abram Kardiner and Lionel Ovesey, *The Mark of Oppression*, New York, Norton, 1951.

families in order to investigate socialization practices. We developed an interview schedule titled "An Adoption Interview Schedule" aimed at getting a description of some of the attitudes held toward child-rearing in the New Orleans community. In addition to getting information directly pertinent to testing the "self-hate" hypothesis of Kardiner and Ovesey, we collected information relating to other aspects of child-rearing. We reasoned that by asking questions in the context of a potential "child adoption," some of the more strongly held feelings of our respondents would be displaced, and thereby permitted expression. The results of this study have been described, in summary fashion, in the main body of the text.

SAMPLE. A "block-sampling" procedure was used with 105 Negro women householders serving as respondents. They represented a random sample, stratified by "social class." The class stratification was proportional to that existing in the Negro population in New Orleans, as described in the 1950 census data. Variables used to identify "social class" were home ownership and median home rental per month.

PROCEDURE. An "Adoption Interview Schedule" (copy included at end of this Appendix) was administered individually to the respondents by female Negro interviewers, all of whom were senior students at Dillard University, and enrolled in a social science research class. Prior to the administration of the schedule to the selected sample, each interviewer was required to obtain five interviews, which were used as training devices in individual conferences with her. The schedule contained 41 items dealing with socialization practices, plus several questions eliciting "face sheet data." Since all the questions were presented as referring to a hypothetical adopted child, it was possible to obtain responses to all of them. Because this design was one in which the respondent was asked to assume that she had adopted a child, the questions cover hypothetical rather than actual behaviors of the parent. It is possible that the responses may be idealized or stereotyped to some degree because of this procedure.

Results

INTRODUCTION

Five different analyses were made of the data collected. The first was of the total group responses; the second was in terms of social class, the third in terms of the type of family groupings, the fourth in terms of ethnic groupings, and the fifth in terms of the stability of the marriage life of the respondents.

RESPONSES OF THE TOTAL GROUP

Forty percent of our respondents were "Creole," i.e., persons who spoke a language other than English, or who had a parent or grandparent who spoke a second language. The remaining 60 percent of the subjects were non-Creole.

The interviewers were asked to judge the skin color of the respondent. The largest single group (46 percent), were described as "dark" in color. About one third of the group were "light" in color, and about one fifth of the group were "medium" in color. Fifty-five percent of the respondents were Baptists, 26 percent were Catholics, 12 percent were Methodists, and 7 percent were members of other Protestant sects.

CHARACTERISTICS DESIRED IN THE TO-BE-ADOPTED CHILD. About three fifths of the respondents expressed a color preference in the to-be-adopted child. Of this group, 59 percent would prefer the adopted child to have a skin color like their own, 25 percent preferred a skin color lighter than their own, and 16 percent preferred a skin color darker than their own (Reference: Question 1).

When asked what kind of original parents would be desirable, half of the respondents expressed attitudes that were not related to socioeconomic class, 44 percent expressed upper-class attitudes, and only 6 percent expressed lower-class attitudes (Reference: Question 2). Almost two thirds of the group would prefer to adopt a female child (Reference: Question 9).

CHILD CARE TECHNIQUES. Forty-three percent expressed a permissive attitude toward the frequency infants should be nursed, 42 percent a strict attitude, and 15 percent a moderate, or "adaptive," attitude. The mean and median ages given by the group for the time at which weaning should take place were 17 months and 12 months respectively. The mean and median ages given by the group for the time at which toilet training should be begun were both 10 months of age, whereas the mean and median ages given by the group for the completion of toilet training were 22 and 24 months respectively. Methods of toilet training were described as "moderate" for 39 percent, while 34 percent describe permissive methods, and 27 percent describe strict or harsh methods (Reference: Questions 3 and 4).

CONTACTS WITH OTHER CHILDREN. Mean and median ages given by the group for the age when a child should be allowed to play with other children were both three years of age. Desirable playmates for the child were described by three fourths of the respondents in nonclass terms. The remaining respondents expressed upper-class attitudes; e.g., select children whose parents belong to a specific upper-class social group. About two fifths of the respondents designated some social group from which playmates should be drawn. Sixty-three percent of the group felt that children's play should be more closely supervised when they are young, i.e., under eight years of age. The main reasons given for the necessity of close supervision at this age, were physical danger (35 percent of the group), and to prevent delinquent acts (35 percent of the group).

We were particularly interested in the ways in which training would be given for handling hostility and aggression. Four fifths of our respondents felt that something should be done when a group of children that included their child started to fight. Twenty percent of the group felt that nothing should be done. Of the 80 percent who felt something should be done, about half would talk to their child in attempts to intellectualize and thereby inhibit the aggression. The remaining respondents were

fairly evenly divided between administering physical punishment and depriving the child of privileges. For 72 percent of the
group, the methods of handling the expression of aggression
would not be affected by the age of the child.

Seventy-three percent of the respondents believed that avoidance was the best technique for the child to use if another child
was constantly making trouble for him. (This response may be
related to the New Orleans pattern of color-caste etiquette, although the other children described were always Negro playmates.)

The questions most directly concerned with testing the Kardiner and Ovesey hypothesis were Numbers 27 through 30.
About two thirds of our respondents felt that a child should be
taught ways of getting along with white children. Only one
third of our sample could give a specific age at which such training should be begun. The mean and median ages given by these
respondents, for the time at which training in color-caste etiquette should be begun, were four and one-half years and five
years respectively. *That one third of our sample felt that the
child did not need to be taught ways of getting along with white
children and that if such training was started, it would be
started late in the formative years, would indicate that the
socialization conditions necessary for producing a universal self-
hate feeling among all Negroes were lacking.* With respect to the
methods to be used in teaching the child to get along with white
children, about three fifths of the group expressed a "race
equality" attitude, while the remaining two fifths expressed a
"segregation" attitude. The responses to how a child would
learn techniques of dealing with color-caste etiquette if they
were not taught at home were vague, e.g., "they will learn when
they get older." The significance of these responses is in their
vagueness, revealing as it does the fact that no culturally perpetuated, systematic way of meeting this recurring problem has
been evolved. Such a systematic pattern would have to exist if a
universally learned trait (e.g., "self-hate") was to be found in

the population (Reference: Questions 8 through 11, 24, through 30, and 37).

EXTENDED FAMILY. As a result of intensive study of our original group of subjects we became much impressed with the role of the extended family in the development of the Negro child. Questions were included aimed at exploring further these relationships. Almost three fifths of the respondents would leave their child in the care of some member of the family if they were forced to be absent from home. Of that number, about two fifths would prefer that the child be kept at some family member's house, while about one fourth of the group preferred that they be kept in their own home (Reference: Questions 18 through 21, and 31).

RECREATION FOR THE SCHOOL AGE CHILD. One of the more important activities in which the school age child evolves greater maturity is that of role experimentation. Many of his role experiments are couched in terms of "recreation" and "odd jobs." Sixty-three percent of our respondents expressed a strict attitude about the time at which a school age child should be allowed to attend movies, whereas only about two fifths of the subjects were strict about watching television and about the same proportion were moderate. Suggested leisure time activities were mainly some form of play (34 percent of the group), activities involving a combination of play, work, and education (33 percent of the group), and work (23 percent of the group) (Reference: Questions 12, 13, 32).

The mean and median ages given by the group for the time at which a child should, if necessary, supplement the family income by part-time work were in both cases 16 years of age. The type of part-time occupations considered desirable are most frequently lower-class occupations (41 percent of the group). The type of adult occupations desired by the subjects for their children were for the most part upper-class ones (58 percent of the group) or ones whose choice would be left to the child (36 percent of the group). The responses to the latter question reflect the strength of class mobility strivings within the Negro community (Reference: Questions 21 through 23).

SEXUAL BEHAVIOR. Differences by social classes have been noted by numerous researchers in attitudes held toward sexual behavior. The mean and median ages given by our respondents for the time at which girls *should* have sexual relations were 17 and 18 years respectively. It should be noted that somewhat less than half of all the subjects gave the answer "after marriage" to this question. The mean and median ages given by the group to the time at which girls *can* have sexual relations were 15 and 15.5 years respectively.

The mean and median ages given by the group of respondents for the time at which boys should have sexual relations were 17 years in both cases, whereas the mean and median ages given for the time at which boys can have sexual relations were 16 years of age in both cases.

IDEALIZED ADULT MODELS. These questions were aimed at getting some notion of the relative frequency of occurrence of family versus nonfamily ego ideals. It was reasoned that if "self-hate" were universal the respondents would project the idealized person to someone outside the family grouping. The majority of the group (57 percent) would like an adopted girl to grow up to resemble some family member. About one fifth of the respondents mentioned a nonrelative, and a few said they would like the child to "be herself." The reasons given for selecting a particular model for girls were mainly nonclass bound (55 percent of the group), whereas 45 percent of the group reflected upper-class sentiments. (Again, this is evidence of the relatively greater strength of social class mobility strivings as against caste mobility strivings). A similar pattern was expressed for boys who were to be adopted, with a somewhat greater emphasis being placed on nonrelatives as models, coupled with a greater emphasis on wanting the child to be "himself" (Reference: Questions 33 through 36).

MOST VALUABLE PARENTAL CONTRIBUTIONS. Statements concerning the most valuable contribution that parents can make toward their children's welfare generally reflect dominant values held by a particular subcultural group. Our respondents felt that the most important and valuable things that parents can do for their children were, in the order of frequency: to provide an education (34 percent of the group), to provide subsistence and to maintain health (25 percent of the group), and to give affection, (17 percent of the group).

ANALYSIS OF THE DATA IN TERMS OF SOCIAL CLASS STRUCTURE

The original sample was drawn and stratified in terms of home ownership and median rental. In attempts to analyze our data in a more refined manner, a second stratification index was used, based upon educational level and occupation of the respondent's husband, and/or her own educational level and occupation. In general, upper-class respondents had college degrees and were engaged in managerial or professional occupations. Middle-class respondents had high school degrees, were self-employed, or worked in clerical, sales, or skilled labor occupations. Lower-class respondents were those who had not graduated from high school and were unskilled workers. In our sample, using these criteria, 11 percent were upper class, 18 percent were middle class, and 71 percent were lower class.

For the purpose of this analysis, the twelve respondents who were originally designated as "upper class" were combined with the nineteen in the "middle class." The responses of this combined group were then tested by means of the Chi square distribution against the responses of the 74 "lower-class" respondents. Seven items were found that differentiated these two groups.

1. Middle-class respondents differ from the lower class in that they were more often judged to be "light" in skin color ($p < .05$).

2. Middle-class respondents differ from lower-class respondents

in that they more often expressed class-bound attitudes about the kind of original parents that they would like the adopted child to have ($p < .05$).

3. Middle-class respondents felt that children should be watched more carefully while playing with other children in order to prevent delinquent behavior, while lower-class respondents felt that the major threat was physical danger ($p < .05$).

4. Middle-class respondents more frequently designated some specific social group from which the child's playmates should be drawn ($p < .05$).

5. Middle-class respondents preferred to have their child kept in their own home during their absence rather than a home of some relative or friend ($p < .01$).

6. Middle-class respondents expressed a stricter attitude concerning movie attendance by the school age child ($p < .02$).

7. Middle-class respondents felt that girls should postpone sexual relations longer than lower-class respondents felt they should ($p < .05$).

THE MATRIARCHY

In addition to grouping the respondents by membership in a particular socioeconomic class, they were also grouped by membership in a particular type of family organization. Thirty-two of our respondents reported that they lived in a "matriarchal," extended family, which included in addition to the immediate family the subject's mother, or for an older respondent her married children, and/or grandchildren. The Chi square distribution was used to test for differences between the responses of the matriarchal and nonmatriarchal groups. Six items were found that differentiated these two groups.

1. The matriarchal group less frequently expressed a preference with regard to the skin color of the child that was to be adopted ($p < .05$).

2. Those matriarchal respondents who did express a color preference differed from the nonmatriarchal group by more fre-

quently specifying a desired skin color different from their own
($p < .05$).

3. The matriarchal group felt that toilet training should be begun at an earlier age ($p < .05$).

4. The matriarchal group more frequently preferred to adopt a female child ($p < .05$).

5. The nonmatriarchal group would more frequently turn to professional individuals and organizations if some problem arose concerning their adopted child which they felt they were unable to handle, whereas the matriarchal group would turn to some family member or to the adoption agency ($p < .05$).

6. Matriarchal respondents felt that boys are able to have sexual relations at an older age ($p < .05$). Parenthetically, this expressed attitude probably is related to the deep-seated inadequacy feelings that we found in our intensively studied male subjects reared in matriarchal homes.

ETHNIC GROUP

On the basis of a linguistic criterion, 42 of our subjects were classified as "Creole." Their responses have been grouped and compared, by means of the Chi square distribution, with the responses of the non-Creole subjects. Two items were found that differentiated these two groups.

1. Creole respondents differed in that they were more often Catholic rather than Protestant in religion ($p < .01$).

2. Creole subjects more frequently expressed a "race equality" rather than a "segregation" attitude toward the ways in which their children should be taught to get along with white children ($p < .01$).

STABILITY OF RESPONDENTS' MARRIAGE

An "unstable marriage" group was isolated from the total group of respondents. The unstable marriage group was composed of 21 individuals who reported that they were separated from their husbands, or divorced, or had been married more than once, or were living with common law husbands, or had illegitimate children. By means of the Chi square distribution, the difference between this group and the 81 married or widowed respondents was evaluated. Two items differentiated the two groups.

1. The nonstable marriage group felt that a child should be allowed to play with other children at an earlier age ($p < .02$).

2. The two groups differed with respect to the techniques that they thought their child should use in dealing with another child who was constantly making trouble for him. The stable marriage group favored avoidance. The nonstable marriage group favored more active measures, e.g., telling the parents ($p < .05$).

Adoption Interview Schedule

```
First of all, are you married? _____ If
"Yes," for how long? _____
Number and ages of children, if any?_____
_____
What does your husband do? _____
Do you ever work outside of home? _____
If answered "Yes," What do you do; what kind of
work: _____
Do you rent or do you own your home? _____
Could you tell me about how much rent you have
to pay each week or month? _____
Does anyone live here besides your immediate
family? _____
Education _____ Size of Domicile _____
Education, Spouse _____
Religious preference _____
Est. age of interviewee _____
```

1. Suppose you wanted to adopt a child, describe for me what kind of a child you would most desire. (Probe for sex, age, skin

color, affective disposition. If age of
child mentioned, inquire why this particular
age rather than an older or younger age.)

2. What kind of original parents would you like
   a child you were going to adopt to have?

3. Almost everyone has opinions about the age a
   child should be taken off the bottle and be
   required to eat solid foods; what do you
   feel this age should be?

4. How frequently do you feel that an infant
   should be nursed?

5. When do you feel that one should start
   teaching a child not to soil itself?

6. At what age do you feel that toilet training
   should be completed?

7. What do you feel is the best way to train a
   child in toilet habits? (Probe on the regularity of training procedures; for example,
   should the child be told that it is a nice
   youngster when it indicates that it wants to
   go to the toilet? Should he be spanked or
   scolded every time he wets his pants or only
   spanked if he wets himself several times in
   a row, etc.?)

8. How old do you feel that a child should be
   before he is allowed to play games with
   other children?

9. Suppose you were to adopt a youngster; would
   you prefer a boy or girl?   Whom would
   you like to have for playmates for him
   or her?

10. Are there any ages at which youngsters
    should be more closely watched while playing
    with other youngsters?

11. Why do you feel they should be watched at
                  ? (That particular age. Probe for
    early or late adolescent period and for
    heterosexual playmates.)

12. When should a school age child be allowed to
    go to the movies?

13. When should a school age child be allowed to
    watch TV?

14. At what age do you feel that a girl should
    have sex relations?

15. At what age do you feel that a girl can have
    sex relations?

16. At what age do you feel that a boy should
    have sex relations?

17. At what age do you feel that a boy can have
    sex relations?

18. If you found it necessary to be away for a while, whom would you most likely get to look after your child? (If older sibling, suppose the sibling had to be away also.)

19. If a person is named with no indication of family relationship, for example, suppose respondent said, "I would leave the child with Sue," learn the identification of Sue; who is she? Is she the mother, the sister, etc.

20. Where would the child be kept while you were away?

21. Suppose that your family could use some extra money; at what age do you feel that a child should help the family earn money by part-time work?

22. What kind of part-time work would you like him, or her, to do?

23. What kind of work would you like your child to do when he (she) grows up?

24. Suppose your child was playing with a group of other children and they got angry and started hitting one another, do you feel that something should be done about it?

25. If yes, what should be done? (If no mention of reaction to own child, probe specifically for treatment to be given own child.)

26. To what age child would such treatment be given? (If given age is "young," inquire what should be done if child is older; if "older," probe for treatment if younger child.)

27. Do you feel that a child should be taught ways of getting along with white children?

28. If "Yes," How would you go about teaching your adopted child?

29. If 27 "Yes," then, How old should the child be when this training is started?

30. If 27 answered "No," then, If parents don't teach their children how to get along with white children, where will they learn it?

31. Suppose some problem arose with the child you had adopted and you didn't know what to do about it, to whom would you turn for help?

32. Suppose a child you had adopted had nothing much to do, what would you suggest that he or she might do to pass the time?

33. Suppose you had adopted a little girl two years old, what person, other than you or

your husband, would you like this child to
be like when she grows up?

34. What is there about this person that you
chose that caused you to pick him or her?

35. Suppose you had adopted a little boy two
years old, what person, other than you or
your husband, would you like this child to
be like when he grows up?

36. What is there about that person that caused
you to pick him or her?

37. Suppose another child was constantly making
trouble for your child, what should your
child do about it?

38. Did any of your grandparents on either your
mother's or father's side speak any language
other than English?

39. If above question answered "Yes," then repeat the question substituting "parents."

40. And if the parents spoke or understood another language, inquire about the subjects
themselves.

41. What do you feel are the three most important and valuable things that parents can do for their children?

Subjective Impressions and Summary of Interview:

Judgment of Skin Color of Interviewee:

Dialect and Society

The speech of the Negro population of New Orleans is far from homogeneous. The complications of ethnic diversity, currents and cross-currents of migration within the South, and the variegated influences of the urban environment, all contribute to this fact. We may observe at the outset that the basic fabric of New Orleans Negro dialectology is nonetheless American, and patterns drawn from "standard American English" contribute the most important element in New Orleans Negro speech.

In a sample of 52 New Orleans Negroes whose speech we have recorded and analyzed, we examined 363 phonetic traits. The vast majority of these traits (71 percent of the total) are those of standard American speech, and these were shared by all or almost all the subjects. The "traits" are actually alternative patterns of pronunciation of 363 test sounds in a wide range of phonetic contexts. They were selected after close examination of a preliminary sample of the speech of five individuals, and were incorporated into a formal "questionnaire" made to resemble an informational or intelligence test. The subjects were asked to read the questionnaire aloud and were aware that the interview was being recorded. (An alternative question-and-answer form, prepared for use with illiterate subjects, proved unnecessary.)

A significant minority of the phonetic traits (10 percent of the total) were also shared by all or almost all our subjects but are dialectically distinctive within American English. Most of them are traits broadly common to the South. Over half of them relate to the disappearing "r" or the shortening of the final "y." Taking this general fact together with our previous statement, we may conclude that the common substratum of New Orleans Negro speech is a selection of patterns that may be called General Southern American, and that some four fifths of the phonetic features of New Orleans Negro dialects are drawn from this substratum. Our primary concern here is with the remaining fifth.

On about 19 percent of the traits there is a marked division within our sample. These are all phonetic dichotomies in which one third or more of our subjects dissent from the majority usage. In most cases the division of the sample is close to fifty-fifty. These variable usages were provisionally classified by a linguist as Southeastern, Orleanian, and Other. There were 23 Southeastern traits, 13 Orleanian, and 37 Other, the latter apparently weighted with Middle Western usages, among other things. The frequency distribution of these traits is given in Table 4.

On the basis of the frequency distributions we divided the sample into "speakers" and "nonspeakers" of the three dialects by breaking each distribution at or near the median (as indicated on Table 4). Our first concern was to establish whether the dialects were mutually exclusive. We found that only three subjects were speakers of both Southeastern and Other and only three were speakers of neither (Chi-square 27.77; $p < .01$). These two dialects thus correlate negatively with each other. Orleanian proved to be related to both of the other dialects and was significantly differentiated from neither. Thus our data reveal only two dialects differentiated from one another with some measure of clarity. (We explored the correlation of Orleanian with various social variables anyway, but without results.)

A social placement questionnaire that was completed at the time the dialect recordings were made enables us to compare the dialectology with a number of social variables: color, sex, age,

TABLE 4. Frequency Distribution of Selected Dialect Traits in a Sample of New Orleans Negroes

No. of Traits	Southeastern	Orleanian	Other
0		1	
1		1	
2		3	
3		4	
4	2	3	3
5	3	15	0
		——Median	
6	3	6	1
7	3	7	0
8	2	4	1
9	3	5	2
10	8	1	2
11	2	1	2
	——Median		
12	5	1	4
13	7		2
14	5		6
15	2		3
			——Median
16	0		1
17	4		0
18	2		4
19	0		0
20	1		3
21			6
22			1
23			3
24			2
25			1
26			1
27			1
28			2
29			1
Total	52	52	52

class, education, ethnicity, residence, and religion. The correspondences between these social variables and the two dialects isolated can be stated very briefly. Southeastern speech is associated with light skin color; Other speech with dark. The Other dialect is also correlated with membership in the middle class, occupationally defined. These findings are statistically significant

TABLE 5. Dialect and Social Position of Sample
of New Orleans Negroes

| | Southeast | | Other | | |
	Speaker	Nonspeaker	Speaker	Nonspeaker	Total
Color					
Dark	9	15	15	9	24
Light	13	10	10	13	23
Unknown	4	1	1	4	5
Sex					
Male	13	13	12	14	26
Female	13	13	14	12	26
Age					
Over 30	18	13	13	18	31
Under 29	8	13	13	8	21
Class					
Lower	14	14	8	20	28
Middle	12	12	18	6	24
Reference Class					
Lower	8	12	13	7	20
Middle	15	14	13	16	29
Don't know	3	0	0	3	3
Education					
Elementary	9	6	5	10	15
Higher	17	20	21	16	37
Ethnicity					
Creole	4	10	10	4	14
Non-Creole	21	16	16	21	37
Don't know	1	0	0	1	1
Residence					
New Orleans	11	11	10	12	22
South	13	9	9	13	22
Other	1	6	7	0	7
Don't know	1	0	0	1	1
Religion					
Catholic	4	8	8	4	12
Protestant	19	14	14	19	33
Other	2	2	3	1	4
Don't know	1	2	1	2	3

($p < .05$). (We distinguished objective class placement from subjective class definition, but the latter proved to be uncorrelated with either dialect.) The relationship between the dialects and the various social variables is given in Table 5.

In one sense the findings reported seem a meager result from a rather intensive and expensive research effort. On the other hand, the results are a rather clear answer to an important question. If we assume that some shared linguistic usages should result from segmentation of society, we can only conclude from our data that the Negro society of New Orleans is not clearly segmented, and that only in relation to occupational class is there any clear relationship between sub-units of the society and general dialect features. The test words distinguishing Southeastern from Other speech are given in Table 6.

The apparent lack of cluster to the dialect features we have examined suggest the usefulness of reëxamining some of our initial assumptions. While we have not pushed this reëxamination to a rigorous test, the suggestion seems implicit in our sample that there is relatively little stability to the dialect pattern in each individual. In 25 cases, for example, our "traits" were duplicated: the subject pronounced the same word in two different parts of the record. These revealed an average of 10.8 percent variability, that is, on the average 10.8 percent of the subjects pronounced the word differently the second time. The most unstable words proved to be: *on, half, a, four, can,* and *eggs.* The most stable were: *children, happy, light, knife, noise,* and *house.* The instability seems to correspond in a general way to the existence of real choice, since there was little agreement among our subjects on the pronunciation of the first (unstable) group of words, but virtual unanimity on the second. On 25 pairs of different words presenting an identical phonetic context, the inconsistency of pronunciation averaged 27.4 percent. These findings would seem to raise some question about whether there is any dialect consistency to individual speech in our sample that is not strictly limited to particular phonetic contexts. In short, it seems possible that the individual's choice of one alternative for a given phoneme in a given phonetic setting may be independent of his choice about any other phoneme not phonetically related to the first.

This disquieting suggestion cannot be easily tested in our data, presenting as it does a formidable problem of tabulation and

TABLE 6. Diagnostic Features of Southeastern and Other Speech[1]

Written English	Southeastern	Other
ten	tin	ten
air	aeh	er
ride	rahd	rayd
time	tahm	taym
afraid	əfred	əfreyd
boiled	bɔyl	bɔyld
scrambled	skraembl	skraembəld
second	sekən	sekənt
mad	maeyd	maed
sad	saeyd	saed
tomorrow	təmɔrə	təmarow
over	owvə	owvər
thing		θiŋ (θeeyn)
get		get (git)
a		ey (ə)
dinner		dinər (dinə)
can't		kaent (kaeyn)
bread		bred (breyd)
nine	nahn	nayn
blind		blaynd (blɑhn)
child	chahl	chayld
night		nayt (nɑht)
point		pɔynt (pəynt)
join		jɔyn (jəyn)
worms		wərmz (wəymz)
Florida		flɔridə (flɑridə)
Washington		wašiŋtən (wašintən)
Birmingham		bərmiŋhaem (bəhminhaem)
morning		morniŋ (mohnin)
sink		siŋk (zeyŋk)
have	haehv (haev)	
again	əgen (əgeyn)	
man	maeyn (maen)	
men	maeyn (men)	
yellow	yelə (yelow)	
window	wində (window)	
found	fawn (fawnd)	

[1] Dialect transcription follows George L. Trager, and Henry Lee Smith, Jr., *An Outline of English Structure*, Norman, Oklahoma, Battenburg Press, 1951. Unless it appears in the alternate column, the principal alternative to the diagnostic pronunciation given is indicated in parentheses.

matrix analysis. Out of curiosity, however, we could not refrain from sampling the data on the point. A preliminary analysis of the percentage correspondence between pairs of individuals on all traits seems to indicate that any two individuals selected at random will have about 73.6 percent common traits. (It will be noted that the average dissimilarity between phonemes paired for phonetic context—27.4 percent—leaves room for an agreement of 72.6 percent!) We calculated the dialect correspondence between four pairs of individuals carefully matched for all the social variables we have used. The percentage agreement between pairs was: 70.4, 76.5, 80.7 and 68.7; average: 74.1. The same index for a pair of individuals who differed from one another in *every* social characteristic is 73.8. The correspondence between two individuals known to have at least some traits of geographically distinct dialects in common is 71.7! The form in which the data were recorded make these calculations very laborious, so that we have not been able to make a more extensive analysis. These preliminary figures, however, strongly suggest a general lack of the linguistic and cultural patterning usually associated with the term "dialect."

Index

343